Contested Common Land

Contested Common Land

Environmental Governance Past and Present

Christopher P. Rodgers, Eleanor A. Straughton,
Angus J. L. Winchester and Margherita Pieraccini

London • Washington, DC

First published in 2011 by Earthscan

Earthscan Ltd, Dunstan House, 14a St Cross Street, London EC1N 8XA, UK
Earthscan LLC, 1616 P Street, NW, Washington, DC 20036, USA

Earthscan publishes in association with the International Institute for Environment and Development

For more information on Earthscan publications, see www.earthscan.co.uk or write to earthinfo@earthscan.co.uk

ISBN 978-1-84971-094-7

Typeset by JS Typesetting Ltd, Porthcawl, Mid Glamorgan
Cover design by Susanne Harris

A catalogue record for this book is available from the British Library

Library of Congress Cataloging-in-Publication Data

Contested common land : environmental governance past and present / edited by Christopher P. Rodgers ... [et al].
p. cm.
Includes bibliographical references and index.
ISBN 978-1-84971-094-7 (hardback)
1. Environmental policy. 2. Environmental policy–International cooperation. 3. Environmental education. I. Rodgers, C. P. (Christopher P.)
HC79.E5C619 2010
333.2–dc22

2010028007

At Earthscan we strive to minimize our environmental impacts and carbon footprint through reducing waste, recycling and offsetting our CO_2 emissions, including those created through publication of this book. For more details of our environmental policy, see www.earthscan.co.uk.

This book was printed in the UK by TJ International, an ISO 14001 accredited company. The paper used is FSC certified and the inks are vegetable based.

Contents

Preface

This book presents research arising from an interdisciplinary research project, 'Contested Common Land: Environmental Governance, Law and Sustainable Land Management *c.*1600–2006', which was funded by the Arts and Humanities Research Council as part of its Landscape and Environment programme between 2007 and 2010. The research project sought to investigate the sustainable management of common land in historical context, placing contemporary concerns surrounding common land in England and Wales in historical perspective and highlighting the multifaceted social, historical and legal factors relevant to the successful development of an appropriate and effective strategy for the future management of our common lands.

Common land has a distinctive legal identity, and is subjected to multiple and potentially conflicting land uses. In exploring the tensions and contests inherent in the distinctive character of common land, this book offers an interdisciplinary perspective on shifting concepts of 'sustainable' land use and the interplay between these conceptions and the governance and management of common land since circa 1600. It focuses, in particular, on the evolution of property rights and changing instruments of governance, their enforcement, and their role in both creating and protecting the distinctive and unique landscape and environment of common land in England and Wales. The key historical questions addressed in the book thus concern how the concept of 'sustainable' management has been articulated, interpreted and applied to common land since circa 1600, and how instruments of legal governance and notions of 'sustainable' management have both reflected and determined cultural values and property rights. The future of common land is currently under debate following the Commons Act 2006. The 2006 Act provides for new forms of commons governance and places the 'sustainable' management of our commons at the centre of public policy for their future. Questions of immediate contemporary relevance are discussed in the following chapters, including the quest for an understanding of the most appropriate models of self-regulation for the delivery of the 2006 Act's objectives for the future environmental management of common land.

These research questions have been addressed at two levels: first, by studying the evolution of legal and cultural conceptions nationally; and, second, by examining the development of governance mechanisms at the local level. By focusing on four case studies, the research presented here seeks to marry historical understanding drawn from local archive sources with contemporary research data gathered through a complementary and carefully focused qualitative research methodology using semi-structured interviews and focus groups with stakeholders. The research project also developed an iterative and collaborative approach to the generation of knowledge, complementing its archival and qualitative methodologies. Two research symposia were held under the aegis of the project at which the research findings at different stages of its work were presented and discussed with invited participants – including policy-makers, stakeholder groups and academics from relevant disciplines. And in the concluding phase of the project, the research outcomes were presented at stakeholder workshops in each case study, which provided an opportunity for two-way dialogue with stakeholders on key issues emerging from the historical and contemporary research, and facilitated the further refinement of the project's conclusions.

In Part I, the chapters charting the history of common land (Chapters 2 and 3) were written by Angus Winchester and Eleanor Straughton, and those discussing the modern issues (Chapters 4 and 5) by Christopher Rodgers and Margherita Pieraccini. All four authors have contributed to the writing of the case study chapters in Part II (Chapters 6 to 9). Final editing for publication was undertaken by Christopher Rodgers and Angus Winchester. The law is stated as at 31 March 2010.

Christopher P. Rodgers
Angus J. L. Winchester
September 2010

Acknowledgements

In presenting the findings of the Contested Common Land project, the authors wish to acknowledge the financial support of the Arts and Humanities Research Council, without which this research would not have been possible. We should also like to record particular thanks to the director of the Landscape and Environment programme, Professor Stephen Daniels, for his support and encouragement throughout the three years of the project. Two interdisciplinary research symposia were held as part of the project, at Lancaster University in September 2008 and at Newcastle University in September 2009, bringing together scholars from a wide range of disciplines and representatives of government agencies and other bodies involved in policy relating to common land in England and Wales and crofting in Scotland. Discussion at the symposia contributed to our collective thinking and we should like to record our thanks to all those who participated in them.

In focusing the research to specific commons located in four distinct geographical areas we have incurred debts of gratitude to a large number of people, notably the landowners and commoners who participated in our interviews, in focus group meetings and in stakeholder workshops. The historical research was facilitated by the courtesy and efficiency of staff in specialist libraries and record offices, particularly those of The National Archives at Kew; the Cumbria Record Offices at Whitehaven and Carlisle; West Yorkshire Archive Service at Leeds; the North Yorkshire County Record Office at Northallerton; the National Library of Wales, Aberystwyth; Powys County Archives, Llandrindod Wells; Norfolk Record Office, Norwich; and Gloucestershire Archives, Gloucester. We are particularly grateful to Mark Fox of the Eskdale Commoners' Association; Dr John Farrer of Clapham; John Metcalfe of Ingleton; Michael Rolt and Alec Baker at the Elan Estate Office; and Belinda Holland of Dderw for granting us access to records in their possession. We also gladly record our thanks to the custodians of the respective Common Land Registers for allowing us access to this essential material: Anne Wallace (Cumbria); Linda Wishart (Norfolk); Jenny Griffiths (Powys); and Chris Stanford (North Yorkshire). Others who contributed to the local research presented in this book included members of the Ingleborough Archaeology Group, who carried out archaeological field surveys of common land in Ingleton parish as an adjunct to our archival research; Messrs J. S. Metcalfe (Ingleton) and H. C. Bargh (Chapel-le-Dale), who contributed their knowledge of the management of Scales Moor since the 1930s; Erwyd Howells of Capel Madog, who generously shared his wealth of knowledge on the hill farming culture of mid-Wales; and George Parry of Scolt Head and District Common Rightholders' Association, who facilitated access to copies of records held by Brancaster Parish Council. We are also conscious that our research stands on the shoulders of previous work and should like to record our debt to the following: Julia Aglionby, Sara Birtles, David Johnson, Robert Silvester, Maurice de Soissons, Richard Suggett and Tom Williamson.

The contemporary research would also have been impossible without the collaboration, support and encouragement of a wide range of stakeholders and organizations. We are grateful to those landowners and commoners who took part in the focus groups and semi-structured interviews. Thanks are also due to the Eskdale Commoners' Association, the Ingleton Commoners Association, the Scales Moor Stintholders, Cwmdeuddwr Commoners Association and the Scolt Head and District Common Rightholders' Association for their cooperation and assistance in organizing meetings and supplying valuable source documentation (including copies of minute books and other unpublished sources). The National Trust provided useful information and assistance with the organization of the research in Eskdale and Norfolk, as did the Elan Trust in the Welsh case study. The heads of common land policy at Natural England (Graham Bathe) and at the Countryside Council for Wales (Buddug Jones) gave access to a wide range of valuable data and policy documentation, and made valuable contributions to the research as it progressed. Thanks are also due to the Natural England staff at Kendal, Leeds and Brancaster, who gave their time for interviews and meetings, and provided source material not otherwise available online. The Countryside Council for Wales staff at Llandrindod Wells also contributed useful policy documentation and data for the Elan Valley case study. Special thanks are also due to Julia Aglionby for providing copies of the draft agricultural management rules adopted by the Shadow Commons Council for Cumbria. These are cited in the text as Defra (2009b) and will be published by Defra in due course with the final report of the Shadow Commons Council Research Project.

We should also like to record particular thanks to Tim Hardwick at Earthscan for his encouragement and patience, and Chris Beacock, who prepared most of the maps for publication. Grateful acknowledgement is made to Natural England and the Countryside Council for Wales for permission to reproduce the maps of common land in England and Wales (Figures 1.1 and 1.2), and to Ben George Photography for the image of Brancaster Marsh (Figure 9.1). The other images were taken by Angus Winchester.

List of Acronyms and Abbreviations

AONB	Area of Outstanding Natural Beauty
CAP	Common Agricultural Policy (of the European Union)
CCW	Countryside Council for Wales
CL	common land unit
CLR	Common Land Register
CPR	common pool resource
CRA	Commons Registration Act 1965
CRO	Cumbria Record Office
d	penny/pence; 12d = 1 shilling; 240d = £1
Defra	Department for the Environment, Food and Rural Affairs
EEO	Elan Estate Office
ELS	Entry Level Stewardship
ESA	Environmentally Sensitive Area
GA	Gloucestershire Archives, Gloucester
GAEC	good agricultural and environmental condition
HLS	Higher Level Stewardship
LU	livestock unit
MAFF	Ministry of Agriculture, Fisheries and Food (now Defra)
NFU	National Farmers Union
NLW	National Library of Wales, Aberystwyth
NRO	Norfolk Record Office, Norwich
NYCRO	North Yorkshire County Record Office, Northallerton
NYRCL	North Yorkshire County Council, Register of Common Land
OELS	Organic Entry Level Stewardship
OLDSI	operation likely to damage the special conservation interest
PCA	Powys County Archives, Llandrindod Wells
s	shilling(s): 20s = £1
PRO	The National Archives, Public Record Office, Kew
SAC	Special Area of Conservation
SDA	Severely Disadvantaged Area
SPA	Special Protection Area
SPS	Single Payment Scheme
SSSI	Site of Special Scientific Interest
SWES	Sheep and Wildlife Enhancement Scheme
WAG	Welsh Assembly Government

WES	Wildlife Enhancement Scheme
WYRO	West Yorkshire Record Office, Leeds
YAS	Yorkshire Archaeological Society

1

Introduction: Common Land as a Contested Resource

Over 500,000ha of common land survive in England and Wales,[1] the vast majority consisting of marginal land beyond the limits of cultivation, characteristically clothed in semi-natural vegetation. Commons include large tracts of the mountains, hills and moorlands of upland England and Wales, the sandy heaths and wetlands of lowland England, and open spaces on the margins of settlements, from the large metropolitan commons around London to small patches of rough ground on the edges of villages (Hoskins and Stamp, 1963, pp104–110, 134–136; Everitt, 2000). Today, they fulfil a range of roles: many continue to serve a function in the agricultural economy as grazing grounds; most are important as open spaces for recreation; in ecological terms, many are deemed to be fragile environments with a high conservation value; some serve particular purposes – for example, as grouse moor or for military training. Historically, these 'wastes', as they were termed, formed an integral part of the traditional rural economy, not only as grazing for livestock, but also as sources of fuel (in the forms of firewood, peat or vegetation such as gorse) and a wide range of other resources, as diverse as fish, berries, nuts, sand, clay, gravel, stones, bracken, heather, rushes and reeds (Neeson, 1993, pp158–184; Woodward, 1998; Winchester, 2000, pp123–142).

Surviving commons represent only a fraction of the land subject to common rights in England and Wales before the 19th century. Almost all surviving commons are to be classed as 'manorial waste', semi-natural land, usually lying on the margins of a community's landed resource, but common land in the early modern period also included the open arable fields and meadows, productive farmland held in unenclosed strips in private ownership but subject to common grazing rights after the crop had been taken or when lying fallow. A long process of land reform, culminating in a great surge of enclosure by acts of parliament in the century between circa 1760 and circa 1860, swept away almost all of the open fields and much of the manorial waste, extinguishing common rights over 2.75 million hectares of land – 21 per cent of the total land area of England – and reducing the surviving extent of common land in England and Wales to circa 554,000ha (Turner, 1980, pp178–181; Aitchison, 1990, p273).

Most of the common land which survived the tide of privatization and enclosure may thus be thought of as 'leftover' land, incapable of conversion to intensive agricultural

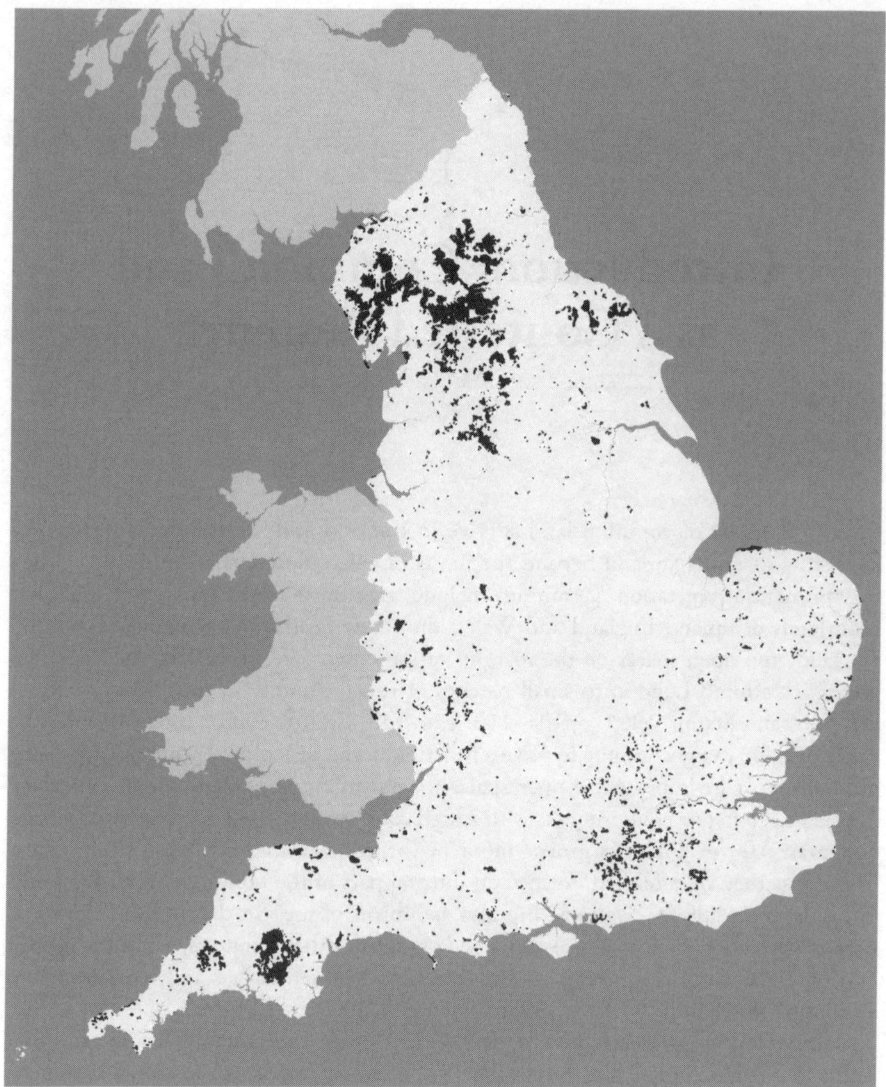

Figure 1.1 *Registered common land in England*

Note: The map excludes commons in the New Forest and Epping Forest (which were exempt from registration) and the Forest of Dean, to which the Commons Registration Act 1965 did not apply.

Source: © Natural England (2010). Material is reproduced with the permission of Natural England, http://www.naturalengland.org.uk

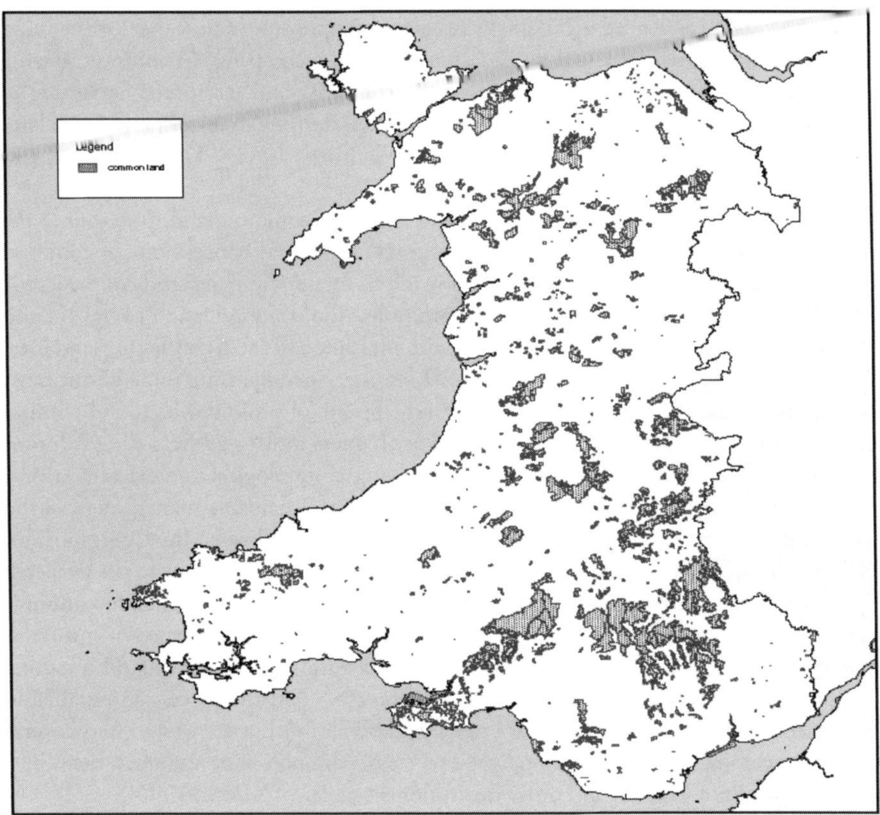

Figure 1.2 *Registered common land in Wales*

Source: © Countryside Council for Wales (2010). Reproduced with the permission of the Countryside Council for Wales[2]

use. The distribution of surviving common land (see Figures 1.1 and 1.2) shows a strong geographical pattern and falls into a number of distinctive types of terrain. Most extensive are upland environments in the hills and mountains of northern England and Wales and the moorlands of south-west England, where, in terms of acreage, the bulk of common land lies. Wetlands, including both peat fen and coastal marsh, form a second distinctive environment in lowland England. Others include the mixed woodland and heath of former royal hunting grounds, such as the Forest of Dean (Gloucestershire), the New Forest (Hampshire) and Ashdown Forest (Sussex), and the small settlement-edge 'greens' scattered across East Anglia. Most surviving commons may thus be conceived of as the last fragments of 'wilderness' – wild or untamed land on the margins of settlement, lying beyond the cultivated land and dwelt-in spaces. But human use, especially the grazing of livestock, is central to determining their character. Within the spectrum of British commons, two opposite trajectories of ecological and land-use change have dominated recent history. Most upland commons remain an important resource in pastoral farming economies and experienced increasingly heavy grazing pressures across the 20th century, often leading to environmental degradation through overgrazing. In contrast, grazing has ceased on many lowland commons since circa 1950, and traditional harvesting of vegetation for fuel and other purposes has petered out, leading to reversion to scrub land and the loss of the open heathland character (Gadsden, 1988, p1.17; Aitchison and Gadsden, 1992, pp166–167).

The theme of this book is the 'contested' nature of common land. It examines the interplay between law, land management and wider cultural conceptions of common land across time, and in so doing seeks to provide an interdisciplinary study of the iconic and often controversial landscapes of the commons. The common land of England and Wales has long been an important resource with multiple and often conflicting land uses. As an important agricultural and recreational resource encompassing some of our most ecologically sensitive environments, it has been the site of profound legal and cultural changes over several centuries. The following chapters aim to address the evolution of common land governance since 1600, providing chronological context at a critical moment in its history. The challenges of re-establishing sustainable management of the commons are to be addressed in the next ten years and beyond when the Commons Act 2006 has been fully implemented. The 2006 Act has introduced reforms to the property rights regime for common land and to the management structures applied to common resource governance, that will significantly strengthen sustainable environmental management and provide a more equitable basis for future access to the land resource. The book offers an assessment of the impact of the 2006 Act, and places the sustainable management of the common lands of England and Wales within the wider international debate concerning the environmental governance of common pool resources, including the work of Elinor Ostrom and other institutional scholars (Ostrom, 1990).

This study takes an interdisciplinary approach, linking historical research in archive sources with qualitative research on modern commons governance undertaken with contemporary stakeholders. It employs case studies in four unique landscapes in England and Wales to illustrate changing patterns of land use, and the differing management principles and regulatory mechanisms applied to common land from circa 1600 to the modern day (see Figure 1.3). Three cover upland commons, in the Lake District of Cumbria, the Pennines of North Yorkshire and the hills of Mid-Wales; the fourth, which includes coastal marshes and a lowland heath in Norfolk, has been chosen to represent surviving common land in lowland England (see Chapters 6 to 9). The case studies inform the book's broader examination of shifting notions of 'sustainability' and of the environmental governance of common land.

The legal framework: Common property rights

Unlike many traditional commons in continental Europe, common land in England and Wales is neither communally owned nor 'no man's land' (*terra nullius*); rather, it is privately owned land over which others possess use rights, giving them legally recognized access to particular resources. Its use was underpinned from the 13th century until the Commons Registration Act 1965 by a firm and stable framework of property rights, which vested ownership of 'waste' in the hands of the lord of the manor, while recognizing the use rights of the local community. The legal framework can be traced

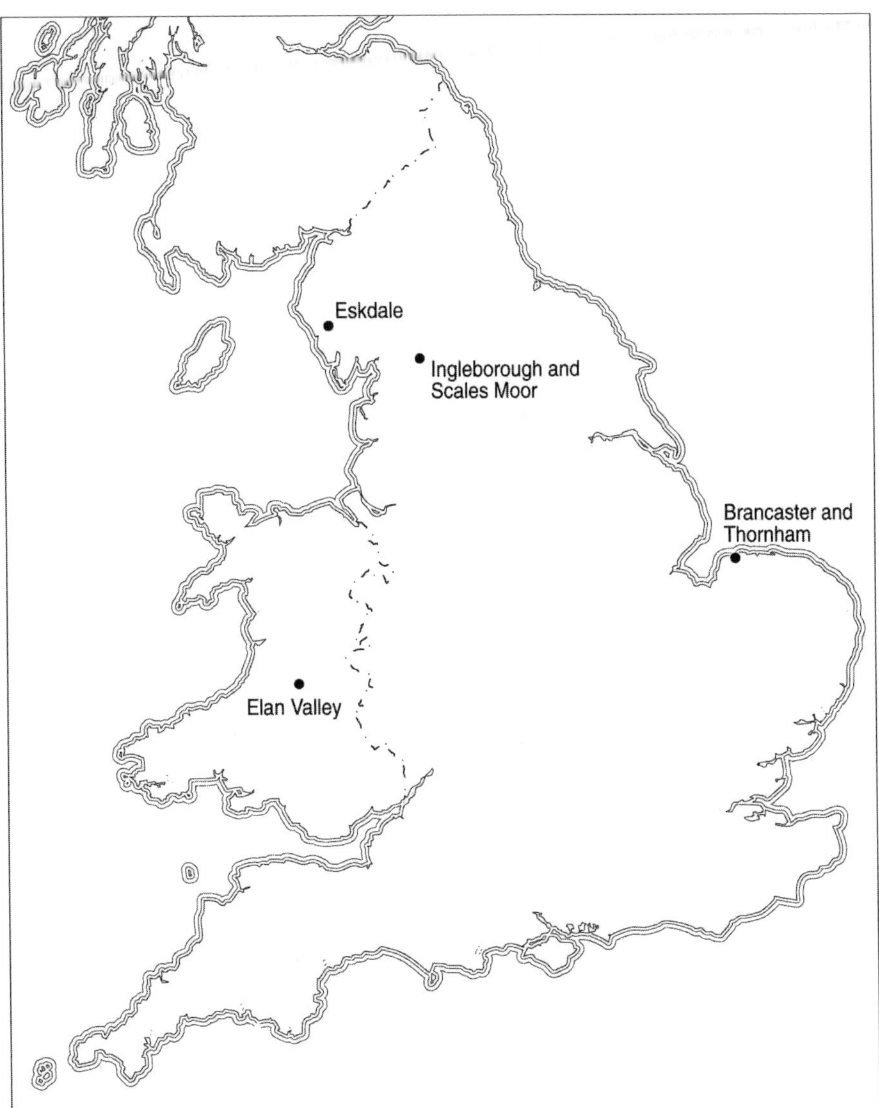

Figure 1.3 *Location of case studies discussed in this book*

Source: Authors

back to the statutes of Merton (1235) and Westminster II (1285), which confirmed the lord of the manor's rights in the soil of the manorial waste (described by Merton as the 'residue' of the manor), but also required lords to respect the use rights of free tenants within the manor.[3] Lords could approve the waste (i.e. enclose sections of it and rent them out for agricultural use), but the statutes restricted their freedom by recognizing the legal validity of the use rights of commoners. As owners of the soil, lords generally retained a wide range of property rights, including mineral and game rights, and a right to any residual grazing over and above the use rights of commoners.

English law developed a sophisticated classification of commoners' use rights, describing both the basis of the right and its nature and purpose. Most rights were 'appurtenant' – that is, attached to a landholding (the 'dominant tenement') as a subsidiary right. It was also possible, however, for an individual to hold common use rights independently of a holding of land. These are known as common rights 'in gross' – 'a separate inheritance, entirely distinct from any landed property, [which] may be vested in one who has not a foot of ground in the manor' (Blackstone, 1792, ii, §34). It has been accepted since the mid 19th century that rights in gross are freely alienable and can be transferred by the rights holder to anyone (see Gadsden, 1988, §3.43). In legal terms it is therefore an anomalous category of right – a right over land that is, in itself, a personal right of the holder and (unlike a right appurtenant) not attached to land that it is intended to benefit. Where they do subsist, however, rights in gross cause problems for the sustainable management of common land, as we shall see in subsequent chapters.

The law also recognized the customary use of common land by people from neighbouring settlements (known as common *pur cause de vicinage*). In legal terms this was a permissive right that applied where two or more contiguous commons usually intercommoned with each other. It was a customary right, and so was implicit in any individual common right (whether appurtenant or in gross) held over either common. The right did not give the holder the right to place his livestock on a contiguous common: rather, it recognized that animals may stray, and protected the common rights holder from an action for trespass where his stock strayed onto the waste of a neighbouring manor. The right could be unilaterally extinguished at any time by the landowner enclosing the common, for example, by fencing it to prevent the straying of stock from one common to another.

The common law recognized six categories of common right (see, generally, Gadsden, 1988, §3.28–3.85; Sydenham 2006, §3.2.1–3.2.7). These are not exclusive categories, however, and in principle any product of the soil, any natural product or wild animal could be the subject matter of a right of common. Many rights that are encountered in practice (including a number discussed in the case studies of commons governance in this book) are difficult to place within one or more of the established categories.

Of the six legal categories of use rights, by far the most significant was *common of pasture*: the right to graze livestock on the common. This right was, and remains today, centrally important to the rural economy in upland areas of England and Wales. The management of the collective grazing over large agricultural commons was, prior to the Commons Registration Act 1965, organized around one of two principles in most areas – by the application of the principle of levancy and couchancy, or by the imposition of 'stints' as a measurement of permitted grazing. The rule of levancy and couchancy determined the number of grazing livestock allowed on the common by reference to the capacity of the land to which the rights attached to feed stock over the winter months. This was not expressed in a numerical form. Stints, on the other hand, permitted a fixed number of livestock to graze the common resource. These mechanisms, and their function in relation to notions of 'sustainable' governance, are considered in more detail in Chapters 3 and 4.

The two other common rights most commonly encountered are common of turbary and common of estovers. *Common of turbary* gave the right to take peat or turf for fuel, and, in principle, must always be attached (appurtenant) to a building or house. The right is limited to taking what is necessary for heating the dominant tenement, and cannot be divided or apportioned between parts of the latter (e.g. if it is divided and sold in separate lots). *Common of estovers* is similar and gave the right to take wood or other vegetation for necessary purposes. It fell into three sub-categories. 'House bote' was the right to take timber for repairing houses or as fuel; 'plough bote' to take timber for making or repairing agricultural implements; and 'hay bote' was the right to take timber, shrubs or brush to make or repair hedges and fences. The right also extends to taking animal bedding (e.g. bracken or rushes), gorse, heather and reeds. In order to be valid, a claim to estovers must be limited by reference to what is necessary for the maintenance of the dominant tenement to which it is attached, and which it is intended to benefit, or be limited in quantity. It is generally accepted that a right of estovers (and, by implication, the similar right to turbary) cannot be severed from the land it benefits, even if the right is quantified (e.g. if the right gives a right to take two carts of peat per annum from the common) (see Gadsden, 1988, §3.67; Sydenham, 2006, §3.2.4). There is no right to sell estovers or put them to another use other than those recognized by the law.

Other rights of common, less frequently encountered in practice today, are the *right of pannage* – the right to graze pigs in woodland or forests – and rights to take fish, wild animals and the soil itself. Brief descriptions of the latter categories will be offered here, as both are encountered in the case studies presented in this work, notably in Norfolk (see Chapter 9). *Common of piscary* is the right to take fish from a lake, river or stream belonging to another. Any land covered with water may be registered as common land, provided it is not foreshore vested in the Crown. The right will normally be registered as appurtenant to a house or land, and in this case it will be limited to what is necessary for the needs of the household it is intended to benefit. There is no reason, in principle, why a right of piscary should not subsist in gross, however, and (somewhat unusually) this is the case with the rights in the Norfolk case study. Rights to take minerals or constituent parts of the soil itself are recognized as *profits à prendre* in law and can also be the subject matter of a right of common. Most rights to take soil will be appurtenant to land and subject to the restrictions mentioned above in reference to turbary and estovers; but they may also be rights in gross, as in our Norfolk case study. A seventh category is the right to take wild animals (*ferae naturae*) from the land of another. This can subsist as a *profit a prendre* in English Law, and can therefore exist as a right of common (Gadsden, 1988, §3.86). It may be difficult to distinguish this category of common right in many cases from instances where a licence or contractual right to take wild animals has been given, such as is given by a right to shoot, hunt or wildfowl over another's land.

Contested common land

Common land thus has a special legal identity and is also a local material resource. But in cultural terms it has much greater significance than this. As Kenneth Olwig has put it, a common is 'not simply an institution, but also a symbol of the ideals and values necessary to the maintenance of such institutions' (Olwig, 2003, p18). An underlying theme of this book is the impact of changing cultural values and perceptions of common land upon the way in which it has been managed across the centuries: the common as a site of multiple, contested ideals and interests. The very existence of common land represents an unfinished contest between ideals of cultivation and wilderness. The lands above or beyond the cultivation line have been variously seen as terrifying, sublime, picturesque or romantic, the subject of legends, literature and art (Thomas, 1983). Without cultivation, vestiges of past human activity often survived on common land where they would otherwise have been destroyed, making the common waste a place where the present confronted the past. Notions of its uncultivated state and marginality might be transferred to the people living among and using the waste: these people might also therefore be defined as somehow wild and uncivilized, picturesque or romantic – the 'outside' lands and peoples being assigned the same characteristics, reinforcing their sense of otherness (Thomas, 1983; Pollard, 1997).

To the medieval mind such landscapes were liminal places, where humanity might encounter the supernatural. The otherness of the wilderness can be seen in early medieval Scandinavian cosmology, where the *utgård* (the same term was used of the common waste beyond the farmland) was inhabited by monsters and was dark, in contrast to the human world of settlement and cultivation (Altenburg, 2003, pp187–188). A similar perception is seen in the Anglo-Saxon era, when saints such as Guthlac deliberately sought to confront demons in the Fens (Colgrave, 1985, p89). The association of wilder spaces beyond cultivation with spiritual or mythical sites is a global phenomenon, reflected in the widespread occurrence of sacred groves and forests, or revered mountains and rivers, often subject, a least historically, to communal forms of guardianship (Thomas, 1983; Schama, 1996). Such sites are not necessarily empty of human intervention; indeed, the beliefs with which they are endowed make them 'extremely humanised landscapes' (Arora, 2006, p61). The wastes on the margins of English villages were similarly humanized landscapes, endowed with meaning. Their role as boundary zones, where the territories of adjacent communities met, gave common wastes a heightened importance as a border to be protected – even as places of potential danger and threat. They were spaces where ritual, such as the 'beating of the bounds', with its attendant claiming of boundary markers, took place and folk memory played a vital part. Minor features in the landscape, both natural and man-made, along the open boundaries across common land were claimed and named. Symbolism was often powerful: the liminality of the common waste was reflected in its association with the dead, notably as the place of gallows and gibbets (Whyte, 2009).

The idea that common land is a 'wild' place where the past is preserved and may be encountered has led to the perception that it existed within a temporal limbo. It has been viewed as a historic relic or artefact, a timeless space surviving cheek-by-jowl with modernity, and somehow escaping centuries of dramatic social, agrarian and landscape change. Even W. G. Hoskins and L. Dudley Stamp, authors of the report of the Royal Commission on Common Land, could claim that common land in England and Wales was 'still hardly changed from Anglo-Saxon times', echoing the view of the Victorian commons campaigner George Shaw-Lefevre, who believed that commons 'remained in their original state of nature' (Hoskins and Stamp 1963, p3; Shaw-Lefevre, 1894, p3). Common land was celebrated as a survival in a national landscape which had been utterly transformed during the era of enclosure, linking contemporary England and Wales with their past.

The 'timeless' view obscures the dynamism of common land: patterns of land usage and practices have changed considerably over time. Indeed, seemingly ancient 'common' land may only have achieved the legal status of common land as a product of modern statute (e.g. the Commons Registration Act 1965), although its redefinition as 'common' is in itself an interesting historical question. Casting surviving communal regimes in a 'primitive' light has a tendency both to obscure historical change in common property rights and governance mechanisms and to create an assumption that common property regimes are a pre-modern relic, rather than 'historically specific ways of managing land and labor under certain socioeconomic and ecological conditions, including resource scarcity and the local conflicts it generated' (McCay and Acheson, 1987, p18).

Another dimension to the culture of common land lies in the evolving perceptions of its value. The purpose of common land – and therefore how and for what ends it should be managed – has been viewed differently by different stakeholders at different periods of time. Since 1600 common land has existed within multiple cultural and legal paradigms, subject to both 'soft' customary manorial regulation and 'hard' statute law; it has been treated as an agrarian resource, but also as a recreational space, as a public utility, or as a political landscape where ideals of improvement, public freedom and wilderness can be tried. Over this period, rights have become increasingly privatized and standardized; paradoxically, the land itself has become increasingly public, and perceived as part of a national landscape. Most rights in common land were traditionally local in that they were tied to the property rights and interests of the lord and tenants of a particular manor. Since the 19th century, the conception of a national and public interest in common land, whether for recreation or for conservation, has come to the fore. Shifting perceptions of common land and of the values attached to it reflect a wider dichotomy in values placed on the environment: the material value of resources, on the one hand, and wider cultural values, as diverse as the spiritual and recreational, as well as conceptions of the stewardship of nature, on the other. In the terms coined by T. C. Smout (2000), an enduring tension between 'use' and 'delight' underpins cultural attitudes to the environment across time.

The variety of uses of common land, and the layers of perception that have endowed it with a symbolic place in national culture, lie at the root of the multifaceted array of contests over common land which form the central theme of this book. At the heart of all communal resources lies an inherent tension between individual self-interest and the communal good. This, of course, is the conflict at the heart of the 'tragedy of the commons', assumed by Hardin (1968) and many others to lead inevitably to the destruction of the resource in question. Notwithstanding the body of literature which has demonstrated that sustainable management of common pool resources (CPRs) is possible, the inherent contest between individual and communal interests remains a key feature of common land, distinguishing it from other property regimes. On common land there exists an essential paradox: no one individual can take sole control or dispose of the resource; yet the interests and actions of each individual are immensely powerful – potentially destructive – and must be carefully balanced by the community of users if the common is to be sustained.

These inherent tensions frequently gained substance in day-to-day contests over the use of common land. Indeed, the property rights regime on common land contained within it a set of tensions between the rights of the owner of the soil and those having communal land-use rights. Not infrequently, the lord of the manor's rights to game or minerals came into conflict with the tenants' rights to grazing or to take vegetation. Managing a common as a breeding ground for game was not necessarily compatible with managing it for grazing; quarries could destroy pastures (e.g. Aldred, 1990, pp76–78, 124–126, 157–159); mining could lead to subsidence. Furthermore, different common rights were not always mutually compatible: the exercise of turbary rights could potentially conflict with pasture rights, as digging peat and turf could destroy the vegetation cover, for example, or lead to waterlogging. Even different aspects of the exercise of a particular common right might lead to tension, as in the conflicting demands for bracken, where the careful harvesting of fronds for thatching could be sabotaged by wholesale harvesting for animal bedding or for burning into potash. Such tensions and conflicts were rarely far from the surface, as the case studies in Chapters 6 to 9 of this volume demonstrate. They also lie at the heart of the quest for successful governance regimes for common land, as discussed below in Chapters 3 and 5.

A third arena of contest lies in the law of property and the multiplicity of legal codes to which common land in England and Wales is subject. The examination of the complex intersection of formal and informal normative rules applied to common land, viewed in historical context, requires a multifaceted and flexible approach that takes account of the concept of 'legal pluralism', and recognizes the role of both 'formal' state-sanctioned legal rules and normative rules of informal status (see Moore, 1973).

Common land occupies an ambiguous middle ground between private and communal property, in which legal and idealized concepts of 'ownership' commonly intermingle, as the formal legal framework of property rights intersects with changing cultural perceptions. As Schama (1996, p61) suggests: 'once a certain idea of landscape, a myth, a vision, establishes itself in an actual place, it has a peculiar way of muddling categories, of making metaphors more real than their referents; of becoming, in fact, part of the scenery'. On one level common land is a symbol of communality, a popular and egalitarian resource; while on a formal legal level, and often in reality, it has been a place of exclusivity and jealously guarded rights. At the heart of this ambiguity lay the powerful and enduring influence of custom. Manorial waste was subject to the 'customs of the manor', a body of local customary law which had evolved since the medieval period to govern local agrarian practice. Custom grew by its nature out of, and was adapted to, local circumstance – and was resistant to attempts to rationalize rights and provide a standard national basis for regulating common land (as discussed in Chapter 2).

Since the 16th century, lawyers have attempted to codify the law of common land with only partial success: there has consequently often been a disjunction between legal theory and the practical reality. Property rights exercised according to local custom might not map satisfactorily onto legal structures imposed by statute, and 'formal' law often attempted to standardize local customary practices that were, in fact, anything but standard. This has posed a challenge to legislative attempts since the 19th century to confine common land and rights within the bounds of accepted legal frameworks and practices. The 'burden' of ancient and complex land-use rights has complicated and sometimes defeated schemes of improvement, appropriation or change.

An attempt to establish a definitive nationwide statement of common rights was recommended by the Royal Commission on Common Land, established in 1955 to make recommendations for the protection and future of common land. In its 1958 report, the Royal Commission recommended the establishment of statutory registers of all common land – a 'modern Domesday Book' of the commons (Royal Commission 1958, para 404ff; Shoard, 1997, p341). This recommendation was implemented by the Commons Registration Act 1965, which provided for the entry of all common land, the rights exercisable over it, and the persons claiming to be owners (both of land and rights) on statutory registers maintained by the county councils. The act provided two registration periods within which land and rights had to be provisionally registered (the final date for registration being 31 July 1970). Land that was not registered within this period was deemed not to be common land, and rights that went unregistered ceased to be legally exercisable (1965 Act, section 1(2)). The registration provisions are explained further in Chapter 4.

Objections to the registration of land and/or common rights were referable to specially appointed commons commissioners for decision (1965 Act, sections 6, 18). Objections could be made to a provisional registration; but if none was made then the registration became final at the end of the period for objections – typically two years from initial registration of the land and/or common rights (1965 Act, sections 5(2), 7(1)). Although the 1965 Act is now widely criticized, it should be remembered that commons registration was merely the first of several stages in the action plan recommended by the Royal Commission for the preservation of the commons. The latter also recommended the introduction of statutory rights of access for the public to all common lands, and the establishment of statutory management associations to oversee schemes for their improvement and management. Completion of this strategic plan for the future of the commons was subsequently delayed. Public rights of access to registered common land were not granted until the passage of the Countryside and Right of Way Act 2000 (2000 Act, section 1), and the Commons Act 2006 introduced measures to facilitate the establishment of statutory commons councils to manage common land (as explained further in Chapter 5).

Many of the flaws in the process for commons registration under the 1965 Act are thrown into relief by the research presented in the case studies in Chapters 6 to 9. A common theme, as we shall see, is that (despite the compulsory registration of common rights) local custom and expedience continue to hold sway, and the commons registers established under the 1965 Act are, in practice, routinely ignored or subverted.

Sustainable governance

This study of environmental governance on common land in England and Wales finds a place within a global and interdisciplinary arena. Research into common pool resources (CPRs) is a young and growing field, with subjects ranging from forests and pastures to radio waves and the 'knowledge commons'. It was Elinor Ostrom, seen by many as the pioneer of CPR research, who first established that management regimes on CPRs, which had previously been deemed inherently unstable, destructive and anachronistic, had the potential to be successful, long enduring and sustainable. Her major volume *Governing the Commons*, appearing in 1990, revolutionized both research and practice, particularly among practitioners working in the developing world. It also encouraged historians, studying common land regimes in the 'Old World', to look at their ancient, enduring CPRs with fresh eyes (Winchester, 2000; De Moor et al, 2002).

Box 1.1 Elinor Ostrom's design principles for successful common pool resource management

By a 'design principle' is meant 'an essential element or condition that helps to account for the success of these institutions in sustaining the CPRs and gaining the compliance of generation after generation of appropriators to the rules in use'.

1 The CPR has clearly defined boundaries and clearly defined membership of use-rights holders.
2 Congruence exists between appropriation and provision rules and local conditions.
3 There are collective choice arrangements (individuals affected by operational rules can participate in modifying them).
4 There is monitoring by appropriators or by monitors who are accountable to the appropriators.
5 Graduated sanctions are applied for infringement of operational rules (appropriators who violate operational rules are likely to be assessed graduated sanctions by other appropriators or their appointees).
6 There is access to low-cost conflict-resolution mechanisms.
7 There is external recognition of self-organization (the right of appropriators to devise their own institutions is not challenged by external authorities).
8 Multiple layers of nested enterprises exist if the CPR is part of a larger system.

Source: Ostrom (1990, p90)

Ostrom gathered examples of successful management of the commons in different geographical contexts, from mountain grazing and forests in Switzerland and Japan to irrigation systems in Spain and the Philippine Islands, in order to identify design principles that characterize enduring CPRs (Ostrom, 1990, p88ff). In all of these contexts, the CPR institutions were considered to be robust, meaning that the rational appropriators 'designed basic operational rules, created organizations to undertake the operational management of their CPRs, and modified their rules over time in light of past experience according to their own-collective choice and constitutional-choice rules' (Ostrom 1990, p58).

Ostrom's institutional insights have since inspired a spectrum of CPR research, as an exploration of the Digital Library of the Commons shows. Here, key themes include resource management, indigenous knowledge and practices, conservation strategies and protected areas, and the interaction of multiple layers of rules and governance. The areas covered are representative of every continent, and the library is particularly rich in literature relating to the commons of Asia and Africa. The theoretical field has also expanded beyond institutions and material resources towards a greater recognition of the cultural construction of commons and the non-material roles that they play.[4]

In her desire to identify and explain the reasons for success, Ostrom perhaps underestimated the complex web of cultural and political factors which shape and interact with a CPR over time and which form the central themes of this book. Nevertheless, there is still much to be gained from her original institutional approach to environmental governance on common land, and her thinking has continued to evolve to encompass complex institutional factors and 'contextual variables', as the title of her recent volume, *Understanding Institutional Diversity*, implies (Ostrom, 2005). In this she concludes:

> *Now that we know that those dependent on these resources are not forever trapped in situations that will only get worse over time, we need to recognize that governance is frequently an adaptive process involving multiple actors at diverse levels. Such systems look terribly messy and hard to understand. The scholars' love of tidiness needs to be resisted. Instead, we need to develop better theories of complex adaptive systems focused on overcoming social dilemmas, particularly those that have proved themselves able to utilize renewable natural resources sustainably over time.* (Ostrom 2005, p286)

This study into the common land of England and Wales is one such attempt to 'develop better theories'. Like many existing CPRs around the world, common land in the UK has survived and endured innumerable 'social dilemmas' and near tragedies, and, indeed, many of these commons have suffered periods of severe social-ecological degradation – some have lost every 'common' attribute save for their legal label. Nevertheless, that there are still commons and active commoners in England and Wales today is proof of the possibility of successful commons management. In a context where global natural resources seem under ever more strain, it is remarkable, and perhaps reassuring, that these pockets of land, layered with multiple – often incompatible – use-rights and cultural values, have survived into the 21st century. A study into the means by which these resources were sustained over 400 years thus has application beyond the individual commons.

The focus of this book is on the 'sustainable' management of the commons, in historical context. 'Sustainable development' is a multifaceted concept: it is now customary to view it as comprising three dimensions – the economic, the social and the environmental. The origins of this tripartite approach are commonly attributed to the Bruntland Report, which defined sustainable development as 'development that meets the needs of the present without compromising the ability of future generations to meet their own needs' and to the principles of the 1992 Rio Declaration (WCED, 1987, p43; United Nations, 1992). The 2002 World Summit on Sustainable Development in Johannesburg explicitly recognized three interdependent and mutually reinforcing 'pillars' of sustainable development – economic development, social development and environmental protection (United Nations, 2002, Resolution 1, para 5.2). Working in an historical context, Turner et al (2003) term these elements the 'three Es': the ecological, economic and equitable. The constituent elements are, moreover, mobile: whereas environmental sustainability is now arguably the dominant paradigm in law and policy, in previous centuries ensuring economic sustainability and equitable access to common resources were the key aims.

The multifaceted approach to defining sustainability was reiterated by the 2005 United Nations World Summit Outcome (United Nations, 2005, para 1(10)). It contextualizes environmental protection within the socio-economic dimension, and stresses the complementarities of the different elements (social, economic and environmental) for realizing sustainable development. Sustainable *management* involves a balancing process, taking into account the economic, social and environmental protection elements of sustainability. A particularly difficult question in the context of contemporary commons governance concerns the extent to which the protection of ecosystems and natural habitats can be balanced against the exploitation of economic resources. Theories of 'weak' sustainability attribute limited weight to protecting natural capital when balancing the needs of development and environmental protection (see Pearce, 1993, 13ff). A weak sustainability approach can be seen in many of the land management instruments applied to promote nature conservation on common land (as described in Chapter 4). The balancing function between differing contested land uses that is implicit in the operation of these legal mechanisms often requires the needs of the environment to be traded off against economic development (Bosselmann, 2008, p52).

Building on this threefold distinction, the research presented in this study focuses on three aspects of sustainable management which are seen as especially pertinent to common land:

1 sustaining the common resource for present and future generations;
2 protecting its environmentally sensitive ecological and landscape features; and
3 ensuring fair and equitable access to the land resource.

These involve balancing the competing demands of common resource users and the wider public inherent in the shared nature of the legal interests in common land.

This study considers how these interests were addressed through governance institutions (such as manor courts and commoners' associations), practices of rule-making and enforcement, and through control mechanisms based on number, space and time. The tripartite cultural approach to sustainability is particularly helpful in the present research context, which conceptualizes past, present and future sustainability on common land. It allows for time-depth, and a wider range of values and determinants than the purely ecological or resource led – encompassing also the desire to sustain the 'cultural' tradition or customs of a land-based community and to sustain social relationships (both potentially significant motives for regulating the use of the commons, above and beyond the simple need to preserve resources).

The successive reforms to European agricultural policy initiated since 1992 have also seen the European Union, Common Agricultural Policy (CAP) move from an emphasis on production towards a greater emphasis on sustainable land use, wildlife protection and, more recently, the preservation of culturally important and historic landscapes. Inevitably, this has meant introducing a sense of time and history into the sustainability agenda. In early discussions sustainability was often forward-looking, intrinsically linked to 'development'; now, there is also a backwards glance. Increasing use of the label 'cultural landscape' reflects an understanding that many of our most ecologically and aesthetically important environments have been created and sustained over several centuries through human effort and ingenuity. This does not mean that all historic practices or agrarian traditions were inherently positive or benign; but it recognizes that human land use and long-term ecological processes are indivisible. Common land is a supreme example of a cultural-ecological landscape, and its endurance and sustainability can only be understood in the context of a long time-depth.

Moreover, environmental sustainability is not itself a static concept. Our expanding scientific understanding of ecological processes has greatly changed, and continues to change, the terms of the debate. The redefinition of peat moorland as vast carbon stores is a case in point: this marks a relatively new addition to the sustainability agenda, emerging out of a growing understanding of climate change and carbon processes. It will be one of the most significant drivers of sustainable policies and land-use practices in the 21st century; yet it was little discussed even as recently as ten years ago. Similarly, landscape management will need to adapt to the effects of sea-level rises. This can already be seen in experiments in 'managed retreat', currently being undertaken in many lowland coastal zones in the UK, including the north Norfolk coast. There are also attempts to reverse historical processes. As the current lively debates over the possible reintroduction of lost predator species, such as wolves, or the reversion of farmland to wild scrub or forest ('re-wilding') show, the dialectics of productivity *versus* wilderness and culture *versus* nature – tensions at the heart of changing cultural conceptions of common land – remain potent.

The complexity caused by the intersection of multiple legal codes is magnified in a modern context if we consider the relationship between common property rights and legal instruments targeted at implementing sustainable land management. The provisions of modern environmental legislation frequently sit uneasily with the distinctive property rights applicable to common land. This raises further tensions – for example, between state-sponsored land management standards and locally derived customary land practices. The close identification of the 'public interest' in modern commons management with nature conservation and the protection of important landscapes also reflects the changing perception of common land as a communal resource, referred to above. It introduces a further point of tension (or contest) – in this case between the 'public' interest in promoting sustainable management for the protection of wildlife and landscapes (reflected in statutes such as the Wildlife and Countryside Act 1981 and the Commons Act 2006), and what are now conceptualized as 'private' law interests (typically the property rights of appropriators and landowners).

The modern legislation on environmental protection primarily impacts upon common land and its management in two ways:

1 through the imposition of legally enforceable land-use controls in sites designated for protection under English law; and
2 through the use of management agreements to encourage the adoption of environmentally friendly land management.

These environmental governance mechanisms are applied, however, irrespective of the nature of the property rights in the land to which they apply, whether it is freehold land, tenanted or common land. In the case of common land this causes further tensions between the unique property rights regime that applies (and the resource allocation that it represents), and the public interest in nature conservation represented by the conservation legislation. In many cases the result is that the complex property rights in common land inhibit or frustrate the pursuit of the nature conservation objectives sought in the public interest (see Chapter 4).

Conclusions

The challenge for producing a paradigm study of the principles governing the sustainable management of CPRs is complicated by the fact that no two commons are the same. Although similar 'contests' between different interests and interest groups can be detected in the history and modern governance of many commons, their relative importance and the interplay between them varies from one CPR to another. It is a complex picture and one with no easy resolution. The case studies presented in Part II of this study will highlight the challenges for achieving sustainable management by focusing on CPRs in four localities, in which the interplay of governance mechanisms and land use, past and present, are often materially different. Before the case studies, however, we consider the framework of governance principles applied to common land in England and Wales in historical context, and the institutional forms within which contests over the land resource have been resolved. This will require a consideration of the nature and role of custom and of common property rights, alongside an examination of the manner in which concepts of 'sustainable' management have been captured and reflected in customary and legal norms since the early modern period. This is the subject of Chapters 2 to 5. Chapter 5 also considers models for the future 'sustainable' management of the commons offered by the Commons Act 2006.

Notes

1 There is no common land in Scotland or Northern Ireland. The enclosure of commons in Scotland during the 18th and 19th centuries was so complete as to remove any vestige of land comparable to the common lands of England and Wales. Land within the Scottish crofting system does, however, present some similarities and is subject to its own system of land tenure and legal protection (see Shoard, 1997, pp348–349).

2 Produced by CCW on 26 August 2005. OS base maps reproduced with permission of HMSO. Crown copyright reserved. CCW licence no. 100018813.

3 The framework established in the statutes of Merton and Westminster II (Section 46) was confirmed by the Act for the Improvement of Commons, 1549 (Statutes 3 and 4, Edw. VI, c. 3).

4 The Digital Library of the Commons is at http://dlc.dlib.indiana.edu/dlc/ (accessed 23 April 2010).

Part I

Custom, Property Rights and Sustainable Management

2

Custom and the Culture of the Commons, 1600–1965

In his influential essay on the role of custom in early-modern England, E. P. Thompson (1993, p97) noted that 'at the interface between law and agrarian practice we find custom'. Nowhere is that more pertinent than in relation to common land and the variety of interests and use-rights that were claimed over it. The legal framework of property rights on commons (outlined in Chapter, pp4–7) provided a skeleton, capable of being shaped and fleshed out according to circumstance. Legal principles were mediated by local custom, with the result that patterns of property rights on common land differed in detail from one locality to another, while changing perceptions and priorities exerted different forces at different times. Local custom and informal practice are thus central to understanding the place of common land in English culture, and they have continued to flow as a strong current even in modern times. This chapter therefore seeks to look behind the formal legal principles to explore the interface between custom and more formal conceptions of rights by examining the cultural dynamics which have moulded conceptions both of 'ownership' and of the perceived rightful use of common land since the 16th century.

These evolving conceptions reflect the successive cultural lenses through which common land has been viewed since 1600. In outline, a late-medieval focus on custom and tradition as the touchstones for determining right usage of common land was increasingly supplanted from the 17th century by an obsession with 'improvement' and its corollary – the view that common land was there to be reclaimed for more productive use. This, in turn, was succeeded from the 1860s by a desire to preserve surviving commons for public access, recreation and wildlife conservation. These changing paradigms created a dynamic in which each added another layer of meaning to existing perceptions of common land.

The standard work on the law of common land interprets modern governance rules as being the product of 'centuries of gradual absorption of manorial custom into a standardised common law' (Gadsden, 1988, § 1.02). Customary law had deep roots and was essentially local, the medieval 'custom of the manor' varying from place to place (Bonfield, 1996). It was also an evolving body of regulation, which continued to develop in response to changing circumstances. Indeed, custom played a vigorous part in relations between the plebeian and the elite in the 17th century, providing a moral and political foundation from which to defend the status quo against challenge (Wood, 1997). Custom was thus the touchstone at the heart of decision-making about the right ordering of common land in the early-modern period. At the core of custom lay the concept of 'good neighbourhood', the maintenance of friendly relations between neighbours. This was ultimately a moral and spiritual precept, flowing from the recognition that living and working alongside others required the acceptance of mutual obligations and, hence, the fettering of individual liberty (see Wrightson, 2007). In the agrarian world, the heart of 'good neighbourhood' was in the day-to-day behaviour of individuals in an environment with many shared resources and few physical boundaries, where the actions of one individual were likely to impinge directly upon others. Maintaining 'good neighbourhood' involved the control of livestock and the upkeep of fences, to keep animals out of the growing crops of corn and hay; it also required the neighbourly management of common land, involving matters such as herding practices and the marking of livestock (Winchester, 2000, pp45–47). In order to determine what constituted 'good neighbourhood', communities turned to 'ancient custom', the way things had been done in the past, illustrating both the indivisibility of the two principles and that the taproot of regulations governing the use of common land ran deep.

Local custom continued to interact with formal law until the capture of property rights in a fixed and static form as a result of the Commons Registration Act 1965. Meanwhile other national cultural fashions also became influential. From the 17th century, the ethos of 'improvement' became an organizing principle across both moral and physical spheres, ushering in a new frame of reference for views concerning land. Concern that common wastes were 'wasteful', in that they were capable of being reclaimed for cultivation and, hence, for profit, can be traced back to the 16th century: as early as circa 1576 a call was made for the compulsory division and cultivation of wastes for both individual profit and the national wealth. By the mid 17th century, the culture of improvement was strong: in the idealism of the English republic, it could be claimed in 1657 that 'Those who are against improvement are Enemies to the Commonwealth'. Puritans saw common land as one of the 'great Nurseries of Idleness and Beggary', a view reflecting the association between the commons and the poor, which was already established by 1618, when John Norden commented that places 'where great and spacious wastes, Mountaines, Woods, Forests and Heaths are' attracted squatters living idle and godless lives (Norden, 1618, pp111, 114; Shannon, 2009, pp94, 97–98).

The concept of improvement gathered momentum in the 18th and 19th centuries, when it was expressed in a wide breadth of activities, from increasing the industriousness of the labouring poor to redesigning private parkland. Agricultural improvement included the introduction of new techniques and new crops, improved livestock breeds, drainage and reclamation, ideas which were spread through agricultural societies and a burgeoning literature that applied scientific reasoning to farming. In the gathering national momentum, the restrictions on use inherent in the status of common land were presented as the major block to improvement, requiring private and, eventually, parliamentary schemes of enclosure (Thomas, 1983; Wilmot, 1990; Wade Martins, 2004; Tarlow, 2007). Central to the improvement ethos was the narrowing and hardening of property rights. This was seen as a process of modernization, a narrative of progress in which human civilization was presumed to be moving along a trajectory from 'primitive' open access resources without a developed concept of property, towards modern private property systems. The argument rested on the binary opposition of 'common' (symbolizing archaic inefficiency, communalism and custom) and 'improvement' (symbolizing modern efficiency, private individualism and science). Improvement possessed 'a moral value and a social desirability far beyond mere enhancement of profit' (Tarlow, 2007, p35).

The place of common land in national life changed again from the mid 19th century, as the essentially local concerns of land management for farming purposes were replaced by wider issues of environmental conservation and public access. The sea-change occurred in the middle decades of the 19th century, prompted initially by the desire for recreational access to suburban commons. The Commons Preservation Society, founded in London in 1865, sought to reinterpret the public interest in common land by seeking a communal recreational right of access, in contrast to the traditional individual right to use and take resources (Cowell, 2002). The result was a groundswell of opinion against further enclosure to retain the common land that had survived the age of improvement as a national resource. Recreational access remained a dominant driver across the 20th century, culminating in the Countryside and Rights of Way Act 2000, which gave a public right of access over most registered common land. Conservation of the semi-natural ecosystems which characterized much remaining common land also became a powerful force. By the later 20th century, the twin aims of environmental protection and public access – both implicitly conceiving of common land as 'a sort of national property' (to coin Wordsworth's famous phrase) – had come to dominate debates over the management of surviving commons.

Private rights and public 'ownership'

Conceptions of the 'ownership' of common land are thus culturally loaded and subject to shifts of emphasis over time. The formal legal framework recognized the lord of a manor as owner of the soil and of manorial rights to game and minerals, and the commoners as holders of use-rights giving them access to certain resources from common land; but it existed within a changing context in which custom played an enduring role. The meaning of 'ownership' often looks different when viewed through the lens of the 'soft' law of custom rather than the formal law of property, and the history of common land may be thought of as a contest between cultural conceptions.

The opposing forces of private rights, on the one hand, and public 'ownership', on the other, form a theme running across the centuries. There was also a shifting boundary between what constituted common land and what did not: areas that were tantamount to common land in terms of their use and ecological character did not always possess the legal persona of common land, and land which was common at one point in time is sometimes found not to have been such at another period. Before exploring the opposing forces of private rights and public 'ownership' on land that was indisputably recognized as common, it is worth touching on these grey areas along the margins of what was defined as common land.

Two categories of land were for all practical purposes almost identical to manorial waste – areas of semi-natural vegetation over which grazing rights were shared – and yet were legally distinct. The first were defined sections of waste, particularly in former hunting forests or chases in the uplands, which were deemed to be private seigniorial pastures in the medieval period. Grazing rights over such land originated as agistment or licensed use, rather than common rights *sensu stricto*, although the distinction had often been forgotten by the 16th century and the waste in question was treated in the same way as other categories of common land (Winchester, 2000, pp84, 94). Examples of such private wastes are encountered in the case studies presented in this volume. In Eskdale (Chapter 6) the high mountain tops were claimed as the lord's private deer reserve by the late-medieval period, giving them a legal status separate from the surrounding common, while in Brancaster (Chapter 9) areas of sand dune and saltmarsh were claimed as the lord's several lands in the 17th century, although they had come to be classed and registered as common land by the 20th century.

A second category of land on the margin of 'true' commons consisted of those sections of manorial waste which had been separated by a physical enclosure for use as a communal cow or ox pasture, a type of land found in numerous communities by the 16th century. They represented a distinct category of communally used land, in which individuals had rights to graze specific types of livestock. In many cases, rights in such shared pastures were legally 'sole rights', as opposed to common rights, as the lord of the manor retained no residual interest: the land had been granted away and the grazing rights represented fixed shares of the whole (Gadsden, 1988, §1.27–1.28, 1.60–1.61). In the Ingleton area (see Chapter 7, pp114–16), for example, the commoners' informal process of enclosing sections of the wastes and converting them to stinted pastures appears to have continued for many years without challenge, such that the lords' interests in the waste was said in the early 19th century to have lapsed through lack of use. Thus, lands which were once common came to be held in severalty, or were classed as stinted pastures with rights of sole pasture.

Property rights and custom

If the boundary of land that constituted true common could shift across time, so too could conceptions of property rights over land that was unquestionably common land. Taking the long view, the balance between the rights of landowners and use-right holders is found to have possessed a degree of complexity and fluidity. Within these shifting sands it is possible to discern opposing patterns, both of increasing privatization and commodification of rights, particularly during the era of 'improvement', and persistent and widening conceptions of public 'ownership'.

While the 18th and 19th centuries saw the disappearance of much common land, the culture of improvement impinged even upon commons that survived enclosure. One aspect of this, which contributed to the evolution of property rights, was the spread of stinting, the articulation of grazing rights in numerical terms (discussed further in Winchester and Straughton, 2010). This involved a spectrum of processes from informal agreements (e.g. Scales Moor, Ingleton – see Chapter 7, pp116–17), through to more formal stinting schemes under the legal mechanism of enclosure (e.g. Thornham Common – see Chapter 9, p168). Elsewhere, statutory powers were used. Some enclosure acts included clauses that allowed commoners to privatize their rights – generally through stinting – while continuing to manage the land as shared unfenced pasture. The General Enclosure acts of 1801 and 1836 included provision for laying allotments together to form shared pastures, 'stocked and depastured in common' by the proprietors, while that of 1845 made provision for commons to be stinted or 'regulated'.[1] In such cases, the stinted land may no longer have been technically 'common' and the nature of the property rights may have changed; but the grazing was used and conceived of as a communal resource; indeed, some were subsequently registered as common under the 1965 Act and are therefore classed as common today.

Where a common became stinted, the very act of expressing a grazing right in terms of a stint could change its legal character. By the mid 19th century the precise legal nature of stinted rights (often termed 'cattlegates' or 'beastgates' in the vernacular) was being debated by the courts of law: since they gave a tenant a form of exclusive possessory right over a fixed share of the common pasture, it could be argued that they gained a substance and a quantifiable value quite different from an unstinted common right (Getzler, 1997, pp218–220). Once quantified, stints could be sold separately from the dominant tenement to which they had originally been attached. In northern England, trading in stints which were not attached to land is recorded by the 17th century; in lowland England, grazing rights which had formerly been attached to cottages were being separated by the 18th century (Neeson, 1993, pp83–84; Shaw-Taylor, 2002, p74; Winchester and Straughton, 2010). On urban commons, in particular, rights were often shared, leased or sublet, further distancing the user from the legal commoner (Bowden et al, 2009, p3). Grazing rights belonging to the town of Clitheroe, Lancashire, for example, were in theory attached to properties in the town; yet a flourishing trade in 'beastgates' had developed by the late 18th century, to the extent that few of those exercising grazing rights also possessed property to which a right was attached (French, 2003).

The consequences of severing pasture rights from land could fracture the communal basis of use-rights on the common, with the result that a common might cease to 'belong' to the neighbouring resident community in any real sense. Severance paved the way to monopolization, enabling an individual to buy up stints to acquire a controlling share in the use-rights. In extreme cases, a common could cease to be common land in all but name and might be subject to a major change of use, as alternative management strategies were imposed. Instances of this can be seen in commons in the Pennine hills of northern England during the 19th and 20th centuries, when stints were bought up with a view to gaining control of the common in order to convert its prime purpose from communal pasture to heather moorland managed for the raising and shooting of grouse. Quantification of grazing rights could thus have far-reaching consequences through altering the legal conception of the right.

A second area in which a tendency towards privatization of rights over common land is visible was where local systems governing the exercise of common rights led to the allocation of a defined section of a common to an individual for a particular purpose. The legal orthodoxy was – and remains – that common pasture rights applied to the whole common, and not to limited areas of it (Gadsden, 1988, §4.30), yet the practice could be quite different. The spatial limitation of individual rights created an invisible web of boundaries – not physical enclosures, but acknowledged lines across the open wastes – dividing the common into sections used by different commoners. By gaining exclusive rights, a commoner might start to treat that section as private property. In Eskdale, for example, the allocation of parts of the common as cow pastures 'belonging' to individuals from the late 16th century enabled many tenants to enclose parts of the lower hillsides by 1700, converting them to private property and reducing the area of the common (see Chapter 6, p96). Presumably through collusion and the willingness of the lord of the manor to turn a blind eye to these encroachments, the allocation of defined areas of common land for individual use led to a partial privatization of the common resource. Comparable spatially defined use-rights were found widely in the hills of mid-Wales, where it had become the custom by the 18th century for each holding to have exclusive grazing rights for sheep over a section of the common, which was recognized as the 'sheepwalk' belonging to that holding (see Chapter 8, pp141–144). Exclusive use-rights and the precision with which it was possible to draw sheepwalk boundaries led to some being registered under the Commons Registration Act of 1965 as separate units of ownership, creating 'a series of sub-commons, each with one rights holder' in some areas (Gadsden, 1988, §3.108–3.112). Even where the practice of dividing the common into territories has not been deemed sufficient to give commoners a claim on the ownership of the soil itself, it evidently comprised more than a mere convenience, and points to a strong sense of customary property rights operating below the level of law. There is thus an important distinction to be drawn between tangible property rights which would stand before the law and a sense of ownership over a specific part of a common, which was no less real to those who held it but received no formal recognition in common law or in property rights.

Informal conceptions of 'ownership'

That distinction is equally true when considering the constituencies of people 'belonging' on common land, where, once again, customary interpretations and legal codes did not necessarily coincide. Formally, those with a legal interest in common land were the owners of the soil and the holders of legally recognized use-rights. Yet wider constituencies – whose influence has been integral to the history of common land – have claimed a sense of ownership over commons, despite falling outside the orthodox legal framework. They covered a broad spectrum, from local residents (particularly the poor), through marginal mobile groups, such as travellers, to the wider public of the nation at large.

The first area of uncertainty concerned the rights of the landless poor, significant numbers of whom lived in common-edge cottages, which had sprung up as squatter settlements in the population explosion of the 16th and early 17th centuries (Everitt, 2000, p218). Most use-rights were formally appurtenant – that is, attached to a holding of land; yet in many areas custom dictated that access to the resources of a common might belong to 'the inhabitants': in other words, by virtue of residence rather than landholding. These less formal conceptions of 'ownership' did not sit comfortably with the legal basis of use-rights on common land. The law attempted to exclude them, Gateward's case of 1607 ruling against rights claimed by inhabitancy (see Thompson, 1993, p130). Yet the concept of common rights by residence survived, and grazing rights belonging to landless cottagers in lowland England continued to be recorded in the 18th century (Neeson, 1993, pp61–62, 68–69; Shaw-Taylor, 2002, pp71–72). Women and children played an important but often hidden role as active commoners, relying on common land for grazing, fuel and materials rather than turning to charity or the poor law: it has been suggested that 'the widow and her cow were probably as common in reality as they are in fairy tales' (Humphries, 1990, p38).

In Norfolk some parish authorities actively sanctioned access to the resources of common land by the poor – particularly for fuel, but also for limited grazing – even where the paupers in question did not possess a formal entitlement (Birtles, 1999, pp83–86, 91–94). Informal custom, operating outside the law, was almost certainly more widespread. On the forest commons in Northamptonshire, cottagers assumed and exercised fuel-gathering and grazing rights, even though only a minority dwelt in common-right cottages. Furthermore, the resources of a common might be exploited by the poor as raw materials from which to make a livelihood – for example, 'furze' (i.e. gorse, *Ulex* species) as fuel for sale, rushes from which to weave mats, or medicinal herbs for sale to townspeople (Neeson, 1993, pp176–177; Everitt, 2000, pp216–217; Cowell, 2002, p151). As Steve Hindle (2003, p48) puts it, the poor were often 'agents in the fabrication of their own economy of makeshifts: inventing traditions where there were none, claiming rights by virtue of residence, manipulating custom in their own interest'. That wider body of informal custom and practice, lying beneath formal conceptions of common right, no doubt forged the link between common land and the poor which existed in the minds of many commentators. By the 17th century, marginal members of society were associated with land on the margin.

Local immemorial custom could also allow residents to collect seasonal resources from the common, such as vegetation, fruits and nuts, though structures of landownership and governance might not have recorded this activity or recognized it as a legal right. In Ashdown Forest a dispute arose during the years 1876 to 1882 between the landowners and local inhabitants concerning the cutting of litter. It was a conflict between perceptions of custom in the eyes of local communities living around the forest and legal conceptions in the eyes of the owners of the soil. The collecting of litter was seen by inhabitants 'as a tolerated custom' and formed part of the 'moral as well as economic ambience into which working people were born' (Short, 1999, p147). This is also exemplified in north Norfolk (see Chapter 9, pp170–171, 175–177), where the custom of gathering products such as samphire and sea lavender from the foreshore was sufficiently well established in communal memory and practice to be registered as a common right under the 1965 Commons Registration Act, despite receiving no mention in manor court records – and, indeed, being difficult to fit into any of the recognized categories of common right.

It is difficult to capture the meaning and significance of common land to many of the more informal or extra-legal groups because they have left little or no written trace. This is the area of custom which merges into the realm of 'unwritten beliefs, sociological norms, and usages asserted in practice but never enrolled in any by-law' (Thompson, 1993, p100). Occasionally, however, there are glimpses in oral statements taken down during lawsuits, or in testimony emerging from outside the formal bureaucracy. The oft-quoted words of the poet John Clare, expressing the personal sense of loss that enclosure could bring to those who knew a common well though having no legal right in it, record what Jeanette Neeson (1993, p11) has termed 'the breaking apart of customary relationships' in rural Northamptonshire. For Clare, recalling familiar places and features from the landscape of his childhood, enclosure was a 'lawless law', a phrase which neatly encapsulates the antagonism between different conceptions of law and belonging on common land (Summerfield, 1990, p171).

Lying on the margins of communities' territories and often traversed by roads and tracks, common land was the locus of encounters between resident and itinerant groups.

Not only did local inhabitants possess a sense of 'ownership' over common land, many commons were periodically occupied by groups such as travellers attending fairs, show people, and gipsy or Roma communities. Fairs, shows and circuses were a familiar sight on common land, particularly in or near urban centres, and were often of longstanding: the fair still held annually on Midsummer Common in Cambridge was first recorded in a 13th-century charter (Roach, 1959, p7; Bowden et al, 2009, pp74–75). While some fairs had the protection of charters or the weight of custom and popular feeling to support them, others lacked formal recognition and were not necessarily welcomed by landowners. In the early 19th century, the Earl of Bridgewater succeeded in preventing the use of Berkhamsted Common (Hertfordshire) as the venue for the Whitsun fair – 'a common fair since time immemorial' – threatening to bring charges of trespass against local residents, implying that their access onto the common was at his discretion (Cowell, 2002, p154). In the very different cultural climate of the mid 20th century, the Royal Commissioners on Common Land accepted in 1958 that commons had often been used as venues for fairs and amusement shows 'by ancient right or custom' and viewed their activities as mutually beneficial to both the public and the show community (Royal Commission, 1958, pp38, 105).

Attitudes to other itinerants, the gipsy and other travelling communities, hardened during the 19th and 20th centuries. In principle, they seem to differ little from the travelling fairs, who used the common intermittently with no strict 'legal interest' in the land; but it seems that itinerant groups were treated selectively and defined in terms that were implicitly or explicitly moral, and sometimes no doubt founded on prejudice. Gipsy and Roma communities were the target of 19th- and 20th-century by-laws, the very existence of which hints at the regularity and antiquity of their association with common land. By-laws for West Tilbury regulated commons, Essex, confirmed by the Home Secretary in 1895, expressly prohibited dwelling houses on wheels, tents, booths and circuses; the first draft drawn up by local conservators – which was not confirmed – had been even more detailed, prohibiting such activities as mending chairs, sorting rags, washing in the pool and singing sacred or secular songs. Similar by-laws from Skipwith common, Yorkshire, in 1906, included a prohibition on the paraphernalia associated with travellers, traders and fairs, such as huts, booths, platforms, roundabouts, swings, shooting galleries and aunt sallies.[2]

Reporting in 1958, the Royal Commission viewed travellers as a problem, questioning the extent to which they were 'genuine Romanies', the descendants of 'those who rejoiced in the "wind on the heath" over a hundred years ago' (Royal Commission, 1958, p38, para 106). They tended to group them with 'spivs', 'squatters' and 'vagrants', engaged in 'filching' and 'thieving', a discourse remarkably similar to that used by John Norden in the early 17th century. Discussing the commons of London and the Home Counties, Hoskins and Stamp (1963, p148) use a telling phrase when referring to 'The almost traditional use of [a common] as a gipsy encampment'. That the travellers' use is described as 'almost traditional' reveals a deep antipathy towards the longstanding nature of their occupation, the implication being that they were not quite traditional enough to count.

Stringent controls originally designed to exclude gipsies and Romanies, show people, traders and squatters could lead to unforeseen consequences as land uses and cultural attitudes changed. The conservators of Clent Hill, Worcestershire, amended their by-laws in 1922 because the rules established in 1880, prohibiting tents, booths, hirers of horses and so on, were affecting a nascent tourist trade by, for example, preventing local people from offering donkey rides to the rising numbers of 'artisan class' visitors from the Black Country.[3] Rapid socio-economic change could create new legal paradoxes on common land.

Beyond the uncertain boundaries which defined the limits of resident or itinerant communities' rights over common land lay a wider conception of interest in the commons, that of the nation or the public at large. Although not recognized in law until the battles over public access to common land in the mid 19th century, the notion that commons in a sense 'belonged' to all had a long history. Perhaps most famously, during the upheavals of the English Civil War, the 'Diggers' or 'True Levellers', led by Gerrard Winstanley, made a settlement on common land at Walton-on-Thames, Surrey, cultivating the soil and making shelters – a pattern that would spread to other commons in the south of England and the Midlands. The Diggers contested the legal orthodoxy of property rights, arguing that the removal of the monarchy had restored common lands to the people of the Commonwealth. In 1649, Winstanley and his colleagues appealed to the House of Commons to answer 'Whether the Common-people shall have the quiet enjoyment of the *Commons* and *Waste Lands*; Or whether they shall be under the will of *Lords* of *Manors* still.' The notion that common land belonged to the local community was made explicit in a Digger tract of 1650, explaining why 'the poor Inhabitants' of Iver (Bucks) had dug up the common 'belonging to the aforesaid Inhabitants' (Thomas, 1969, p61). The Diggers were thus attacking the 'Norman yoke' of manorial lordship, an impulse that can be interpreted as political and moral, but which also arose out of economic circumstance, the pressure on land and tensions provoked by squatter encroachments on common land: here again, the association between common land and the poor can be seen (Hill, 1973, pp26–31, 38–39, 111, 118–119; Thomas, 1969, p58). They were part of a wider upsurge in radical thinking and, though their direct action on common land died out, the notion that waste lands should be taken over by the state to be actively improved was earnestly proposed to parliament during the 1650s (Shannon, 2009, pp98–99). As a political movement, the Diggers were ahead of their time; but their very existence in the heady early days of the English republic demonstrates that perceptions of common land as public property existed in the 17th century.

From at least the early 19th century it was argued that the public at large had a moral right of access to common land not for food production or a place to live, but for open space, fresh air and recreation – elements that were considered of no less importance than food in the overcrowded and polluted industrial landscapes of 19th-century Britain. By the 1860s, the idea that the wider population had a moral right of access to common lands, either through long custom of recreation (tacitly accepted but not recognized in law) or through simple need, was seen to overrule traditional property rights. In an argument not dissimilar to Winstanley's in the mid 17th century, the preservation campaigner George Shaw Lefevre questioned the idea of 'absolute ownership of Lords of Manors in the waste lands of their districts', and argued for the restoration of a presumed pre-Norman community sense of ownership, akin to 'ancient Saxon folk land'. He went on to suggest that the interests of the public now outstripped those of both lords and commoners: common lands 'concern the people of the district, and the public generally, even more than the Lords of the Manors and their commoners' (Cowell, 2002, p157).

By the later 20th century a notion of public 'ownership' of common land had become so ingrained and durable that it gave rise to the popular misconception that common land is 'common' because it has always belonged to, or allowed access to, all peoples. As Paul Clayden (2003, p1) notes: 'Ask ten people in the street who owns common land, and nine will probably reply "the Queen", "no one" or "everyone".' For him, the wider public interest and sense of belonging can be read as a natural development from the traditional recreational uses of common land once made by local communities.

In summary, customary, informal and moral definitions of belonging have interacted with 'hard', formal legal definitions of property rights on common land for many centuries. Contests over the 'ownership' of common land often encompassed more than a legal battle concerning formal rights and included a wider political battle which centred on the conception that common land belonged to the common people (Allen, 1997, p65). On one level, the freehold ownership of common land is a straightforward legal question and those with property rights over it can also usually be established relatively easily. But seen from the perspective of local custom, the received legal understanding of common landownership could be described as a convenient narrative, sometimes verging on fiction, in an attempt to apply standard common law principles to complex customary interactions. Historical evidence points to an evolving and variable relationship between landownership and use-rights, in which custom played a major part. Without straying further than the four case studies described in Chapters 6 to 9, it is possible to find significant aspects of the 'ownership' of common land which do not sit easily with formal conceptions of property rights. The sheep heafs of Eskdale and the sheepwalks of mid-Wales represent longstanding allocations of exclusive use-rights to individual commoners, yet they could not be recognized under the terms of the Commons Registration Act 1965 and remain invisible in formal law. Conversely, the customary gathering rights on the Norfolk saltmarsh commons were registered under the 1965 Act, even though they do not fit easily into formal categories of use-rights. Such examples illustrate a more complex interplay of rights and conceptualizations of 'property' than can be comprehended by reference to the formal law of property alone.

Productivity and wilderness: The culture of the commons since circa 1860

What was common land for? For much of its history this question would perhaps seem redundant: common land was for the extraction of necessary resources in the form of food, fuel and other domestic and building materials. However, the multiple use-rights and the tensions between private and public senses of 'ownership' meant that it could signify different things to different groups at any given time. To commoners, common land might mean grazing for livestock and the provision of fuel – and perhaps the difference between survival and insolvency at the margins of production. To landowners, it might signify a place to exercise game rights, a potentially profitable source of minerals, timber and stone, together with prestige, status and power. To nearby inhabitants, the common might be a place to walk and play and to collect wild foods. In a more abstract context, common land has expressed a range of cultural ideas: a mythic landscape, a political metaphor, a utopian community.

Although common land was historically a landscape of production and extraction, the interplay between the pursuits of 'wilderness' and 'cultivation' runs as a theme through debates over common land since the mid 19th century. Within the formal property rights regime lay a tension between the lord's rights to wild game and commoners' rights to graze domestic livestock. On the grouse moors of the Pennines and other upland commons, landowners have sought since the late 18th century to create a managed wilderness in order to harness a wild species for sport, a process which has involved modification of the landscape (Done and Muir, 2001). Although the quarry was ostensibly wild, certain types or densities of vegetation suited gamebird species more than others, and the cultivation of game habitats could bring graziers and hunters into direct conflict, as occurred in Eskdale in the 19th century, and on Ingleborough in the 20th century (see Chapters 6 and 7, pp92, 122). The historic tension between the role of common land as a source of wild game for the landowner and a resource for domestic livestock and materials for commoners is still evident today on grouse moor commons (Natural England, 2008a, ppxxxiii, xliv), and is paralleled elsewhere in the desire to create favourable conditions for wild species for conservation purposes rather than for sport.

For much of its modern history, the overriding question was not whether common land should produce agrarian or extractable goods in the form of food, fuel, minerals, materials and game, but, rather, how far that productivity could be improved, by whom, and by what means. This was the overarching discourse of the era of 'improvement' and parliamentary enclosure. Yet, that period of intense agrarian activity and enclosure contained within it a paradox. Even as enclosure commissioners were laying out new field boundaries, the wild and rugged unfenced prospects of the wastes were becoming the sublime object of writers, artists and, increasingly, tourists. It is tempting to see a direct causal relationship, the widespread loss of commons stimulating a new aesthetic appreciation of open landscapes. Keith Thomas suggested that this 'ability to derive pleasure from scenes of relative desolation represented a major change in human perception' which rested, ultimately, on having achieved a stable and sufficient supply of food from the cultivated lands: 'Only when the threat of starvation receded could such an attitude prevail' (Thomas, 1983, p264). In urban areas, commons often played a dual role as agrarian pasture and unofficial recreation ground: the era of improvement saw the conversion of some urban commons into formal public parks with 'improved' landscaped vistas, arboretums, promenades and carriage drives (Bowden et al, 2009, pp57–60). It was a period of contradictory land-use policies: the general Inclosure Act of 1845 expected enclosure commissioners to consider the need for recreation grounds and allotments for the poor; but the lack of actual provision made for the public was later described as 'most inadequate' and a 'great scandal' (Shaw-Lefevre, 1894, p275). Certainly, the popular interest in common land was moving beyond mere resource extraction, and as the acreage of unenclosed land diminished with each annual enclosure bill, campaigners began a concerted effort to preserve the remainder.

The influential Commons Preservation Society was launched in 1865, and the Metropolitan Commons Act 1866 followed, giving greater protection to commons lying within London's Metropolitan Police District and making provision for management mechanisms, such as boards of conservators. But pressure to preserve access was building beyond the metropolis: in 1866, the Commons Preservation Society employed over 100 men to remove the fencing on Berkhamsted Common (Hertfordshire), erected by the lord of the manor, which prevented commoners and members of the wider community from gaining access to parts of the common for resources and recreation. The change in public opinion was making enclosure increasingly difficult to justify at national level, and in 1869, the House of Commons Select Committee on the Inclosure Act called a temporary halt to the enclosure commissioners' work. Court battles against the enclosure of numerous individual commons followed and subsequent legislation, such as the Commons Acts of 1876 and 1899, was primarily aimed at regulation and preservation of commons rather than wholesale enclosure. Local acts of parliament, such as the New Forest Act of 1877 and the Malvern Hills Act of 1884, sought to achieve the twin aims of preserving common rights and providing recreational access for the public at large (Cowell, 2002; Hurle, 2007, pp125–126; Straughton, 2008, pp33–68).

Thus, in a remarkable cultural shift, by the end of the 19th century, common land had acquired a new function and identity as a public or civic space, a place for recreation and respite for the masses, in both urban and rural environments. In 1897, Robert Hunter, a prominent common land preservation campaigner and one of the founders of the National Trust, summed up the importance of commons in and around the crowded London environment, describing them as 'a play ground for the greatest aggregation of human beings the world has ever seen'. He argued that 30 years of campaigning to preserve surviving commons had been 'a very potent factor in the maintenance of the health – not only of the bodily, but of the mental, I might almost say the spiritual, health – of the town population' (Hunter, 1897, pp392, 403). The subsequent purchase or receipt of large acreages of rural common land by the National Trust – for which specific provision was made in the National Trust Act, 1907[4] – underlined the importance of open spaces to the public. Agrarian landscapes, subject to private property rights, could also be iconic public spaces and, hence, be transformed into 'national' property. A significant step in the process was taken by the Law of Property Act 1925, which gave public access to metropolitan commons and commons lying wholly or partly within urban district areas. One consequence of the latter provision was to secure public access to parts of the central Lake District fells, which lay within the Lakes Urban District, though a general right of public access to common land was not achieved until the Countryside and Rights of Way Act 2000.

If public access seemed to promise the wholesale preservation of commons, pressures for more utilitarian uses in the 19th and 20th centuries suggest an alternative conception of common land as public property. Commons were still often perceived as 'uncommitted' land which could be committed to a new purpose or emergency. Upland common lands might be prime sites for water gathering grounds, reservoirs, forestry or military training areas (Hoskins and Stamp, 1963, pp83–85; Bowden et al, 2009, pp41–55; Ritvo, 2009; and see Chapter 8). But this was a divisive issue: was the national interest in defence, water supplies and timber, or in agriculture, landscape preservation and the more intangible spiritual and aesthetic aspects of landscape? Two World Wars consolidated the use of common land as military spaces or emergency development zones. The military legacy is often still in evidence, whether in major long-term installations such as those at Greenham Common or Fylingdales Moor, or in minor structures surviving as gaunt concrete remains from World War II, such as the coastal radar station on Barrow Common, near Brancaster, which took advantage of the common's hilltop location to patrol the Norfolk coast. Some, such as extensive parts of Dartmoor, remain militarized spaces today, serving as firing ranges and training grounds. Urban commons, in particular, although highly valued as green spaces, were nevertheless subject to multiple uses and pressures in an expanding built environment, providing space for new housing, workhouses, prisons, hospitals, barracks, cemeteries, railways, reservoirs, sewage works and rubbish tips, among other civic incursions (Bowden et al, 2009, pp41–43, 56–57).

By the middle of the 20th century there was a growing sense of uncertainty surrounding property rights to common land, compromising schemes for improvement and change in use. In 1955, the Royal Commission on Common Land was established to enquire into the use, status and law of commons, its membership including the landscape historian W. G. Hoskins and the architect of the Land Utilisation Survey, L. Dudley Stamp. The commission concluded that there was continuing confusion over common landownership and rights (the exact acreage of common land in England and Wales was still unknown); that statute law was largely inadequate in helping landowners and commoners in the management of common land; and that many commons were suffering an institutional vacuum since the fading of traditional governance through manorial courts. They pointed to a continuing need for agrarian improvement on common land; but this was expected to coexist with the new ideals of landscape preservation, recreation and – increasingly – wildlife conservation. The commission moved the debate further in the direction of public access, turning on a modern understanding of what common land was for and who belonged on it: a right of public access was one of the commission's key recommendations for the future of common land. The commission called for a register of all surviving common lands and rights, provisions for schemes of management and a statutory right of public access – thereby giving formal recognition to a transformation in property rights and cultural attitudes (Royal Commission, 1958, pp129–131). Although the recommendations concerning access and management were not realized until the 21st century, the commission's call for a common land register led directly to the formalization of property rights effected by the Commons Registration Act 1965 (see Chapter 4, pp54–57).

Conclusions

On common land, possibly more than any other category of land, ideas of private and public space, productivity and wilderness, custom and law have existed in a dynamic interaction since the medieval period. Paradoxically, the dangerous and disorderly 'wild land' beyond the reaches of cultivation has come to be celebrated and identified as the most valuable of landscapes, highly prized as a place where the public can walk and play, and a reserve of native flora and fauna that have been lost on more intensively cultivated ground. Although most commons are not truly wild or totally given over to nature, many today fulfil an important role as being at least symbolic of such places, of being an approximation to wilderness in a landscape of intensive farming and crowded built environments. As liminal spaces, they have since 1600 attracted ideals and idealists, while notions of 'ownership' have been subject to misconceptions and the reinvention of tradition.

In attempting to recapture the place of common land in the lives and minds of past generations, it is necessary to look beyond the confines of the legal literature. The social reality, built on custom and pragmatism and varying according to the character of the local environment, might be rather different from what legal treatises and statutes suggest. The framework of property rights determined who, in law, could and could not use the land; but in practice this has been regularly subverted, ignored or actively contested. The Diggers questioned the authority of 'old Norman laws' in a world turned upside down, and John Clare defined enclosure as a 'lawless law'. In his pursuit of free public access to common land, Shaw Lefevre questioned the relevance of manorial property rights in a modern world. Property rights in common land may be conceived of as cultural conveniences, which have been given varying degrees of credence and importance at different times and by different people. An individual's or group's interest in common land might not be questioned or considered relevant for substantial lengths of time – graziers might use their sheepwalks without questions of ownership arising, or villagers might walk across or play games on common land entirely undisturbed – until a change in circumstances brought matters to the fore. In the context of an enclosure award or improvement scheme, or a statute such as the Commons Registration Act 1965, it became necessary to codify interests in a defined area of land and to enforce hardened rules of exclusion and inclusion. But in whose interests might this be done, and to what end? Did the legal settlement accurately reflect what had gone before? This does not mean that the law always works in favour of the more powerful levels of landowner or state. It seems likely that foreshore rights in north Norfolk (see Chapter 9, pp170–171) were not, strictly speaking, legally recognized common rights before registration; but it suited the local community to register them as such, thereby recording, preserving and, in the process, redefining their customary practices. Property rights have become hardened since the era of enclosure, and even more so in the wake of the Commons Registration Act 1965, but custom and subversion have continued nevertheless. It is against this backdrop of a complex cultural history of 'ownership' that the management of common land and changing notions of sustainability since 1600 must be viewed.

Notes

1 41 Geo. 3, c. 109, s. XIII; 6 & 7 Will. 4, c. 115, s. XXVII; 8 & 9 Vict., c. 118.
2 PRO, HO 45/10457/B18343/1-4; HO 45/10316/126241/9.
3 PRO, HO 45/11466.
4 7 Edw. VII, c. 136, sec. 29, 36–7.

3

'That our common moore be not wronged': Sustainable Land Management in a Historical Context

Literature on the management of commons over the past 20 years has seen a productive cross-fertilization between historians and scholars working on contemporary common pool resources (CPRs). In the search for examples of sustainable management institutions, CPR researchers often look to the past for evidence and experience that may inform the present (e.g. Ostrom, 1990, pp58–88). Conversely, historians have used Elinor Ostrom's CPR design principles as a framework for analysing governance systems in the past (e.g. Fleming, 1998; Winchester, 2000; De Moor et al, 2002; Straughton, 2008). Enduring management regimes were a feature of commons across Europe from the medieval period until the mid 19th century and, in some cases, beyond: a recent survey concluded that few regions in Europe 'did not fulfil most of the criteria laid down by Ostrom for long-enduring, self-managed commons'. Universal features included quantitative limitations and seasonal restrictions on resource exploitation, monitoring systems, and a scale of penalties against those who broke the rules (De Moor et al, 2002, pp250–251). Management systems governing common land in England and Wales were no exception.

Since common land supplied necessary agrarian and domestic products which underpinned a community's economic stability, sustaining the resources of a common was the underlying objective of governance systems. When exploring past management of common land, it is helpful to bear in mind the three interconnected facets of sustainability: economic, environmental and equitable (above, pp13–14; Turner et al, 2003, pp126–127). Environmental sustainability for its own sake is essentially a modern concept and is very rarely mentioned explicitly in historical sources. Nor is congruence between past management and ecological benefit necessarily clear cut. On the one hand, environmental sustainability is often implied in measures taken to promote economic sustainability: it goes without saying, for example, that livestock would provide a greater return from a fertile pasture than from an exhausted one. On the other hand, the careful management of a resource might cease as a community's use for it waned (as occurred with bracken and gorse in the late 19th and 20th centuries), regardless of the ecological consequences. Even actions which seem directed towards environmental sustainability can also be interpreted as examples of 'efficiency' or 'risk-sharing' (De Moor et al, 2002, p250). A common was, ultimately, a complex matrix of material resources, which fluctuated in importance over time. It is therefore important to view sustainability in a historical context as a dynamic process, a continuous cycle of changing pressures and responses, rather than an attempt to maintain a particular ecological balance.

Any exploration of sustainability in a historical context is thus faced with challenges of interpreting evidence and identifying the motives of past generations. Unable to observe day-to-day practice or to measure the direct impact of a particular management tool or decision, historians cannot be sure whether commoners were consciously acting to sustain their resource, or whether they succeeded. But this does not mean that the past is out of bounds. The existence of institutions of governance and of management tools is evidence both of a desire to sustain a resource and of the means to do so. The language of regulations and customary rules also has much to tell: positive terms, such as managing a resource in a 'husband-like manner', and negative terms, such as 'overcharging' or 'over-pressing' the common, shed light on the thinking behind management systems. The following discussion takes a long time-depth, from the 16th century to the mid 20th century, to reveal the complex reality of rule-making and enforcement, and to identify theoretical questions that may help to see contemporary sustainability in a more nuanced light. The past does not present a blueprint for the future; rather, the historical evidence provides a rich source of experience and evidence, which can inform contemporary discussions of common land management.

'Good neighbourhood' and sustainability

As we saw in Chapter 2, the customary concept of 'good neighbourhood', which underpinned agrarian life in the early modern period, meant the maintenance of peaceable relations between neighbours who relied on a range of finite, and potentially exhaustible, resources. 'Good neighbourhood' was not an unchanging state of harmony, but rather an ideal standard of community relations which needed to be constantly redefined and reinstated as social-ecological conditions changed. Users grappled with perennial temptations which might threaten both the resource and social cohesion (Ostrom, 2005, p288). In the pursuit of 'good neighbourhood' on common land, three main underlying drivers can be identified: first, the need to sustain a physical resource so that it could continue to provide food and materials for rights holders; second, the need for just and equitable access to minimize resentment and preserve cohesion; and, third, the need to negotiate and balance conflicting demands.

Sustaining the resource

Historical records provide evidence of an implicit awareness of the potential loss of a resource and a desire to take action to preserve it. This is perhaps most obvious in the litany of presentments in manor courts against individuals accused of 'overcharging' or 'over-pressing' a common by grazing more animals than they were entitled to. The infringement was at its heart a legal one, relating to the abuse of property rights; it may not have resulted in any obvious destruction of the pasture. Yet the language of the court records suggests an additional dimension: it is often labelled as a 'wrong' done to the common, an offence against custom, or an offence against fellow commoners, factors which have an obviously social dimension and emphasize the sustaining of 'custom' itself. Entries in the record of the manor court of Eskdale (Cumbria) provide a vivid illustration of this theme. Grazing rights were limited by 'our Antient Custome' (as it was put in 1679), which was built on the rule of levancy and couchancy. Buying in supplementary winter feed was forbidden; therefore, when a commoner bought hay and brought it into the manor in 1720, the result was 'to oppresse his neighbours' – the core of the offence being that he gained an unfair advantage over other commoners by boosting the number of stock he could over-winter and thus graze on the common in summer. It is in this light that an order of 1694 should be seen. This required each man's stock to be counted in winter, so that 'our Comon moore be not wronged and our Customes not abused'; a similar order of 1701 was made so that 'our Comon be not overcharged'.[1] The idea that common land could be 'wronged' strongly suggests a concept of sustainability extending beyond the mere policing of property rights.

Similar conceptions of good stewardship (and its antithesis: poor stewardship) are encountered in manor court orders and presentments concerning other common rights. Those exercising turbary rights were expected to dig peat in a 'husband-like' manner, ensuring that worked-out turbaries were not waterlogged and that the vegetated sod was replaced: they were to 'bedd, cover and levell again' the bottom of their peat diggings, as it was put in an order from Clapham (Yorkshire) in 1704.[2] A similar concern over environmental impact in the same area of Yorkshire is found in attempts to limit physical damage to the surface of common lands through the removal of soil and turf. Again, the language of manor court records suggest a clear conception of sustainability: 'Great abuses and much damage', 'injuring the surface of the Common', a 'great Injury' done to the common, 'destroying the herbage'. All indicate a direct concern for the physical condition of the common.[3]

More generally, an awareness of the potential impact of environmental damage on the local economy is found in regions as different as the Lake District mountains and the Cambridgeshire fens. Orders aiming to prevent the loss of grazing and the danger posed to livestock through the flooding or erosion of upland peat diggings, or the drowning of fen pastures through failure to maintain banks and drainage ditches, or through poaching by the hooves of livestock show local management regimes seeking to foster beneficial environmental practice for the common (economic) good (Winchester, 2000, p132; Ravensdale, 1974, pp64–68). From these appeals to good husbandry and warnings against abuse, damage and injury to the land, it is evident that good land stewardship was a vital component of 'good neighbourhood'. Nevertheless, the reason the cases cited above were brought before the court lay ultimately not in the ecological damage that had been caused but in the impact of the actions of individuals upon the interests of others. Environmental concerns were embedded within a socio-economic context, and, as such, ecological issues cannot be easily separated from concerns about economic value, equitable access and harmonious relationships within the community.

Equitable access

Good neighbourly relations were more likely to be maintained in conditions perceived to be fair and equitable; consequently, the rules established by the manor courts aimed primarily to achieve equitable access to resources for the commoning community. If a commoner encroached on a neighbour's sheep walk, or dug peat in a neighbour's designated peat digging, or took more gorse than was needed by their household (thus depriving others of their share), then he or she was in breach of this principle. As we have seen, overstocking by one individual was usually expressed as an offence against fellow commoners rather than in terms of explicit ecological harm.

Equitable access did not, of course, mean that each member of the community had the same level of access to a resource: access was determined primarily not by a modern notion of social justice but by proportionality based on property rights and ancient custom. At the root of concepts of equitable access invariably lay the legal notion of 'necessary use'. Where rights were attached to land, they were only to be used in support of the 'dominant tenement', the holding of land to which they belonged. Produce from the common was not to be sold or taken out of the manor and there was a presumption that the quantity of the resource which could be taken should be limited to what was deemed necessary. This was explicit in the case of the common right of estovers, (a term derived ultimately from the Latin *est opus*: 'it is necessary') and was implicit in other rights. It was articulated by the author of *The Law of Commons and Commoners*, published in 1720, whose starting point was that tenants required access to the resources needed to enable them to pay rent and perform services. They could not do this without cattle; cattle required pasture; therefore it was necessary for them to feed their cattle on the manor's waste. Likewise, tenants could not live without fire; therefore it was necessary for them to have access to fuel (Anon, 1720, pp6–7). But that was the limit of their right: a commoner, for example, could not exercise his turbary right in order to dig peat for sale to fuel-hungry townspeople nearby.

Custom often lay at the heart of access to common land by the landless poor, as was seen in Chapter 2. In some areas, the resources of the commons were seen as vital to the poor – hence the role of custom in many lowland manors in upholding access to fuel resources, particularly gorse, for the poor (as in Norfolk; see Chapter 9, pp171–172). Elsewhere, manor court juries, often composed of the wealthier tenants, sometimes sought to marginalize the poor by placing closer restrictions on landless cottagers than on their landed neighbours. This was particularly evident in relation to turbary rights on upland commons, where cottagers were frequently restricted in the amount of fuel they were allowed to cut, or the part of the common on which they could cut it (Dilley, 1991, p317; Winchester, 2000, pp129–133). Orders which prioritized the rights of the landed over those of the landless had the effect of restricting the use-rights of one section of local society. What equitable access meant, in practice, was thus determined by local custom, refining the underlying principles of property rights and leading to variations between localities.

Balancing conflicting demands

Common land has long been a multifunctional resource, where the interests of different user-groups, whether they are in livestock, fuel, materials, game or, more recently, recreation, might make it a site of contest. There was an inherent conflict between the interest of the lord of the manor in exploiting his ownership of the soil and the use-rights of his tenants, while within the community of commoners there was tension between individual self-interest and the communal good. The right to extract one resource had the potential to conflict with another, even though both were entirely legitimate: for example, breaking the soil for minerals, peat, turves, soil or quarry stone had the potential to reduce the area of grassland for grazing livestock. In other cases, legitimate right holders might be in competition for a single resource. Bracken (*Pteridium aquilinum*) provides the most striking example of a single resource with multiple conflicting uses, and therefore requires careful management. The plant had three principal uses in the early modern period: it was used as litter for livestock and as a thatching material for roofing. In both cases, these were 'necessary uses' for the support of the house and land to which the right was attached. But bracken was also exploited commercially by burning it into potash for sale. Although not a 'necessary use' – and thus, strictly speaking, not a valid use of a common right of estovers – the burning of bracken was accepted and was widespread, particularly in the 17th and 18th centuries (Winchester, 2006). The dilemma at the heart of the governance rules applied to common land was that the resources it yielded were subject to an array of conflicting and sometimes incompatible demands and interests, most of which were founded on entirely legitimate property rights. Seen in the abstract, such rights would seem to spell ecological disaster for any given land area. In practice, however, competing rights were understood and exercised within the context of careful mediation, rule-making and monitoring by grassroots management institutions, which might modulate and even override legal interests, if necessary.

Regulation

Local institutions

Before the 19th century, the key institutions in regulating the exercise of use-rights on common land in England and Wales were local seigniorial courts, to which the shorthand term 'manor courts' may be applied. These were local meetings, called by the lord of the manor and presided over by his steward, which those holding land in the manor were required to attend. Decisions were taken by a jury composed of tenants of the manor, their deliberations grounded in the concept of 'the custom of the manor', which governed tenures, land transfers and inheritance, and litigation between tenants (Bonfield, 1996; Poos and Bonfield, 1998). Customary law was formulated in by-laws and orders which sought to maintain order within the manorial community and to foster 'good neighbourhood'. Maintaining good order included overseeing the management of common land, and negotiating a way through the tensions between the conflicting demands of different uses and interests which were a perennial feature of its history. Manor court by-laws and 'presentments' of offenders against local customary law provide a rich body of historical evidence for the management of common land from the medieval period to the 19th century (Ault, 1965; Dilley, 1967; Winchester, 2000) – examples of the evidence they yield are given in the case studies of Eskdale and Brancaster, pp94–97, 171–173 in this work).

But it is often necessary to delve behind the formal records of manor courts in order to locate the wellspring of local custom. The manor did not always coincide with the unit of agrarian organization (a village might be divided between two manors, or a manor might embrace several villages), so the roots of decision-making often lay elsewhere than the manor court. Non-manorial village meetings are recorded in midland open-field England during the later medieval centuries. Manor court records use phrases such as 'the common ordinance of the whole township' and 'by the common consent of all the neighbours', implying that the village community might act separately from the manor, even if regulations were subsequently recorded by the manor court (Ault, 1960; 1965, pp40–54). Indeed, manor courts sometimes devolved the power to make day-to-day orders to officials, as, for example, at Cononley (Yorkshire West Riding) in the early 17th century, when 'bylaw men' were appointed each year to govern the township's open fields and were required to bring their orders to the court (Gulliver, 2007, pp23, 30–31). In much of upland northern England, where manors were frequently large overarching units covering several settlements, there is evidence of informal local decision-making by groups of farmers at grassroots level through a body known as the 'byrlaw' (or a variant, such as 'burlaw' or 'bireley'), which appears to have had its roots as a folk institution, originally separate from the seigniorial courts (Winchester, 2000, pp42–45; 2008). The body of customary law governing the use of common land thus probably evolved orally through local meetings of villagers long before being recorded in the records of the manor courts.

The efficacy and longevity of manor courts varied greatly between individual manors; but manorial activity tended to diminish nationally across the 18th century, with a widespread collapse by the end of the 19th century (Dilley, 1967, pp130–132; Straughton, 2008, pp124–134). The failure or collapse of the manor courts had complex causes. Weak and inefficient manorial administration played a part, particularly as customary tenures declined in the face of leasing or enfranchisement and the courts lost their role as registers of tenancies. In Cumbria during the 18th century, a spiral of collapse in manor court control over common land has been identified. Confidence in the courts ebbed away, turning comparatively quickly into contempt and a refusal to accept the regulations that they imposed. As a result of this collapse, severe problems of overgrazing on the commons paved the way for enclosure and privatization (Searle, 1993, pp135–144, 149; Straughton, 2008, pp124–160). But even where courts continued to be held, their records often grow silent on agrarian matters, suggesting that active formulation of by-laws and the effective policing of rules ceased. One consequence of the fading of the manor courts was that, on many commons, the historical evidence for land use and management dies away some time before the 20th century. The final death-knell of most manor courts was sounded by the Law of Property Act 1922, which abolished copyhold and customary tenancies, and was seen to remove any residual incentive for the lord of the manor to call regular courts (Royal Commission, 1958, pp46–47).

In a context of inactive or fading courts, many commons in England and Wales entered a new era without a formal management body, though informal recourse to custom may often have continued, even if largely undocumented. In some cases, however, alternative management bodies emerged. Parish councils occasionally assumed responsibility for commons within their boundaries. Statutory mechanisms for enclosure or regulation also provided a means to adapt property rights (e.g. through stinting) and to restructure land management (Straughton, 2008, pp165–169, 192). For example, where an enclosure award was directed towards stinting (rather than fencing) of a pasture, this might be accompanied by the establishment of a stint-holders' management committee, as at Thornham in 1797 (see Chapter 9, pp173–174). From the 1860s onwards, legislation was often directed towards regulation in support of preservation and recreation, rather than enclosure, and commons and forests that were subject to individual regulatory acts, or which came within the terms of the Metropolitan Commons Act 1866, were given new management structures and bodies. In addition, between 1879 and 1919 some 36 commons in England and Wales were regulated under the Commons Act 1876, from semi-urban commons and popular beauty spots to vast upland pastures stretching over thousands of acres. On regulated commons, boards of elected 'conservators' were given powers to make by-laws, sanctioned by the Home Office, but this process was not without controversy, as commoners and officials disagreed over whether the central object of by-laws was agrarian management or public order (Straughton 2008, pp204–241). In 1899, a new Commons Act introduced mechanisms for district and parish councils to regulate and manage common land; again, this was aimed primarily at those commons which had civic, recreational value rather than agrarian uses. Some 200 commons were placed under provisions or schemes of regulations under the 1899 Act.[4] The Commons Act 1908 did make provision for agrarian management, but for a highly specific function: to control the turning out of entire animals onto common land. Only the recent Commons Act 2006 provides comprehensive legislation designed to assist management with 'statutory commons councils' (see Chapter 5).

Alternatively, commoners and landowners established grassroots associations or meetings, which did not have the legal powers of statutory bodies, but might carry with them the continuing weight of custom and locally derived authority. Some can be traced back to the 19th century: for example, an association of stintholders and a 'management committee' were established to govern the Solway marshes at Burgh-by-Sands (Cumbria) in 1838, a decade before an enclosure award set up a formal stintholders' committee.[5] Similar grassroots bodies were found in the stinted pastures of the Pennines, such as those in the Ingleton area, where records of annual meetings of a stintholders' committee for Scales Moor survive from 1884, and for Ingleborough from 1927 (see Chapter 7, pp119–121). Informal commoners' associations proliferated in the late 20th century, particularly in response to the need to organize the registration of rights under the Commons Registration Act 1965 and to coordinate involvement in later agri-environment schemes. However, whereas manor court rules were legally binding, those made by commoners' associations had no legal status and depended on informal acceptance by those holding rights.

Taking the long view, a persistent theme in the governance of common land in England since the medieval period is the role of local, often informal, grassroots bodies. In the hey-day of the manor courts, decisions taken at village meetings in lowland England or hamlet 'byrlaws' in the north lay behind the formal proceedings of the seigniorial court. Their existence and the tradition of self-governance they imply perhaps paved the way for the informal local bodies which succeeded the manor courts. The trajectory of change in the process by which commoners and landowners moved from traditional manorial court management towards a new institutional framework has been complex. The timescale and nature of these institutional changes has varied from common to common, in some cases resulting in a temporary lapse or permanent absence of formal management bodies; in others leading to the emergence of a specialist single-issue institution, such as a commoners' association or stint-holders' committee. Some of the post-manorial institutions were founded on a statutory model, others on more informal, locally derived structures.

Rule-making

In Ostrom's estimation, good management of commons requires a combination of social norms of reciprocity and trust, and of rules of a more formal legal character (Ostrom, 2005, pp287–288). How, then, did the local (often informal) bodies which oversaw the management of common land in England and Wales go about formulating rules that were 'fair, effective and legitimate'? The corpus of customary rules recorded by manor courts, either explicitly in the form of orders and by-laws or implicitly in the wording of presentments against offenders, dates largely from the 16th and 17th centuries, when the courts enjoyed a flowering, (Harrison, 1997; Winchester, 2000, pp33–42). Published examples of manor court by-laws (see, for example, Cunningham, 1910; Hallam, 1963; Ault, 1965; Winchester, 2000, pp152–175) show the courts seeking to uphold 'good neighbourhood' in the use of common land by putting in place systems of regulation to govern such mundane practical matters as herding practices, the marking of livestock, and the gathering of vegetation and other resources. The by-laws are usually regarded as indigenous systems of governance, tailored to fit local circumstance and thus fulfilling key aspects of the design principles for sustainable management of CPRs proposed by Ostrom (see Box 1.1, p12).

However, external influences also played a part in fashioning local customary law. First, it is clear that the wider folk culture of the countryside, extending beyond the shores of Britain to other regions of north-west Europe, contributed a body of common custom, resulting in the repetition of a core of agrarian regulations across many communities. The exclusion of infectious livestock from the common; the requirement that pigs should be kept ringed to prevent them from grubbing and, often, 'bowed' or 'yoked' to prevent them breaking through hedges; rules to prevent loose livestock from damaging crops; rules controlling rams on the common – these and other regulations are repeated regularly in manor court records and show that different communities met the challenges of managing the use of common land by formulating similar regulations (Winchester, 2008).

Then there was the interplay between custom, whether local or more general, and statute. In the mid 16th century, courts leet were given specific statutory responsibilities and powers relating to the management of common resources. For example, the Act Concerning the Breeding of Horses 1540, laid down a minimum size for stallions put to graze on commons in order to preserve and enhance the quality of horses. It also forbade the putting of diseased horses on common land. Presentments and reiterations of by-laws concerning these topics in manor court records after 1540 can be interpreted as absorbing statutory responsibility into the body of local law. However, the story is more complex than that: there are good grounds for thinking that the statute was incorporated into formal law regulations which were already part of local custom. The statutory requirement to keep scabbed horses off the common had a long history before 1540; so did the desire to prevent poor-quality stallions from breeding: late-medieval orders from Fountains Abbey's estates in Yorkshire required that only stallions above a specified minimum value could be put to the common (Winchester, 2000, p103). The interplay between local custom and statutory control of common land is a central theme in the later history of English commons, but it appears to have been complex even in the 16th century.

A third external influence on local customary law lay in the machinery of manorial administration, specifically the role of the officers of the manor court. Many of the lists of by-laws which proliferated across the 17th century appear to represent an active attempt to capture the body of customary law by collecting and writing down the 'ancient pains' which governed the deliberations of the manor court. Two examples from Cumberland illustrate what was almost certainly a widespread process. The surviving 'pain' list from the manor of Isel in 1662 is prefaced by a statement by the jury confirming 'these paines and amerciaments followinge (among many others) to have been anciently used time out of minde'; and the same 53 pains were ratified in 1688 as the 'antient paines Bylawes & Orders belonging to this Mannor'.[6] This was a careful selection of local law, formally recorded and confirmed, and signed on both occasions by the full manor court jury and local gentlemen. A similar process is visible on the Aglionby family's estates near Carlisle, where the hand of the steward was much in evidence. In 1683 the steward prepared a volume of by-laws containing abstracts of orders and presentments recorded in court rolls since the early 16th century, followed by a list of orders and by-laws 'collected out of ancient court-rolls' in 1641 by the then steward and a draft memorandum confirming these in 1683.[7] Elsewhere, the repetition of almost identical regulations across several manors on a single estate strongly suggest the hand of a manorial administrator (Fraser and Emsley, 1977, pp111–118; 1986, pp154–163; Robinson 1990, pp182–189). These various expressions of the influence of estate stewards suggest a growing professionalization in the running of the manor courts. We can imagine that the power of the printed word would tend to privilege the court-keeping manual over local custom and oral tradition in framing the deliberations of the courts, moving by-law-making one step away from the grassroots.

The by-laws recorded by manor courts in the 16th and 17th centuries were thus the result of a complex interplay between custom, grassroots decision-making and wider culture. At one level these were, indeed, statements of local law, grounded in the need to provide local responses to particular social, economic and environmental challenges. But they should not be viewed in isolation: they were framed within a wider body of common agrarian custom and a clear context of common law, reaching back to the 13th century, if not before. They can only be fully understood in the light of contemporary developments: the role of statute; the growth of the legal profession and the development of legal process; and changing attitudes to land among the landowning classes and their stewards, as the dominant paradigm shifted from 'ancient custom' towards 'improvement'.

As traditional management institutions faded or were replaced, so the rules they issued underwent processes of adaptation and change. Nevertheless, locally devised modern by-laws and rules might borrow from custom, and do not necessarily suggest a complete break with the past. For example, the 'Fell Rules' setting out grazing regulations, issued by Eskdale Commoners' Association in 1980, clearly belong to a long tradition of customary rule-making and by-laws on common land in Eskdale, and can be seen as a modern version of rules created some four centuries earlier in a manor court award of 1587 (see Chapter 6, p101). Local management bodies might also attempt to draw down external powers to help solve local problems, as when graziers on commons regulated under the Commons Act 1876 drafted new agrarian by-laws, even though these were sometimes rejected by the Home Office (Straughton, 2008, pp204–217).

Trial and error in 'the laboratory of experience over the generations' (Turner et al, 2003, p126) presumably played a major part in arriving at sustainable practices on common land. Yet we must not fall into the trap of seeing traditional rules as inherently sustainable or inevitably more successful than centrally designed solutions. For example, the traditional rule of levancy and couchancy, though pivotal for maintaining equitable access to the common, did not take account of the carrying capacity of the common pasture itself. More generally, when courts spelled out their rules in writing, it is not always possible to distinguish between those that comprised a rather empty rehearsal of custom (which might be widely ignored), and those that were actively chosen to have impact. And lest we should assume that manor courts and associations were a benign influence, and an inherent 'good', we should also remember that they were only as fair and effective as the individuals who operated them.

Enforcement

The systems of policing these local regulations and the scales of penalties imposed on those who broke them are further examples of congruence between the historic grassroots governance of common land in England and Wales and the design principles proposed by Elinor Ostrom (see Box 1.1, p12). Manor courts appointed officers to monitor the exercise of common rights and to bring offenders against by-law to court. Fixed financial penalties were attached to each regulation, the size of the 'amercement' (fine) reflecting the seriousness of the offence.

A range of practice is encountered in the appointment of monitors. In northern England manor courts often appointed 'burlawmen' or 'barleymen', usually four in number, forming a small committee to oversee compliance with local by-laws. Alternatively, or in addition, courts might appoint officers with responsibility for specific aspects of communal life: pounders (responsible for impounding stray livestock), 'hedge-lookers' (to ensure that field boundaries were maintained) and 'moss reeves' (to supervise the peat mosses) (Winchester, 2000, p45). In the Cambridgeshire fens a committee of 'fen reeves' oversaw common rights (Ravensdale, 1974, pp67–68). It seems possible that, over time, as the manor courts declined, the role of officers such as these grew in importance. In the fens, the fen reeves continued to function as the primary repository of regulatory authority into the 19th century. In some northern manors, including Eskdale, the appointment of officers outlived evidence of active management of common land by the manor courts: orders and amercements fell away, yet officers continued to be appointed. What is less clear is whether, without the active backing of the manor court, those monitoring the exercise of common rights had real power to enforce regulations.

It is possible to interpret the penalties imposed on those breaking by-laws as a graduated scale, reflecting the seriousness with which the courts viewed offences. For example, in the Pennine manor of Alston Moor during the 16th century, the penalty for failing to 'bed' a peat working was a mere 6d; that for hounding or chasing livestock on the common twice as much (12d); that for marking animals with the wrong mark the much more substantial penalty of 6s 8d (which equalled 80d). When the same court was concerned about pressure on turbary rights in 1679, the swingeing penalty of 39s 11d was placed on those breaking the newly imposed order restricting peat-digging by landless cottagers (Winchester, 2000, pp164, 133). Likewise, it is possible to discern an attempt to make the penalty fit the offence in relation to individual miscreants. For example, when the Brancaster jury in Norfolk was confronted with two men who had dug sea holly roots in the sand dunes in 1625, they amerced each of them 6d and ordered them to desist under pain of 3s 4d each. When one of the men continued to offend, the penalty was doubled the following year.[8]

However, the effectiveness (and, indeed, the purpose) of the financial penalties laid down in the courts' orders must sometimes be in doubt. It is not always possible to be certain that the fines demanded by a court were paid; indeed, the widespread custom of appointing 'affearers', whose role was to mitigate the penalties imposed at the court sitting, could lead to a substantial discrepancy between the amercement fixed by the court and the amount actually paid. The repeated recording of specific offences and named offenders could suggest that the court was failing to stamp out an activity; alternatively, it could indicate that the court saw the 'fine' as something more akin to a licence. In such cases, the activity might be tacitly accepted, provided that those engaged in it paid for the privilege and did not assume that they could undertake it as of right. For example, the eight offenders recorded at Brancaster court (Norfolk) in 1713 were all residents of the neighbouring parish of Burnham Norton, and were presented for fowling and fishing (and, in one instance, digging sea holly) in the lord of Brancaster's liberties and amerced 5 or 10 shillings each. Four years later five of those presented in 1713 and three other Burnham Norton men were named again for similar offences.[9] Rather than attempting to prevent the activities, it seems likely that the court was effectively licensing outsiders to take produce from the common on resource exploitation.

Management mechanisms: Restrictions on quantity, area and time

Quantity

One of the abiding principles of common right was that produce could not be taken from the common for sale or to be taken outside the manor, and the quantity of the resource which could be taken was limited by the concept of 'necessary use'. Inherently flexible and indeterminate, such a principle might break down in conditions of social or environmental stress. In such circumstances, custom and by-law could define – and, indeed, restrict – 'necessary use' by articulating quantitative limits on resource exploitation.

In the case of pasture rights on common land, a further indeterminate concept had come to govern the numbers of livestock which could be turned out on to the common by the later medieval centuries. The rule of 'levancy and couchancy', recorded in court rolls from the 14th century (Ravensdale, 1974, p78), did not impose an explicit numerical limit; rather, by limiting the right to the number of animals that could be over-wintered, it related the size of an individual's grazing right to the productivity of his landed holding. The emphasis was therefore on equity, ensuring proportional access to members of the manorial community. Since it took no account of the amount of grazing available on the common, it is questionable whether the rule of levancy and couchancy could guarantee preservation of the resource for future exploitation, particularly when new methods of improvement increased the over-wintering capacity of farmland. An alternative mechanism was to express pasture rights in numerical terms, each commoner having a 'stint': the right to graze a certain number of livestock. In this system the livestock-carrying capacity of the common could be calculated and then apportioned between those having grazing rights. Although the apportionment of stints between individuals was usually carried out to ensure equitable access (e.g. by linking the size of the stint to the value of the holding), the fact that the global number of stints could take account of the carrying capacity of the common gave stinting an inherent advantage as a mechanism for sustainable management.

Why, then, were numerical limits imposed on grazing rights on some but by no means all commons? As late as the mid 20th century only around one third of common land in England and Wales was stinted (Royal Commission, 1958, p22). First, as might be expected, there is some evidence for a broad correlation between the level of grazing pressure on a common and the system of controlling livestock numbers found there. Where commons were extensive and grazing pressure was low, unstinted commons governed by the rule of levancy and couchancy were frequently found; where livestock numbers were high and the available grazing on the common small, stinting was the norm. Other drivers behind the introduction of stinting systems probably included the greater certainty and ease of policing numerical limits and the fact that, by the 16th century, farming realities (the trading of livestock, purchase of hay as winter fodder, droving, wintering young animals away from the home farm) sat increasingly uncomfortably alongside the assumptions underpinning the rule of levancy and couchancy (that a farm had a fixed stock of animals, over-wintered from year to year on fodder grown on the farm) (see Winchester and Straughton, 2010).

Stinted pasture rights were traditionally expressed in terms of the 'beastgate' or 'cattlegate': the right to graze one horned beast. Conversion formulae were often agreed upon, enabling a commoner to graze other livestock (e.g. ten sheep for one cattlegate). Flexibility could be achieved by varying the entitlement given by possession of a stint in the event of changing circumstances, as discussed in Chapter 7. An illustration of the difficulties which could arise from an inappropriate conversion rate comes from the Lake District manor of Wasdalehead in the early 19th century. In 1807 it was claimed that the recent shift away from cattle rearing towards sheep breeding had resulted in overstocking. Each cattlegate entitled a commoner to put 1 bull, ox or cow or 15 sheep on the common: the common could bear a mixture of stock but when all stints were exercised by sheep, overstocking became a problem.[10]

In the case of materials such as turbary, estovers and stone, limitations on quantity might take the form of a restriction on the means of carrying it, the manpower required to harvest it, or the implements used to gather it. For example, restrictions on the quantity of bracken which could be taken were sometimes expressed in terms of manpower, a frequent limit being one gatherer per holding (Dilley, 1972, pp159–160). Across lowland England, gorse (*Ulex* spp.), also known as 'furze' or 'whin', was a valuable fuel resource, particularly among the rural poor (Neeson, 1993, pp159–160; pp174–176; Shaw-Taylor, 2002, pp75–76). By-laws regulating the cutting of gorse on the common included what seems to have been a widespread customary quantitative restriction, whereby gorse was only to be taken from common land by being carried in bundles; carting it away on a wheeled vehicle was forbidden. Eighteenth-century by-laws to this effect are recorded from Warwickshire, Northamptonshire and Oxfordshire (Thompson, 1991, p145; Neeson, 1993, p175; Shaw-Taylor, 2002, p76), while a series of orders made at Brancaster, Norfolk, suggest that a comparable custom existed there in the 16th century (see Chapter 9, p172).

Area

Complex spatial allocations and restrictions were often introduced for the purposes of day-to-day management, particularly on extensive upland commons, despite the fact that legal theory conceived of use-rights as being general to the whole of a common. Topography and environmental factors could result in marked ecological contrasts between different parts of a common, making some more productive than others or restricting the distribution of particular resources to certain areas. Distance from the holding to which a common right was attached also played a part: there would be an assumption, not always stated explicitly, that it would be most convenient for a commoner to exercise rights on the section of the common closest to his land. Then there were the practical considerations of managing livestock or cutting peat or vegetation on the common. Good neighbourhood could be better served by systematic organization of the exercise of rights – keeping the flocks and herds of individual commoners separate, for example, so as to reduce the potential for conflict.

On some commons in the hills of northern England and in Wales, the allocation of grazing rights had the effect of giving individual commoners exclusive rights over a section of the common (see Chapter 6, pp94–96; Chapter 8, pp141–144). Both the Cumbrian 'heafs' and the Welsh sheepwalks were central to the day-to-day practices of livestock management. Both were reliant on the territorial nature of hill sheep. Preserving the invisible boundary lines between neighbours was achieved by 'keeping a strong flock', involving the inclusion of older wethers (castrated male sheep), who knew the flock's territorial limits and helped to guard the boundaries against intruders (Banks, 1880, p38; Howells, 2005, p65). In both northern England and mid-Wales the necessity of maintaining continuity in the flock, to ensure that territorial instincts were passed down, led to the custom of retaining a 'landlord's flock', which was let with the holding to maintain the territorial integrity of heaf or sheepwalk when tenants changed. In these areas, the common had little integrity as a grazing ground; rather, it consisted of a patchwork of defined blocks, each subject to exclusive use by an individual commoner.

Similar allocations of sections of the common to individuals occurred in connection with rights of turbary and estovers. Where peat formed the principal fuel, as was the case in much of upland Britain until the 19th century, it was usual for a section of the peat diggings to be assigned to each commoner. Rights in these 'peat pots' were exclusive to the individual: no one was to dig peat except in his own allocated place; nor to carry away peat dug on his neighbour's peat pot; nor to allow others to dig peat in his own peat pots. As peat beds were worked out, new peat pots were assigned by officers of the manor court (Winchester, 2000, pp129–130). Spatial allocation of use-rights was also found in relation to bracken. Defined stands of the plant, known as bracken 'rooms,' 'dales' or 'dalts', were allocated to individual commoners, particularly in Cumbria, their bounds sometimes being defined in great detail. These sections of bracken-covered hillsides assigned to individual commoners were protected by the weight of the courts' authority and individuals might be penalized for reaping bracken assigned to the holding of another person (Winchester, 2006).

Time

A third management tool available to local governance bodies was to impose seasonal restrictions by dictating dates limiting when a common right could be exercised. Several factors lay behind the imposition of such restrictions, including the desire to conserve the resource in question, to reduce the potential for conflict (e.g. by synchronizing the movement of livestock), or to ease competition between conflicting demands for a particular resource. In open field areas, the annual rhythm of cultivation and harvest generated a series of dates punctuating the year and dictating the exercise of pasture rights. Fields and meadows would be closed to most livestock until harvest, after which they were thrown open. Manor court by-laws often specified a date (typically Michaelmas, 29 September) before which grazing on the stubble was forbidden, as in the regulations governing common of 'shack' over the open fields at Brancaster in the 16th and 17th centuries (see Chapter 9, p169).

On the common wastes, seasonal restrictions of grazing rights again illustrate the twin aims of optimal management of pasture and the reduction of potential conflict. One of the advantages of shared cow pastures, separated from the remainder of the waste, was the possibility of developing more sophisticated management regimes to maximize the yield of grass. Seasonal restrictions might be placed on the types of livestock which were to use the pasture, typically cattle and horses in summer, and sheep in winter, and by the 17th century many communities instituted a closed season on their cow pastures, usually approximately one month in spring time, when all livestock were forbidden in order to allow the pasture to recover (Winchester, 2000, pp72–73). Comparable management rules survive in the closed seasons found on the stinted commons in the Ingleton area (see Chapter 7, p126).

The precise dates specified in such by-laws were intended to ensure that all neighbours conformed to the same pattern of seasonal movement. This desire to synchronize the movement of livestock was particularly apparent in the transhumance practices which survived in parts of northern England until the early 17th century, involving the movement of livestock several kilometres away from the home farm to graze summer pastures deep in the hills. This was undertaken through a system of tight communal control, whereby the manor court and its officers specified the date, usually in early May, after the corn had been sown, when the whole community was to de-camp with their stock to temporary dwellings ('shielings') on the summer pastures, and the date in late July or early August when they were to return for the hay harvest. The driving force here was not only the need to exploit the grazing resources of distant pastures, but also to ensure that all cattle were removed from pastures around the home farms while the crops of corn and hay were growing (Winchester, 2000, pp85–90).

Seasonal restrictions were also a feature of other common rights: peat-cutting was often forbidden before a date in early May, for example, presumably to allow all commoners to complete their spring farmwork before turning to the peat banks. The inherent tension between different uses of bracken required the formulation of sophisticated rules which drew the distinction between careful harvesting of fronds for thatching, by pulling stems or by cutting them with a sickle, and wholesale gathering for bedding or burning, by mowing with a scythe. In the by-laws from north-west England, approximately one month separated the dates, the shearing of bracken fronds being allowed from late August or mid September, while mowing was forbidden until around Michaelmas (29 September), the intention being to enable those who needed to select fronds for thatching to gather them before the bracken banks were cleared for litter or for burning (Winchester, 2006).

Conclusions: Sustainability, rules and property rights

Sustaining the resources of common land for domestic and agrarian use in the historic context was a complex and dynamic process, involving the interplay between diverse social-ecological drivers: the need to sustain the resource, to maintain equitable access, and to balance competing demands. The local institutions formulating and policing the rules which sought to achieve those ends have evolved over time as manor courts faded and alternative bodies – or, in the case of some commons, an institutional vacuum – emerged in their place. The rules themselves have been fashioned in the context of a legal pluralist landscape, one involving not only the potential collision between customary law and statute but, more fundamentally, persistent underlying tensions between the formal property rights of individuals and informal customary notions of communal interest. Historic management systems were community based, sensitive to local environmental and social conditions, and deeply conscious of custom and tradition, with the result that the management regimes they devised were tailored to specific circumstances and differed from place to place. Thus, the history of common land management defies simple narratives or models: there is not one management tradition, but a plurality of approaches and responses. As Ostrom notes, CPR governance systems 'look terribly messy and hard to understand', and they challenge the 'scholars' love of tidiness' (Ostrom, 2005, p286). Nevertheless, several key themes emerge.

In the sustenance of the physical resources of the common, the ideal of good land stewardship was vital, but it was not seen solely in physical or ecological terms. Sustaining a resource went hand-in-hand with the need to maintain an equitable level of access, and to balance competing demands which might threaten both the resource and social cohesion. What was being sustained and passed on was not merely a piece of land or an array of resources; it was custom itself. During a dispute over the respective rights of lords and commoners in 1823, the jurors of Newby (Yorkshire) claimed that they were acting to preserve and pass the customs of the court and manor on to posterity in their 'Pristine state'.[11] 'Custom' seems to have stood both for the landscape and for an inherited approach to its management: a grounded way of balancing use-rights in common land.

This is also reflected in the multifaceted nature of regulatory systems, which aimed to provide a rounded set of rules sensitive to local conditions. The three aspects of regulatory control – quantitative, spatial and seasonal – could be combined and were rarely used in isolation. A spatial limitation (such as assigning particular peat diggings to individuals), for example, might be supplemented by quantitative rules when the resource came under additional pressure. Or a suite of different rules operating simultaneously might be used to manage multiple uses of a single resource, as in the case of bracken. It is striking that the Commons Registration Act 1965 and many subsequent modern agri-environment schemes failed to achieve this level of complexity. Today, the complex interplay between quantitative, spatial and temporal mechanisms is often reduced to simple numerical right.

Resource-use rules and property rights

In the historic context, the boundary between customary control mechanisms and property rights was a fluid, and sometimes intangible, one. Customary management bodies had a degree of discretion built on community principles, often adapting property rights to suit local conditions. The very fact of stinting a previously unstinted common implies a change not only in management but also in the property rights regime, since expressing a grazing right in quantitative terms could pave the way for it to become a personal saleable asset (see Chapter 2, p23). Manor courts routinely intervened to limit or even temporarily prevent the exercise of a right by dictating when and where, for example, resources such as peat, gorse or rushes could be cut. In many respects, then, the size or timing of a common 'right' was not a fixed, legally defined, state, but was subject to redefinition as management bodies amended rules or drafted new ones. This reflexivity and fluidity extended to permission for activities as well as limitations. Thus, the commercial exploitation of bracken for burning into potash appears to have been accepted as a customary practice, despite the fact that it could not be justified as a 'necessary use'. Rules were devised to accommodate it. This reminds us that institutions and by-laws were not just tools to prevent or limit activities, but could also act as a force for controlled positive change, enabling new activities to take place (Evans et al, 2008, p111). Traditional management regimes stand in contrast to the Commons Registration Act 1965, which gave primacy to the property right itself, viewing it as inalienable and timeless, regardless of social-ecological conditions. As a consequence, contemporary commoners and land managers often find themselves confined within an unyielding legal schedule of rights with none of the fluidity and responsiveness of customary management.

Understanding successes and failures

Manor courts and successor institutions, such as commoners' associations, had multiple tools at their disposal: the question was whether and how they chose to employ them, and for whose benefit. As we have seen, these bodies were not inherently just. Manor courts sometimes worked to exclude marginal groups, with the court jury representing the wealthier members and managing the common in their own interests. Ostrom (2005, p282) lists, among other possible limits to successful self-organized governance systems, the problem of 'local tyrannies', whereby local leaders or power elites dominate proceedings and 'only change rules that they think will advantage them still further'. The history of common land is no doubt littered with local tyrannies, though we might sometimes be unable to detect them from surviving records.

Were these bodies successful? Even commons with a generally strong management tradition might not always be successful in preventing overgrazing, damage to the fabric of the common or social disputes – indeed, by their nature manor court records abound with evidence of things going wrong. On those commons which suffered from ineffectual management and disputes over rights, the result might be a disturbing breakdown of social relations, land stewardship and animal welfare: the very opposite of the ideal of 'good neighbourhood'. The vicar of one Yorkshire parish, writing in support of enclosure in 1844, described 'neighbours quarrelling and fighting and dogging each other's sheep with the most revengeful cruelty, because both were contending for the herbage of the same plot of ground'.[12] In some cases, a breakdown in effective management could spell the end of a common and pave the way for enclosure. It could be argued that sustainable management of common land rests on a belief that the resource itself has a future: if the resource appeared to be doomed (as may well have been the case during the era of parliamentary enclosure), there might have been limited commitment to sustainable management practices. Conversely, as Ostrom (2005, p286) noted, conflict over resource management had the potential to generate better information, and eventually better systems of management. New strategies or management bodies (such as stintholders' meetings) might arise from a lapse in traditional management or from disputes over rights, as was the case at Scales Moor (see Chapter 7, p117).

The survival of common land as a legally distinct category of land is of itself neither a guarantee of its condition, the richness of its biodiversity or livestock carrying capacity – nor is it evidence of successful management in the past. Sustainability operated on different levels. Sustaining the integrity of an area of land as a common with its distinctive legal entity was often a result of external agency: for example, the prohibitive costs of improvement or enclosure during the era of parliamentary enclosure and the national culture of preservation thereafter. The success with which specific resources within a common (pasture, peat, gorse, bracken) have been protected or sustained over time has depended largely on local systems of management; yet, as has been shown, the ends to which past management regimes were directed were often only implicitly those of environmental sustainability. Nevertheless, in reviewing the historic evidence for sustainable land management on common land in England and Wales, there is room for optimism: the sophistication of the regulations put in place locally to govern the exploitation of common land show that stakeholders in a CPR were evidently not trapped in the inherently destructive game that Hardin's 'tragedy of the commons' predicted. Sustainable land management was a complex responsive process: grounded on a bedrock of local custom and tradition, the manor courts and their successors operated within a constantly changing social-ecological context, where needs and interests were often in tension. Indeed, successful commons management could be read as a continuous, adaptive and innovative process of averting local tragedies. As Elinor Ostrom has noted: 'Coping with potential tragedies of the commons is never easy and never finished' (Ostrom, 2005, p286).

Notes

1. CRO, D/Lec, box 94, Eskdale court verdicts.
2. WYRO, WYL 524/179, m. 6v.
3. WYRO, WYL 524/249, Newby Court, 7 April 1796; NYCRO, ZUC 1/4/1, Newby Court, 16 April 1830.
4. See http://www.defra.gov.uk/rural/protected/commonland/acts.htm.
5. CRO, DSO 198/3, 198/4.
6. CRO, D/Law/1/230.
7. CRO, D/Ay/3/2.
8. GA, D2700/MJ19/1, 5 October 1625; 16 October 1626.
9. GA, D2700/MJ19/13.
10. CRO, D/Lec, box 94, draft case, *Grave v. Fletcher* [1807].
11. NYCRO, ZUC 1/4/1, Newby Court, 4 April 1823.
12. *Report from the Select Committee on Commons' Inclosure*, 5 August 1844, p132, para 1661 (House of Commons Parliamentary Paper1844 (583) V.1.

4

Property Rights in the Modern Commons

The contemporary common lands of England and Wales offer an interesting case study in the conceptualization of 'common' rural space. They illustrate many paradigm features of contested common pool resources (CPRs) – they have a multifaceted role as an agricultural resource, are an important source of natural capital providing ecosystem services, and provide a public space for open air recreation and communal enjoyment. These potentially conflicting roles are represented within a pluralist framework of legal and property concepts that are in many ways unique to English law. Part 2 of the Commons Act 2006 has introduced reform of the governance structures for managing common land. This will require both a reappraisal of the orientation of these conflicting land-use demands and a re-conceptualization of property rights in the commons. This chapter will confine itself to a consideration of the unique legal structures for property rights in the modern commons, and will consider the impact, in particular, of the registration of common rights under the Commons Registration Act 1965. It will consider measures in Part 1 of the 2006 Act for clarifying the commons registers and the property rights that they represent. The environmental governance implications of Part 2 of the 2006 Act will be considered in detail in Chapter 5.

Property rights and 'common' land

The modern legal status of common land in England and Wales is, on the one hand, curious in that it manifests attributes of customary law no longer relevant to other forms of land tenure, and, on the other, entirely paradigmatic of the difficulties of reconciling prevalent notions of property rights with new mechanisms for environmental governance. The complex framework of land-use rights over the modern commons can only be understood against the historical backdrop of customary and local governance mechanisms outlined in Chapters 2 and 3.

Common land is not 'common' in the sense of being a community resource with communal ownership and land-use rights. Although usually owned by private individuals, or by public or private organizations, common land is subject to rights of common that entitle the persons possessing those rights to use the land and its products. The legal categorization of these rights has already been discussed (in Chapter 1 above).

In a modern context the most important common rights on large upland 'agricultural' commons are rights of pasture, turbary and estovers (see pp6–7). Much (but by no means all) of the surviving common land was originally the wasteland of a manor. It will usually consist of open land with rights of common grazing exercisable by the owners or occupiers of farms adjoining the common. Most common land in upland areas is also 'access land' over which the public have a statutory right to roam, and local communities frequently also hold additional rights over common land (e.g. a right to fish in standing waters and/or streams and rivers (a right of piscary) or to enjoy recreational access to the common). In the case of lowland commons, and those whose primary land use is now recreational (rather than agricultural), the picture is rather more prosaic. The commons registers for the North Norfolk case study (see Chapter 9) offer a fascinating insight in this regard. There are, for example, 298 entries of estovers and 'samphire rights' on the register for Brancaster Common (Register of Common Land, Norfolk, CL Unit 65). The majority of these entries record rights to 'full' samphire rights as giving a right to take herbage, estovers, samphire, soil, fish, shellfish, bait and wild fowl. Placing some of these rights within the accepted categories of common right is problematic – an issue to which we will return below.

In legal terms, common rights are a form of *profit à prendre* – a right to take part of the land, minerals or crops or wild animals from another person's land ('the right to take something off another person's land': *Beckett (Alfred F.) v. Lyons* [1967] , p482). Rights of common are usually attached ('appurtenant') to the 'dominant tenement' which they benefit. Rights can also be 'appendant'. Appendant rights originate in the customary right of someone who was granted feudal tenure of arable land to graze his cattle – the animals necessary to plough and manure the lord's arable land – on the wasteland of the manor (see *Tyrringham's case* [1584]). They are very rarely encountered today, and there are no examples of appendant rights in any of the four case studies examined in this work.

In areas where the common provides an important agricultural resource the most important common right is invariably that of pasture. As a *profit à prendre*, a right of common of pasture is literally expressed as the right to take grass by the mouth of cattle, sheep, horses or other livestock, depending on the nature of the right (*Samborne v. Harilo* [1621] , p163 (J. Bridgman); *Earl de la Warr v. Miles* [1881], p577 (V.C. Bacon)). An important qualification of the right – and one that flows naturally from its character as a *profit à prendre* – is the rule that common of pasture does not include a right to supplementarily feed animals on the common (*Besley v. John* [2003]). Prior to the introduction of registration for common rights by the Commons Registration Act 1965, the number of animals permitted to graze the common was usually limited by the principle of levancy and couchancy, as described in Chapter 2. The size of the dominant holding, and the quantity and quality of fodder it could produce, were therefore determinative of the number of livestock that the farm could put to the common in the summer months (see *Cole v. Foxman* [1618], p74). The principle was most commonly applied to regulate grazing on large and open unenclosed pastures in the uplands, such as those in the Lake District, North Pennines and central Wales (Winchester and Straughton, 2010). The other common law mechanism for controlling grazing livestock was the practice of stinting (i.e. determining the number of animals to be grazed by reference to a fixed number ('stint' or 'beastgate') allowed on the common from each farm). These principles were expressed as property rights at common law – or, to be precise, as qualifications on the use of the common resource that a common right conferred on its holder.

Property rights paradigms and the commons

Property rights perform several different functions when defining the relationship of the property holder with land. Two closely related, but different, property models are fundamental to understanding the relationship between common property rights and land use:

1 an entitlements-based model of property rights that stresses the role of property rules in defining the legitimacy of land use and ownership entitlements; and
2 a resource allocation model that focuses on the role of property rights in allocating and defining access to the resources that land represents.

The two models are closely related and reflect the differing functions that property rights perform – on the one hand, in defining legally sanctioned rights to land and its produce, and, on the other, as an allocative tool for defining access to the land resource that the entitlement confers. Neither is mutually exclusive. A property entitlement rule will often also fulfil a resource allocation function.

This can be seen very clearly in the case of common land, where there will be multiple land-use rights over the same registered common. The landowner will, by virtue of his freehold title, be entitled to any land-use rights that have not been allocated to common rights holders by the commons registers. This means that minerals and game rights will usually be reserved to the landowner, together with any surplus grazing or other surplus produce (such as peat) remaining after commoners have exercised the full extent of their registered rights to use the land resource. The property entitlement of common rights holders is more limited, and is defined by the terms of the rights section of the commons registers established under the Commons Registration Act 1965. The registered rights of common captured in the commons registers therefore represent both an initial property entitlement and a resource allocation determined by law. It by no means, however, accurately represents the actual distribution of resource entitlement exercisable by those with an interest in common land. A reallocation of the initial resource entitlements fixed by law can be – and in many cases will have been – accomplished by legal and economic instruments external to the property entitlement rules defining the landowner's and commoners' interest in the land (e.g. by environmental legislation restricting potentially damaging land uses, by 'soft law' instruments such as codes of practice, and by economic instruments to encourage land management for nature conservation). The resource allocation role of these instruments is considered further below.

It will be apparent from the mobile nature of 'property' concepts that there is an inherent tension between the entitlement and resource allocation roles of property rules, and this is reflected very clearly in the complex nature of property rights in common land. Property entitlement theories offer a static view of common land and the legal rights subsisting over it, whereas the resource allocation that the rights represent is often complex, shifting and dynamic. Property entitlement rules characterize 'property' as an abstract construct, identified by 'incidents' of ownership and of conceptually abstract 'rights' which make up the essential ingredients of ownership. For example, Honore (1961, p107ff) focuses on the 'rights' which he regards as essential indicators of ownership, though they need not be present together: the right to possession; to use; to manage; to income; to capital; to security; the incident of transmissibility; the absence of termination; and liability to execution. Others see property rights as primarily comprising items that are either the subject of direct trespassory protection by the law, or capable of separate assignment as parts of private wealth (Harris 1996, p140). The focus here is on whether there is a legally protected right to the exploitation and use of land: whether that right is actually utilized (and, if so, in what manner) is of little relevance to an entitlements-based analysis, and it therefore fails to encompass the functional relationship of common property with the environment.

Defining 'property' as constituent primarily of a 'bundle of rights' does not, however, fully capture the dynamic nature of property rights in the commons, or the shifting and often contested nature of the resource allocation that the rules represent (Penner, 1996; Raff, 1998). Ultimately, 'property' rights define the relationship of power that an 'owner' asserts over a resource such as land, rather than the tangible asset itself. Resource allocation models of property rights therefore stress that they represent the elements of resource utility that (taken together) make up a land interest. The bundle of property 'rights' over land that the law recognizes will define, distribute and reflect different elements of resource utility that accrue to the 'owner' of the right in question (Gray and Gray, 1998, pp15, 39). This approach has considerable potential for capturing the dynamic interrelationship between common property institutions and instruments of environmental governance. Whenever legislation alters the allocation of utility rights over land, then a transfer of 'property' in this sense has occurred.

Environmental legislation is fundamentally concerned with the limitation or redistribution of property rights in this sense – as elements of utility – in order to pursue a public policy objective in environmental protection (Rodgers, 2009). It also resonates with economic models for property that stress the dynamic nature of property rights (Bromley, 1991). These see the function of property rights as primarily to provide incentives to internalize the potential environmental externalities that have emerged from the growing technical potential of agricultural production to generate pollution and damage biodiversity (see, for example, Demsetz, 1967, p348). Resource allocation models also facilitate the identification of interactions between the *form* which legal controls on land use take and the *content* of the land-use responsibilities that they introduce. Most situations in which a modification of common property rights (seen as elements of resource utility) occurs involve the use of public law and/or economic instruments. Their impact will be considered below. The common law plays a very limited role, in a modern context, in reallocating resource and utility rights to further environmental protection objectives.

Defining 'property' in the commons: Entitlements

Commons Registration – the 1965 Act

The Commons Registration Act 1965 required the registration of both common land and of rights over common land (1965 Act, section 1(1)). Common land was defined, for these purposes, as *either* land subject to rights of common 'whether those rights are exercisable at all times or only during limited periods' *or* wasteland of a manor not subject to rights of common (1965 Act, section 22(1)). In the case of common rights, it required the registration of rights whether they were exercisable at all times or only during limited periods – rights to pasture animals on the common during fixed periods in the summer months were therefore registerable.

The rights to be registered were defined very widely to include 'cattlegates or beastgates (by whatever name known) and rights of sole or several pasture or herbage or of sole or several pasture' (1965 Act, section 22(1)). All rights that were not registered during the relevant application period[1] ceased to be exercisable over common land registered under the act (1965 Act, section 1(2)). In the case of pasturage rights for animals, the act stipulated that a definite number of grazing animals be stated and that the right should be exercisable in relation to animals not exceeding that number (1965 Act, section 15). The broad impact was to require the registration of fixed numbers of common grazing rights irrespective of whether they had existed *sans nombre* under the rule of levancy and couchancy, or had previously been stinted.

On many commons the majority of rights were registered under the 1965 Act as appurtenant to a dominant tenement. It is generally assumed that rights held in gross are comparatively rare. Gadsden (1988, §3.44) observes, for example, that 'they are the very occasional exception'. It is noteworthy, however, that all four case studies presented in this work throw up examples of rights in gross. There are, for example, two entries in the Commons Register for Eskdale recording rights in gross, and several entries of rights in gross in the Cwmdeuddwr Common Register. In Ingleborough, appurtenant grazing rights attached to a large number of separate holdings were severed in the 20 years prior to the Commons Act 2006 and converted into rights in gross (see Chapter 7 pp125–6). And in the Norfolk case study all the common rights over Brancaster common (CL 65) were initially registered as rights in gross, even though the nature of most of the rights (as estovers and rights to take the produce of the soil, such as samphire and sea lavender) might dictate that they must have originated in customary rights attached to dwellings in the locality. The evidence presented in Chapters 6 to 9 indicates that a revision of the previously held view as to the incidence of rights in gross, and of their strategic role in the sustainable management of the modern commons, might be required. Whatever their customary origins, there is little doubt that many rights in gross were inaccurately registered in the commons registers (see Gadsden, 1988, §3.43; Aitchison and Gadsden, 1992, p174). The same is true of many rights over stinted and regulated pastures, which, not being strictly common land but governed by individual enclosure awards, should not have fallen into the registration system at all (Gadsden, 1988, §1.59, §1.79).

The grazing rights registered against each common bear no necessary relation to the ability of the common to support the number of animals for which rights were registered, or to the 'optimum' level of stocking needed to prevent overgrazing. The 1965 Act made no provision for the appraisal of applications for the registration of common rights against sustainability criteria – either in terms of the capacity of the common against which the rights were to be registered to provide adequate pasture for the number claimed, or in terms of the potential environmental impact of the rights claimed on wildlife habitats present on the common. The registration of common rights should, moreover, have been based on the historic grazing practice on the common concerned, although this was rarely checked by commons registration authorities. As a consequence, grazing numbers were sometimes inflated, and in some cases the rights registered may never have been exercised at all (or only exercised in part), or they may have been exercised at certain periods and not others (for criticism, see Gadsden, 1988, §4.22; and Countryside Commission, 1986, Appendix C, paras 015–018).

The overall result, therefore, was that excessive numbers of grazing rights were registered on many commons, especially on those that were previously regulated by the principle of levancy and couchancy. This has, in the intervening years, caused innumerable problems for the effective management of common land, some of which the changes in the Commons Act 2006, discussed below, are intended to address. The 1965 Act also failed to require the alteration of the register when farms were bought and sold, or where rights were transferred independently of land. The result is that most contemporary commons registers do not accurately identify the current entitlement to the rights that they record. The 2006 Act requires each commons registration authority to maintain registers of common land and common rights, but the registers originally established under the 1965 Act will be the basis of the new registers (Commons Act 2006, section 3). Many of the defects in the registration system will therefore continue to complicate future arrangements for the sustainable management of the commons.

Impact of commons registration on 'sustainable' management

The role of the common law principles of levancy and couchancy, and of stinting, as property instruments for arranging the governance of the commons was effectively destroyed by the Commons Registration Act 1965. Commons registration severed such links as had previously existed between common property rights and principles of 'sustainable' management. An ancillary effect of the requirement for each grazier to register a fixed maximum number of grazing livestock was the removal of any potential for common law principles – and especially those applicable to the stinting of pastures – to perform a meaningful function in relation to sustainable management. Following their registration, common property rights ceased to be inherently reflexive, and were rendered incapable of variation to meet changing ecological conditions. The courts have also held that the requirement to register fixed grazing numbers effectively abolished levancy and couchancy (*Bettison v. Langton* [2001]). And it destroyed the inherent ability of stinting to act as a reflexive mechanism to adjust grazing pressures in response to environmental factors.

By facilitating the excessive registration of pasture rights on many commons, the 1965 Act also ensured that in most cases the property rights reflected in the register will have ceased to perform the distributive functions of the common law property rules in allocating land-use rights equitably between competing users. The allocative function formerly performed by property rights must therefore be exercised by alternative means, such as through publicly funded environmental management schemes. This can be seen, for example, in the Elan Valley and Eskdale case studies discussed in Chapters 6 and 8, where the resource allocation function formerly performed by common property rights is dealt with by the terms of the collective Environmentally Sensitive Area (ESA) management agreements negotiated for Eskdale and Cwmdeuddwr Commons with the public conservation bodies.

In the case of common pasture rights, the status of the legal entitlement conferred by the registration of a fixed number of grazing rights is important, especially as the registered rights over many 'agricultural' commons bear no necessary relation to the land use required for its sustainable management. Where the rights were originally registered under the Commons Registration Act 1965, section 15 of the latter provided that 'where a right consists of or includes a right, not limited by number, to graze animals of any class, *it shall … be treated as exercisable in relation to no more animals … than a definite number*' (emphasis added). Once the registration became final, the right became exercisable 'in relation to animals *not exceeding* the number registered' (emphasis added) and was conclusive proof of the matters registered (1965 Act, section 15(3) and section 10).

The legal effect of this provision on the property rights reflected in the register was considered by the commons commissioner in *Re the Black Mountain, Dinefwr, Dyfed* (1985). In his view the registered number provided only an upper limit on the number of grazing stock permissible. It followed that if, at any time, the number of animals grazing the common was considered to be excessive, then legal redress could be sought, even though the number of animals put to the common by the grazier alleged to be causing the damage was less than his full registered entitlement. This might reopen the question of re-establishing the link between the exercise of common property rights and principles of 'sustainable' management; but the basis on which this might be done remains obscure. It has, for example, been suggested that the common law principle of levancy and couchancy might still have a role to play in limiting the exercise of pasture rights in order to fix the maximum grazing limit for a common (see Gadsden, 1988, §4.23). But this would restrict any evaluation to issues of economic and social sustainability, and close off considerations of the ecological benefits of restricting grazing to numbers below the registered maximum for a particular common – these issues were not recognized at common law. And how this principle might be applied in cases other than pasturage rights is also shrouded in uncertainty. Consider, for example, the case of registered wildfowling rights in the Norfolk case study (see Chapter 9). The registered rights here are un-quantified, and the application of a principle such as that suggested in *Re the Black Mountain, Dinefwr, Dyfed* would therefore be much more problematic – notwithstanding that the unrestrained exercise of the rights could have much greater impacts upon the ecological value of the commons over which the rights subsist.

Form and content of commons registers

Another important consequence of the flawed registration process undertaken under the Commons Registration Act 1965 was a lack of standardization in the manner in which local commons registration authorities recorded entries in the commons registers. There was also little consistency in the manner in which variations and transfers of rights were recorded after the entries became final. Although a question largely of the *form* in which property rights are expressed in the registers, this was nevertheless an important deficiency in the commons registration system established under the 1965 Act. The registers are legal documents that define the ownership of rights and the boundaries of land registered as common land, and they are used to identify rights holders when management changes are being considered or implemented – for example, under agri-environment schemes on common land. It is therefore important that the rights and common land that they record are both identified and expressed with clarity and certainty, and in a manner that gives an up-to-date record of the land-use rights subsisting over each common. The 1965 Act failed to ensure that this was the case, and has been criticized for failing to provide the necessary certainty and clarity required to underpin the management of the commons (Aitchison and Gadsden, 1992; Short, 2008, pp210–211).

There was no requirement to use standard or 'model' forms of entry when registering either common land or common rights under the Commons Registration Act 1965. As a result, there is wide variation in the manner in which common land is identified from one registration authority to another, and in the way in which common rights (and subsequent variations or transfers of rights) have been registered. This lack of consistency was compounded by variations in the practice adopted by individual commoners and commons associations when applying to register rights under the 1965 Act. Since no appraisal was carried out at the time of provisional registration, either as to the historical accuracy of the rights claimed or their sustainability if exercised in full, many registrations became final that record rights in an idiosyncratic manner – and which is also, in some cases, internally inconsistent when considered in the context of the commons register in question.

The commons registers for the four case studies in Chapters 6 to 9 provide ample evidence of these shortcomings in the commons registration process under the 1965 Act. The commons register for Eskdale (Cumberland CL 58) displays inconsistencies in a number of individual registrations of pasture rights for cattle in addition, or as an alternative to, sheep, and in the conversion rates applied to convert registered rights for sheep into rights for cattle (a conversion rate of 1 cow/10 sheep is used in some cases, 1/20 in others: see Chapter 6). In the case of Cwmdeuddwr Common, there are no registered rights to graze cattle – notwithstanding that mixed grazing with cattle was almost certainly practised in the past. In both cases the form in which the register entries are presented is, however, fairly clear. In the Norfolk case study not only is the nature of the registered rights problematic, the form in which the entries are presented is also unclear and unsatisfactory (see Chapter 9 p174ff). A study of Thornham common by the Rural Planning Service in 1985 was highly critical of the 'unreliable', 'incomplete' and 'legally questionable' nature of the registers for CL41 and 56 (Thornham Low Common) (Rural Planning Services, 1985, p67). The same criticism can be applied to the registers for the much larger area of common land comprising Brancaster marshes and foreshore in the Norfolk case study (CL 65, CL 124 and CL 161).

Commons registration: The Commons Act 2006

Revising the commons registers

Part 1 of the Commons Act 2006 makes provision for the amendment and correction of the registers established under the 1965 Act. It requires the commons registration authorities to maintain the registers established under the 1965 Act, which will be rolled over and become registers under the 2006 Act (Commons Act 2006, sections 1 and 2). It does not, however, reopen the registration of either common land or common rights – save for making provision for the correction of incorrect entries or omissions from the register of common land, and for the registration of new common land, changes to registered common rights and the registration of new rights of common created after it comes into force (Commons Act 2006, sections 3(1), 3(3)). It does not reopen the registration of common rights undertaken under the 1965 Act, and some of the problems caused by the flawed registration process under the 1965 Act will remain. Nevertheless, the 2006 Act is intended to introduce much greater clarity and certainty into the commons registers, and to provide a more secure basis for the registration of both common land and common rights.

Part 1of the 2006 Act was brought into force in seven pilot areas on 1 October 2008 (Commons Registration (England) Regulations 2008, regulation 1 and Schedule 1). The pilot commons registration authorities are the county councils of Cornwall, Devon (excluding Plymouth and Torbay), Hertfordshire, Kent (excluding Medway), Lancashire (excluding Blackpool), the county of Herefordshire, and Blackburn with Darwen Borough Council. The transitional period during which revisions to the registers are to be made runs from 1 October 2008 to 30 September 2010. Applications for amendments to the register must have been made between 1 October 2008 and 30 September 2009 (Commons Registration (England) Regulations 2008, regulation 39(2)). Following conclusion of the revisions to the registers in the seven pilot authorities, it was initially proposed that the implementation of Part 1 of the 2006 Act would be rolled out in three stages between 1 October 2010 and 2012.[2]

The Commons Registration Act 1965 did not require the compulsory amendment or updating of the registers when common land or commons rights were sold, although voluntary amendments could be made where rights were apportioned, released or extinguished (1965 Act, section 13). Unsurprisingly, many transactions were not recorded and most registers are now inaccurate and out of date. The 2006 Act addresses this by requiring the updating of the registers with transactions that have occurred since the close of the initial registrations in 1970. Any changes to registered common rights that have occurred since 2 January 1970 must be registered in the updated register during the transitional period for revising the commons registers in each registration area. In the case of the seven pilot areas, this should have been done by 30 September 2010. This will apply to any variation or surrender of a right of common that has occurred since 1970, to any transfer of a right held in gross, and to any severance or apportionment of a right attached to land that has occurred since initial registration (2006 Act, schedule 3, para 2). Any right of common to which this applies, but which has not been registered by the end of the transitional period, will be extinguished (2006 Act, schedule 3, para 3). No variation is required, however, in the case of rights of common that are attached to land that has been sold or transferred (without severance of the rights) between 2 January 1970 and the end of the transitional period (2006 Act, schedule 3, para 2(3)).

New common land can be registered under the Commons Act 2006, and in limited circumstances land that was wrongly omitted from the register during the registration process under the 1965 Act can now be registered under Part 1 of the 2006 Act. Land that was wrongly registered as common land can also be removed from the register in certain circumstances. The 2006 Act does not define 'common land' other than by reference to the pre-existing definition to be found in the Commons Registration Act 1965 and the categories of land that can be registered under the 2006 Act, as described below (2006 Act, section 3). It was noted above that the 1965 Act defined common land as *either* land that is subject to rights or common *or* the wasteland of a manor not subject to such rights. This is important in order to understand some of the technical provisions in the 2006 Act for the correction of incorrect registrations made under the 1965 Act, discussed below.

New common land can come into being, first, when new rights of common are created over land. The Commons Act 2006 provides for the creation of new rights of common by express grant or under statute, provided that the rights are attached to land and the land over which they are exercisable is not a town or village green (2006 Act, section 6(3)). The rights will only be exercisable when the land over which they subsist has been registered as common land, if it is not already so registered. New common rights cannot, after the commencement of Part 1 of the 2006 Act, be created either by prescription or in the form of rights in gross. All new rights must be attached to land, and pre-existing rights in gross will only be exercisable, if transferred, when the identity of the new owner is registered in the common register (2006 Act, section 12). The 2006 Act prohibits the severance of rights where the rights are registered as attached to land, and provides for the attachment of rights *pro rata* to the dominant land from which they benefit (2006 Act, section 9; Commons (Severance of Rights) (England) Order 2006; Commons (Severance of Rights) (Wales) Order 2007). Severance of appurtenant rights is only permissible in limited circumstances defined by the 2006 Act: by a local order, by transfer to the conservation bodies or a commons council, or where they are temporarily leased or licensed, for a maximum of two years (in England) or three years (in Wales).

Second, it is possible to register 'exchange' land under the 2006 Act. The Act enables landowners to apply to the secretary of state or National Assembly of Wales to deregister common land; but if the land to be deregistered is more than 200 square metres in extent the applicant must offer exchange land that is not currently common land to replace the land to be deregistered (2006 Act, sections 16 and 17). When considering whether to consent to the registration of the exchange land in place of the common land released, the authorities must consider the views of people with common rights over the release land, the interests of the neighbourhood and the public interest.

The third situation in which new common land can be registered is where it was omitted from the registers established under the 1965 Act in error. Schedule 2 to the 2006 Act sets out several closely defined circumstances in which land omitted from the registers under the 1965 Act can now be registered as common land under Part 1 of the 2006 Act. This applies, first, where land is recognized as common land under a statutory scheme of management or local Act of Parliament, but was exempted by ministerial order from registration under the 1965 Act (1965 Act, section 11). The secretary of state had power under the 1965 Act to exempt from registration any common land that was regulated under a local act or scheme of management – for example, a scheme made under the Metropolitan Commons Act 1866 or the Commons Act 1899. Such land will now be registered as common land under the 2006 Act. It also applies to allow the registration of new common land where a provisional registration of the wasteland of a manor was made under the 1965 Act, but the registration was later cancelled by the commons commissioner in specified circumstances – for example, because the land had ceased to be associated with a manor at the time of the determination, because there were no longer rights of common subsisting over it, or because the provisional registration was withdrawn by agreement (2006 Act, schedule 2, paras 4(3)–(5)).

These tightly defined registration provisions are intended to reverse mistakes in the registration of common land under the 1965 Act that arose from conflicting judicial decisions as to the legal status of the wasteland of a manor. In *Box Parish Council v. Lacey (1979)* it was held that land still had to be owned by the lord of the manor at registration if it was to retain its status as wasteland of a manor. This enabled landowners to avoid the registration of their land as commons by the simple device of disposing of either the lordship of the manor, or of the land itself (while retaining the lordship). The House of Lords subsequently held, in *Hampshire County Council v. Milburn (1991)*, that land qualified as wasteland of a manor (and was therefore registerable as common land) if it was either currently or *formerly* the waste of a manor. Many provisional registrations had been cancelled by commons commissioners, relying on the *Box Hill* case, by the early 1990s. The closely defined circumstances in the 2006 Act, under which former manorial wastes can now be registered as common land, permit the rectification of the commons registers where this has occurred. Where former manorial waste is registered under these provisions, it will, however, not be possible to register common rights that were formerly exercised over the land, as these will have been extinguished for want of registration under the 1965 Act. It will also be necessary to consult the commons commissioners' decisions in order to make out the facts required by the 2006 Act for re-registration.

Model entries: Clarity and certainty in registration

Part 1 of the 2006 Act takes an important step towards improving the clarity and certainty of the commons registers by providing for 'model' entries which commons registration authorities must follow when recording rights and registering common land. The model entries to be used in the pilot registration areas are set out in Schedule 3, Part 1 to the Commons Registration (England) Regulations 2008. They require every new entry made in the registers – whether relating to registered land, rights of common or the ownership of common land – to follow as closely as possible the relevant model entry with such variations and adaptations as the circumstances may require. This will apply to all updating entries made during the transitional registration period in each registration area, and to any amendments to the registers made subsequently under the provisions outlined above. While not providing for a systematic and complete overhaul of the form and content of the registrations in each register, therefore, the introduction of a standardized system for recording rights and the extent and identity of common land over which they are exercisable should, in time, greatly improve the certainty and clarity of the registers maintained under the 2006 Act.

Sustainability appraisal of new common rights

Finally, the registration and amendment of new common rights will, in future, be potentially subject to a sustainability appraisal. The 2006 Act provides, in section 6(6), that an application to register the creation of a right of common pasturage must be refused 'if in the opinion of the commons registration authority the land over which it is created would be unable to sustain the exercise of the right and … any other rights of common exercisable over the land'. The same principle will apply to an application to vary common rights after Part 1 of the 2006 Act comes into force (i.e. from 1 October 2008 in the seven 'pilot' registration areas identified above). Rights can be varied either by becoming attached to new common land, or by virtue of changes made to the rights themselves (e.g. a change in the number of animals that can be grazed on a common land unit). An application to register a variation of a grazing right must be refused if the land over which it is to subsist would be unable to sustain the exercise of the right (2006 Act, section 7(5)). In both cases the application of sustainability principles is linked to the cumulative impact of the new rights upon the ability of the common to support the continued exercise of the total number of registered grazing rights. The commons registration authority must consult Natural England before approving a registration or variation of rights (Commons Registration (England) Regulations 2008, regulation 36). This would suggest that the ecological impact of the exercise of the additional rights will be an important factor in the appraisal required by the 2006 Act. These reforms should, in time, lead to a strengthening of the link between concepts of sustainable management and the commons registers. The failure of the 2006 Act to reopen pre-existing registrations means, however, that the registration of excessive numbers of grazing rights on some commons will be problematic to the exercise of the new sustainability appraisal requirements, which focus on the cumulative impacts of existing and new rights.

Where the registration of 'replacement land' is proposed in exchange for the release of registered common land, the process for establishing whether consent is given to the proposals will also involve a sustainability appraisal of the impact of the proposals upon the management of the new common land. The commons registration authority must have regard to the 'public interest' when deciding whether to register replacement land, and this is expressly defined to include nature conservation, the conservation of landscape, and the protection of public rights of way and of features of archaeological or historic importance (2006 Act, sections 16(6) and 16(8)).

Property rights, resource allocation and environmental regulation

Common land as communal environmental resource

Modern environmental legislation, and measures introduced to encourage environmentally friendly farming under the Common Agricultural Policy of the European Union, have both had a major impact upon property rights in the commons. A number of legal and economic instruments have been introduced, both through environmental law and rural development policy, that redistribute or restrict elements of resource utility in the commons and thereby effect a redistribution of property rights. The principal legal mechanism for promoting and protecting biodiversity is the designation of geographically distinct high nature value areas for protection, the primary wildlife designations in England and Wales being Sites of Special Scientific Interest (SSSIs), Special Protection Areas (SPAs) and Special Areas of Conservation (SACs).

The impact of modern environment legislation, and of re-allocative instruments employed to pursue public policy, has been particularly marked in the case of common land, in large measure because of its significance as an environmental resource. A large proportion of the surviving common land in England and Wales includes high nature value sites designated for protection under European or national environmental legislation. In England, for example, 210,806ha (approximately 57 per cent of the total area of common land) is in SSSIs notified under the Wildlife and Countryside Act 1981 (Natural England 2008a, Tables 3.1, 3.2). The poor condition of many natural habitats found on common land is a major problem for the implementation of public policy. Common land is also an important component in environmental policy for landscape protection. In England 48 per cent of common land is in National Parks and 30 per cent is in Areas of Outstanding Natural Beauty (AONBs). In total, 88 per cent of the total area of common land in England is to be found within one or more of the principal sites designated either for landscape or habitat protection (Natural England 2008a, Table 3.2).

Environmental regulation: Intersections, interactions and conflicts

The way in which shifting perceptions of 'common' land are reflected in property rights at different periods is an important theme of this work: an equally central theme in the modern context is the nature of the interaction between property rights and instruments of environmental governance. The introduction of environmental legislation not only reflects a new conception of common land as a communal environmental resource; it also introduces the potential for conflict between common property rights and the public interest in nature conservation. The legal provisions in the Wildlife and Countryside Act 1981 for the notification and protection of SSSIs take no account of the fact that a site may include common land. Where a potential SSSI includes common land, this may cause problems both in applying the initial procedures for notifying the site, and subsequently in securing a management scheme to regulate the land use for nature conservation. Similarly, the registration provisions of the Commons Registration Act 1965 and the Commons Act 2006 were drafted without reference to the particular requirements of environmental management.

Natural England and the Countryside Council for Wales ('the conservation bodies') are under a duty to notify an SSSI to every 'owner and occupier' of any of the land affected (1981 Act, section 28(1)). Section 15 of the Countryside Act 1968 gives them the power to conclude a management agreement with any 'owner, lessee or occupier of land' in an SSSI, while section 7 of the Natural Environment and Rural Communities Act 2006 gives Natural England a wide power to conclude management agreements with any person having 'an interest in land' (whether or not within an SSSI; see Rodgers, 2008, Chapter 13). The term 'occupier' was given a wide interpretation by the House of Lords in *Southern Water v. NCC* (1992), and will include most categories of occupier holding common rights over land that is notified as an SSSI. The practice of English Nature, its successor Natural England and the Countryside Council for Wales has for some years been based on a statement originally made in the House of Lords on 17 October 1990 by Baroness Blatch to the effect that for the purposes of the 1968 and 1981 Acts, 'occupiers' of land include both crofters and the holders of common rights (Nature Conservancy Council, 1991). Commoners with registered rights will therefore normally be served with the site notification when an SSSI is established (providing they can be traced), along with the freehold owners and tenants of the relevant land.

Following the notification of an SSSI, the principal protective mechanism applied by the 1981 Act is a statutory consultation procedure before potentially damaging operations can be carried out. The site notification will specify 'operations likely to damage the special conservation interest' (OLDSI) of the site if carried out. The OLDSIs will be selected with regard to scientific criteria, and will be dictated by the need to achieve favourable conservation status for the habitat, or species of animal, bird or plant, for the protection of which the site was notified. The nature of the occupier's land tenure rights will be irrelevant to this exercise, and the OLDSIs will be the same whether the site includes common land or not. It is a criminal offence to carry out any of the specified operations without the conservation body's consent (1981 Act, section 28P). An operation will be lawful, however, if carried out with written operational consent from the conservation body, under the terms of a management agreement or under a management scheme established for the SSSI (1981 Act, section 28E). These provisions are targeted at initiating a statutory consultation when a landowner proposes to carry out a notified operation, and this will often result in the conclusion of a management agreement to protect the site.

The broad effect of the service of the list of OLDSIs is to reallocate elements of resource utility and land use to the state, represented in this case by the conservation body. By prohibiting the carrying out of notified OLDSIs without prior operational consent, the 1981 Act reallocates the land management prerogatives represented by the OLDSIs to the state. Following changes to the law made by the Countryside and Rights of Way Act 2000, the conservation bodies can refuse operational consent to OLDSIs indefinitely, subject to the occupier having a right of appeal to the secretary of state. This represented a further shift in property rights – viewed as elements of resource utility – from the owner or occupier of SSSI land to the state (Rodgers, 2009). The 2000 Act also gave the conservation bodies the power to introduce management schemes in SSSIs in order to promote, for instance, the positive management of wildlife habitats, and to serve management notices on the owners and occupiers of SSSI land if the terms of a scheme are not being complied with (1981 Act as amended, sections 28J and 28K).

Similar land use restrictions are applied in SPAs and SACs designated for protection under the terms of the EC Wild Birds Directive of 1979 or the Habitats and Species Directive of 1992. The Conservation (Natural Habitats & C) Regulations 1994 (as amended) require a statutory consultation on proposed OLDSIs, and also give the conservation bodies wide powers to make by-laws in 'European' wildlife sites (1994 Regulations, regulations 18, 19, 28). There are also more extensive restrictions on the power of local authorities to grant planning permission for development in European sites (1994 Regulations, regulation 48 *et seq*). All four case studies examined in this work include both SSSIs, and SACs or SPAs notified under the 1994 regulations.

The list of OLDSIs will often be extensive, and this has major implications for the exercise of common rights in land. It may prohibit the exercise of some types of common right altogether, and subject the exercise of other common rights to statutory variation by requiring prior consultation with the conservation body. The OLDSIs notified in upland SSSIs, for example, commonly prohibit the digging of peat and thereby override the common right of turbary. Similarly, they may prohibit variations in the number of livestock grazed on common land in an SSSI, subjecting the common right of pasturage to a prior consultation requirement when livestock management changes are proposed. In practice, however, the complexity of the property rights regime applicable to common land is such that the application of environmental controls rarely reflects common property rights fully or accurately. The list of OLDSIs may prohibit management actions that commoners have no legal competence to carry out, such as supplementarily feeding livestock on common land. Similarly, it is not uncommon for common rights holders to be offered payment under publicly funded land management agreements for carrying out operations which have already been 'nationalized' by the service of an extensive list of OLDSIs in an SSSI. Several of the case studies examined in this work illustrate the lack of integration between common property rights and environmental governance mechanisms.

The application of these environmental controls is, however, dependent upon the conservation bodies serving a notice of OLDSIs on commoners when notifying common land as an SSSI or European wildlife site. If the site notification is not served, then the legal controls on OLDSIs will not apply to restrict land uses, and common property rights will be unaffected. Although the conservation bodies have a statutory duty to notify all occupiers within an SSSI, including, in most cases, common rights holders, the complexity of the common property rights regime, together with the unsatisfactory nature of the registers established by the Commons Registration Act 1965, means that it is often impossible to accurately identify the holders of rights in the land affected. This can make it very difficult to apply legislative controls aimed at promoting sustainable management (see Rodgers, 1999). The Norfolk case study examined in this volume provides a good example of these problems, in practice (see Chapter 9).

Economic models for sustainable commons management

The legal and social characterization of common property rights is also fundamentally important if we consider the introduction of 'voluntary' management under publicly funded schemes to encourage environmentally friendly land management. Agreements for the implementation of environmental land management schemes on common land can be offered by the conservation bodies either under their statutory powers to encourage positive management of SSSI land, or under the EC Rural Development Regulation. The Sheep and Wildlife Enhancement Scheme (SWES) is an example of the former, using the power to offer management agreements in SSSIs to target environmental improvement on common land – as exemplified in the Eskdale and Ingleton case studies examined in Chapters 6 and 7. The use of Environmentally Sensitive Area (ESA) agreements to promote environmentally friendly farming techniques is an example of the latter – as exemplified in the Eskdale and Elan Valley case studies (see Chapters 6 and 8).

The changes to the regulatory regime for SSSIs in the Countryside and Rights of Way Act 2000 were accompanied by fundamental changes to the way in which payments for agreements on European sites and SSSI land are calculated (see *Guidelines on Management Agreement Payments and Other Related Matters* (DETR, 2001), made under section 50 of the 1981 Act). The use of management agreements in SSSIs is, under the 2001 guidelines, increasingly focused on habitat protection schemes with management agreements that typically impose obligations to manage land for environmental improvement and habitat recreation, with incentive payments for capital works of conservation benefit, such as providing traditional hedges and dry stone walls, recreating upland heather habitats or recreating wetlands. In England this development is typified by the Wildlife Enhancement Scheme (WES), under which management agreements are strategically targeted to specific habitat restoration objectives, such as heather regeneration in the case of the SWES in Cumbria.

Management agreements for the environmental improvement of common land can also be offered under schemes in the England Rural Development Plan, or that for Wales, irrespective of whether it is within an SSSI or designated European wildlife site. The Environmentally Sensitive Areas programme was funded under the EC Rural Development Regulation of 1999 and its predecessors. Farmers in geographically designated ESAs could be offered management agreements for environmental management of their land, the terms of which were determined by the statutory instrument designating each ESA (Agriculture Act 1986, section 18). ESAs proved to be a very important tool for introducing environmental management into the English and Welsh uplands, and the programme had a major impact upon the economic sustainability of marginal farming in upland areas, many of which typically encompass large tracts of common land. The Eskdale case study in this volume is within the Lake District ESA, for example, and Cwmdeuddwr Common (in the Elan Valley case study) is within the Cambrian Mountains ESA.

The ESA programme was closed to new entrants in 2005 and was replaced by the Environmental Stewardship scheme in England, funded under the England Rural Development Plan 2005–2013. This is a more closely targeted environmental scheme, operating at the farm level with environmental management plans designed on a 'whole farm' basis. Environmental Stewardship is based on a 'public goods model' under which positive management for conservation is purchased by the state (Environmental Stewardship (England) Regulations 2005). Payments for environmental land management are made under one of four optional elements within a stewardship agreement: Entry Level Stewardship (ELS), Organic Entry Level Stewardship (OELS), Higher Level Stewardship (HLS) and (from 2010) Uplands ELS (2005 Regulations, regulations 3 and 5, and Schedule). Entry is dependent on the applicant achieving the relevant points score for management undertakings under each of the three elements of the scheme. Payments under Higher Level Stewardship agreements are made on the basis of specific works under one of a number of closely targeted conservation programmes (e.g. heather regeneration in the uplands).

In Wales, similar objectives have been pursued through the Tir Gofal and Tir Cynnal agri-environment schemes, which (like the Environmental Stewardship schemes in England) are premised on a positive conservation ethic with payments for habitat recreation, whole farm management and payment for capital works of environmental benefit. Eligibility for the schemes requires the applicant to score at least 100 points, with points awarded for a range of habitats, environmental features and farm characteristics. The scoring system can be problematic for commons, given their poor environmental quality and unenclosed nature.[3] However, applications that include SSSI land were awarded fixed point scores, provided that the applicant agrees to carry out any work needed to enhance the SSSI value. This could be advantageous for commons such as Cwmdeuddwr, which (as we shall see in Chapter 8) includes several SSSIs. A draft management plan was drawn up for applications scoring 100 points, and if accepted by the Welsh Assembly Government (WAG) and the applicant, a Tir Gofal agreement would be offered. The agreements have a duration of ten years, with a break clause after five years. Tir Gofal is being replaced from 2012 by a new scheme, 'Glas Tir' – strategically devised to tackle environmental issues at a water catchment and landscape level. Glas Tir includes special provision for the participation of commons, and a key issue for the future of Cwmdeuddwr common will be its eligibility for enrolment in the new scheme (see below, pp156–158). Although participation in agri-environment schemes is voluntary, they are commonly used to deliver the environmental management of conservation features on many SSSIs and European sites in Wales. This is the case in the Elan Valley case study, for example, as explained in Chapter 8.

Characterizing property rights: Conflicts

The legal characterization of property rights is important for the effective implementation of these schemes, and raises a number of difficult tensions and land-use conflicts. As a legal instrument for promoting environmental management, land management agreements require an economic exchange by which a landowner or farmer trades property rights in return for payment from the state. Clearly, a farmer can only exchange property rights in a form that is legally recognized – and in a contemporary context this will be reflected in the commons registers maintained under the Commons Registration Act 1965. The latter are often inaccurate, however, and fail to identify either the holders of rights or the extent of the right claimed, accurately or fully. And although agri-environment agreements can be made available to groups of commoners for the management of a CPR, such as a large extensive upland common, the property rights regime reflected in the registers makes it extremely difficult to achieve the necessary consensus between all potential appropriators in order to secure an agreement. The agreement of all common rights holders will be required in order to secure the legal enforceability of a collective agreement, and it can often be difficult to identify all potential commoners with property rights in the common. And if they can be identified, achieving a comprehensive consensus in a legally binding agreement can be difficult and time consuming. The ESA agreements negotiated for Eskdale Common in 1995, and for Cwmdeuddwr Common in 2001, exemplify the problems to which the complex common property rights regime can give rise in this regard (see Chapters 6 and 8 below).

Finally, the legal characterization of the land use permitted by a common property right will also impact upon the utility of agri-environment schemes as a tool for promoting the environmental management of common land. Measures under the EC Rural Development Policy are only available for applicants engaged in 'farming', and are therefore inapplicable if a common is not put to an agricultural use. The determining factor here is the economic use to which commoners put their rights, rather than the nature of the rights themselves – only common rights holders who are registered as farmers for the receipt of European Community subsidies can claim agri-environment payments under schemes such as ESA, ELS or HLS.

It follows that agri-environment schemes such as HLS have no potential application for the management of 'recreational' commons or those whose primary feature is (paradoxically) their high nature value rather than their value as an agricultural resource. The North Norfolk case study provides a good example of this phenomenon (see Chapter 9). The common land units in this case study offer an example of one of the most important wildlife areas in the UK, with migrating wildfowl populations of European-level significance – but on which there is virtually no contemporary agricultural use, although historically this has not always been the case. Schemes such as HLS are therefore inapplicable as a tool for managing the common resource, and for the manipulation of common property rights to promote the sustainable management of the commons in this ecologically sensitive area of the English coastline.

Resolving these conflicts between common property rights and the public policy objectives sought by environmental policy and rural development initiatives requires a flexible re-conceptualization of property rights, one that recognizes the functionality of property concepts and their role in the protection of the resource and its environmental features. It also requires a reconsideration of the governance structures within which commons governance is implemented by appropriators and other stakeholders. We will consider these issues in Chapter 5.

Notes

1 Two periods for application for registration were prescribed by regulation 5 of the Commons Registration (General) Regulations 1966 (SI 1966/1471), each with a subsequent period for objections to provisional registrations. The relevant application periods were, first, 2 January 1967 to 30 June 1968 (objections to provisional registrations to be made by 30 September 1970); and, second, 1 July 1968 to 2 January 1970 (objections to provisional registrations to be made by 31 July 1972).

2 The projected implementation timetable is as follows:

- October 2010: *Area 1* – South-East, South-West, East of England, London (comprising 101,948ha registered common land; 2265 town or village greens);
- October 2011: *Area 2* – West Midlands, North-West (comprising 141,353ha registered common land; 752 town or village greens);
- October 2012: *Area 3* – East Midlands, Yorkshire and the Humber, North-East (comprising 130,193ha registered common land; 1353 town or village greens).

See www.defra.gov.uk/wildlife-countryside/protected-areas/common-land/registration.htm. At the time of writing (August 2010), this timetable has been postponed.

3 Semi-structured interview, Welsh Assembly Government, March 2009.

5

Contemporary Governance of the Commons: The Quest for Sustainability

Modern priorities for sustainable governance of the commons have been pursued using a variety of legal and economic mechanisms that often fail to resolve tensions between public interest values in sustainable governance and property rights in the commons, between recreational land-use and environmental governance priorities, and between private legal obligations (such as those between landlord and tenant) and the legal obligations on commoners reflected in modern environmental legislation. This chapter will examine the self-regulatory models proposed for the commons under the Commons Act 2006, and their potential as mechanisms for sustainable management. The 2006 Act introduced measures to facilitate the establishment of statutory commons councils. This chapter will argue that, in opting for a 'managerial' reform model based on the self-regulation of commons through commons councils, the 2006 Act has ignored a number of deep-rooted problems arising from the unique nature of the property rights subsisting over common land (and discussed in Chapter 4). It will use qualitative data to examine the prospects for the successful introduction of self-regulatory management through statutory commons councils under the 2006 Act, and will compare and contrast these with other self-regulatory models that are currently used to manage the modern commons.

Commons governance

Although the Common Registration Act 1965 introduced substantive reforms aimed at establishing registers of common rights and common land, it did not seek to establish governance models for the management of the commons that were registered under that Act. Many commons are governed by collective bodies of commoners and landowners, and in some cases this has been the case for many years (for examples, see Chapters 6, 7 and 9). The legal models that have been developed are varied, both in terms of the legal structures deployed to give legal effect to management decision-making and their efficacy in ensuring the sustainable management of the commons.

The manor courts ceased to play a meaningful role in common management in many areas long before the abolition of copyhold tenure by the Law of Property Act 1922. Nevertheless, some manor courts have continued in existence and regulate individual commons, but with very limited powers that are now circumscribed by statute. The Administration of Justice Act 1977 provides that manor courts can continue to sit and to conduct such business as was customary prior to the coming into force of the 1977 Act, but they no longer have power to hear and determine legal proceedings (see 1977 Act, section 23). The manor courts to which this applied are specified in Schedule 4 to the 1977 Act, and in the case of those courts listed in Part 3 of the schedule, the customary business of each court is recorded and described. This includes, in many cases, the power to regulate the management of the common in question. It is difficult to see, however, how management could be carried out effectively without the power to hear and determine legal proceedings (see Gadsden, 1988, §12.145ff).

In practice, self-regulation by commoners' associations, and by associations of graziers is today of far greater importance. Some of these have evolved from manorial institutions, while others are organizations established to manage individual commons and to represent the collective views of the common graziers. Some commons associations came into being as a response to the need to collectively agree the basis for the registration of common rights under the Commons Registration Act 1965. This was the case in Eskdale, for example, where the Eskdale Commoners' Association was formed in 1967 primarily to arrange the registration of rights under the 1965 Act – although a wider role in the maintenance of the common was also envisaged, as explained further in Chapter 6.

Other commons associations have come into existence in response to specific situations requiring a collective response (for example, in response to the need to negotiate a collective management scheme or management agreement for the common). This was the case in another of the case studies examined in this book, Cwmdeuddwr Common in Powys, where the commons association was formed in the early 1990s to negotiate a management agreement for the common under the Environmentally Sensitive Areas programme (see Chapter 8). One of its primary functions today remains that of receiving payments under the agri-environment scheme from the Welsh Assembly Government and distributing them among its members.

Since a commons association is an unincorporated body, it lacks legal personality and is therefore unable to enter into legal transactions, or to initiate legal proceedings, in its own right and in its own name. The principal drawback of unincorporated associations as tools of collective management is that they have no power to bind a dissenting minority. This will be the case whether or not all commoners are members of the association. In the many cases where not all of the commoners participate in the association, then its managerial powers will be even further circumscribed. The members, even acting by a majority decision, have no power to pass resolutions binding a person who dissents – and neither does a majority have power to bind a dissenter to make financial contributions towards management. A commons association cannot grant easements over the common (*Paine & Co. v. St. Neots Gas and Coke Co.* [1939]). This power is vested in the owner of the soil, but cannot be exercised in a manner that interferes with the exercise of the common rights. The acquiescence of the commoners in granting easements is therefore important, but cannot be expressed in a legally binding form (see Gadsden, 1988, §12.151). Gadsden (1988) points out that it is common practice for commoners to enter into an agreement not to sue the grantee of an easement, such as a right of way over the common. This is not entirely satisfactory, however, and would probably not bind individual members of the association.

The natural corollary to this unsatisfactory position is that the unanimous participation of all commoners is required if a legally binding scheme of management is to be introduced in order to regulate livestock and make changes in the land use permitted on a common. This can be time consuming and frequently leads to substantial difficulties. Cwmdeuddwr Common was, for example, one of only four commons in Wales to enter the Environmentally Sensitive Areas agri-environment programme. The negotiation of the management for the common was complex and time consuming, requiring the identification of all commoners with grazing and other common rights, and required a substantial effort to ensure their acquiescence in the proposed scheme. The negotiation of the ESA agreement for Eskdale Common was, similarly, rendered more complex and time consuming because of the necessity to secure the participation of everyone with rights registered against the common, whether they were active grazers or not (see Chapters 6 and 8).

The difficulties are sometimes magnified by the consequences of the flawed nature of the registration process under the 1965 Act. In both Eskdale and Cwmdeuddwr it was possible to identify, from the commons registers, who the current rights holders were, and then to seek their participation. In many cases, however, where transactions in land and/or common rights have taken place since 1970, it is simply impossible to discover from the registers who the current holders of common rights are. The registers in the Norfolk case study (see Chapter 9) provide a very good example of this phenomenon. At the very least, the failure of the 1965 Act to require that the subsequent sale and/or leasing of common rights be registered will render the process of identifying the current holders of common rights more complex: at its worst, it may render this an impossible task and, as a result, prevent the accomplishment of a satisfactory management scheme for the common.

Prior to the Commons Act 2006, there was no 'model' form of legal structure for the collective management of the commons. The problems posed by attempts to organize collective management through unincorporated commons associations have been avoided in some cases by the adoption of bespoke institutional arrangements for individual commons. The management of Ingleborough, a common divided into two registered common land units, presents an interesting case study of such an initiative (see Chapter 7). One section is managed by an unincorporated association of the kind discussed above (in this case, a stint holders' meeting), whereas the commoners with registered rights on the other have formed a company limited by guarantee that has the responsibility for managing the common grazing. This affords it legal personality, and enables it to take management decisions, enter into legal agreements and to initiate legal action in its own name on behalf of its members. Its powers are, in practice, further enhanced by the fact that the absentee landowner has given the company a power of attorney to exercise all the functions and powers of the owner of the soil in relation to the management of the common. The combined effect of this unique legal structure is to collectively give the commoners, acting through the company, exclusive and unlimited control of the management and use of the common.

Managing the modern commons

The Commons Act 2006 addresses these management deficiencies by making provision for the establishment of statutory commons councils – corporate bodies that will have power to make legally binding decisions as to the management of a common. The size, nature and regional jurisdiction of each council will vary, and the Act does not lay down a template model for all commons councils. Their adoption will not be compulsory, and there must be local support for the establishment of a commons council. The establishment of a commons council will not, moreover, override the rights of landowners. Nevertheless, the new model for collaborative management presented by the 2006 Act has the potential to be a major step forward in establishing more effective forms of collective organization of commons management. It is also a key development in the quest for more sustainable commons management.

The 2006 Act provides that the secretary of state or Welsh Assembly Government can, by order, establish a commons council for any land that is registered as common land, or as a town or village green that is subject to rights of common (2006 Act, section 26 (1), (2) and (4)). The secretary of state (or if the common is in Wales, the Welsh Assembly Government) must publish a draft of the proposed establishment order and invite representations from the public on it. It may also hold a local inquiry on the proposal (2006 Act, section 27 (2) and (3)). The authority cannot make an establishment order unless it is satisfied, having regard to the representations that have been made, and the result of any local inquiry, that there is 'substantial support' for the establishment of a commons council – and particular regard must be paid to the views of persons having legal rights over the common (including, for instance, the owner of the soil), the common rights holders themselves, and others with legal functions which relate to the management and maintenance of common land (see 2006 Act, section 27 (4) and (5)). Local authorities in the area concerned may, for example, have statutory functions in relation to the common under development control law or in relation to public rights of way.

Commons councils will be established by order, and will be corporate bodies (2006 Act, section 26 (3) and (4)). A commons council, if established, will not be classified in legal terms as a servant or agent of the Crown, and neither will it enjoy any status, immunity or privilege of the Crown (2006 Act, section 28 (1) and (2)). It will be an 'occupier' of any of the common land it administers that is within a Site of Special Scientific Interest (SSSI), and the legal controls on land use in SSSIs set out in the Wildlife and Countryside Act 1981 will apply to it (2006 Act, section 52 and schedule 5, para 3). It will not, however, be treated as a 'public' body with the additional duties that public bodies have under the 1981 Act to promote the conservation of the flora and fauna of special interest in an SSSI (2006 Act, section 28 (3); for the duties of public bodies with regard to SSSIs, see 1981 Act, section 28G). As we shall see below, however, it has to consider the 'public' interest when exercising its functions and this includes taking account of nature conservation when exercising the new powers to pass regulations for managing the common.

The Department for Environment, Food and Rural Affairs (Defra) has published a draft 'model' establishment order (Defra, 2006a). This posits a suggested membership of between 10 and 12 members for a commons council governing a group of three separate common land (CL) units. A balanced representation is suggested, with three representatives appointed by active graziers on the largest common, and two and one, respectively, for the other two notional CL units. This model would permit informal commoners associations governing specific commons to continue as before, while nominating members to act on their behalf in a statutory commons council established for the group of commons in question. An 'active' grazier is defined for these purposes as someone who has grazed animals on one of the commons for a period of 12 months immediately preceding the date of coming into force of the establishment order (Defra, 2006a, draft regulation 2(i)). The balance of the council's membership would comprise one non-active grazier, two landowner representatives, and (if the common lies with a National Park) one representative of the local National Park authority – plus up to two co-opted members (Defra, 2006a, draft regulation 3(2)). Defra has also promulgated a draft constitution for commons councils in England, which will be applicable unless varied by the terms of an establishment order made under the 2006 Act (Defra, 2006b; Commons Councils (Standard Constitution) (England) Regulations 2010).

Defra has also sponsored research into the feasibility of establishing statutory commons councils by sponsoring three pilot 'shadow' commons councils, with a view to testing the issues that would arise during the establishment of commons councils in the pilot areas. The three pilot shadow councils were Cumbria, Minchampton common (Gloucestershire) and Bodmin common (Cornwall). Each of the three pilots went through the process that would be involved in establishing a statutory commons council, once Part 2 of the 2006 Act has been brought into force. Of the three pilot councils, the shadow Cumbria commons council has resulted in a proposal to establish an 'umbrella' statutory council on a county-wide basis, with representation from the many local commoners' associations across Cumbria that currently manage individual commons in the county.

The Cumbrian model combines informal governance by commoners' associations, in which all stakeholders participate, with a formal governance structure (the proposed commons council) with a more limited and closely defined membership that can introduce legally enforceable management rules. This raises an interesting historical parallel with the relationship in previous centuries between informal 'byrlaw' meetings and the more formal proceedings in the manor courts (see Chapter 3). The Cumbria model posits a commons council of 15 voting members (Defra, 2009a). There would be ten representatives of active graziers, with one drawn from each of ten regions in the county; two representatives of non-active graziers; and three owner representatives chosen (one each) by the representatives of owners with recreational interests, sporting interests and agricultural interests. The Cumbrian proposal defines active graziers for these purposes as commoners who have grazed a hefted flock for at least the previous two years. The management of individual commons in Cumbria would remain with local associations under delegated powers, and the statutory council would only make a decision relating to an individual CL unit (e.g. a particular common) if there was a majority of 75 per cent of commoners from that unit in favour of the proposal. In this way it is proposed to maintain local control of day-to-day management in the hands of the commoners' associations for each individual CL unit, while achieving both the power to make legally binding rules and economies of scale through the use of a county-wide model for the statutory council. The Federation of Cumbria Commoners has agreed, in principle, to proceed with the establishment of a council on this basis, subject to resolution of a number of outstanding issues.

Implementing sustainable management: The potential role of commons councils

The Commons Act 2006 could facilitate a move towards a more dynamic model for common property rights that promotes sustainable management as a key objective for the commons. This will depend, however, upon the willingness of commoners and other stakeholders to use the new statutory powers to initiate self-regulation by establishing statutory commons councils. This is by no means certain to materialize. The other two pilot 'shadow' councils sponsored by Defra, for example, both failed to produce concrete proposals for the establishment of a statutory commons council.

The promotion of sustainable management is central to the role of commons councils. When exercising their statutory functions, they must have regard to 'the public interest', which is defined to include nature conservation and the conservation of landscape, the protection of public rights of access to land, and the protection of archaeological remains and the historic features of common land (2006 Act, section 31 (6), (7)). They must also have regard to any guidance issued by the secretary of state or Welsh Assembly Government when exercising their statutory powers.

The powers conferred on commons councils by the 2006 Act are potentially extensive, but not unlimited. A commons council will have the functions and powers conferred upon it by the order that establishes it (2006 Act, section 31 (3), (3)). An establishment order can confer one or more of three possible functions on a commons council: the management of agricultural activities on the land for which the council is established, the management of the vegetation on the land, and the management of common rights. The functions that an establishment order can confer are elaborated upon to include the power to introduce binding regulations in order to regulate agricultural activities on the common, regulations as to the management of vegetation and as the exercise of common rights on the common (2006 Act, section 31 (3) (a), (4)). The commons council's powers cannot override the legal rights of the owner of the soil, however, or those of any other person having a legal interest in the land over which the rights are exercised, other than a right of common (2006 Act, section 33 (1)–(3)). Where the consent of the owner of the soil is required before a rule-making power can be exercised, or action taken to enforce a rule already in place, the 2006 Act enables the commons council to give notice of its proposed actions to the owner, who will be deemed to have given consent if they do not object to the proposal within the time allowed in the council's notice (2006 Act, section 33 (6)). The commons council's notice of its intention to exercise these powers must give at least 28 days in which the recipient can respond (2006 Act, section 33 (5)).

The commons councils can be given power to establish 'live' registers of common rights (2006 Act, section 31((3) (b) and (c); and for an example, see DEFRA, 2006a, draft regulation 8). A 'live' register is one that will give an accurate picture of the entitlements affecting a common, the current holders of those entitlements, and the manner in which they are being exercised (e.g. the number of animals stocked on the common by each commoner). A 'living' register of this kind would be similar to that regulating livestock grazing on Dartmoor under the Dartmoor Commons Act 1985, a model that is widely accepted as highly beneficial. Grazing rights on Dartmoor are governed by a separate system of registration in the Dartmoor Commons Act 1985. This operates quite differently than the Commons Registration Act 1965, most notably in requiring changes in the ownership and use of common rights to be notified and entered in the public registers established by the Act.

Action by a commons council to establish a living register would require the compulsory registration of all formal and informal transfers of grazing entitlements, and the supply of information as to stocking numbers by adjoining landowners turning stock out onto the common. It could also require details for the number of animals grazed on the common by each grazier and the mark, tag or other means by which ownership of the animals is identified. The register of grazing would be open to public inspection. A commons council can also make rules governing the leasing or licensing of common rights (see 2006 Act, section 31 (3) (b)–(f)). In the case of grazing rights, for example, this power might be used to restrict the licensing of rights to a shorter period than that permitted by law (two years in England, three years in Wales)[1] and to require anyone temporarily transferring rights in this way to register the transfer with the secretary of the commons council. If the commons council is given power to maintain a register of grazing, any temporary transfer of this type would also be registrable on the 'live' grazing register. A commons council can also be given power to remove animals illegally grazing the common and to remove unlawful boundaries and other encroachments (2006 Act, section 31 (3) (f); Defra, 2003, proposals 1–7; Defra, 2006a, draft regulations 5 and 6).

The agricultural management rules can include provisions limiting the periods when animals can be turned out onto the common, prohibiting the grazing of 'entire' (i.e. un-castrated) male animals, stipulating standards of husbandry and controlling the supplementary feeding of animals on the common (Defra, 2006a, draft regulation 6). The express inclusion of a provision concerning supplementary feeding in Defra's draft establishment order provides a further example of the lack of integration between land management powers and property rights, as common rights of grazing – being merely *profits à prendre* – do not confer a legal right to supplementarily feed grazing livestock (see *Besley v. John* [2003]).

The Defra Shadow Commons Council Project has produced land management regulations for the Cumbrian commons that would have legal effect under the terms of the proposed establishment order for the Cumbria Commons Council (Defra, 2009b). This provides an interesting template of the type of detailed management that could be implemented on 'agricultural' commons where the common gazing provides a valuable economic resource for appropriators. It enlarges upon the rules in the Defra draft establishment order in a number of respects. It contains detailed rules, for example, restricting the turning out onto the common of certain types of animal – some in order to preserve the quality of livestock reared on the common (hence, restrictions on the introduction of bulls over the age of six months, or rams and ram lambs between 31 July and 10 November annually), and others to preserve the quality of the vegetation (e.g. restrictions on shod horses or ponies) (see Defra, 2009b, draft regulation 10). The regulations would also prohibit the release of any stallion or other animal considered by the council to be a danger to persons or animals. The draft regulations also contain provision for the marking of animals for identification purposes, and prohibit the release of animals that are not hefted in accordance with local livestock management custom and practice (Defra, 2009b, draft regulations 4 and 5). They provide for the removal of dead commonable animals by their owners, and for the appointment of a reeve who will have power *inter alia* to remove unauthorized animals from the common and detain them (Defra, 2009b, draft regulation 12). These powers can be delegated to a local commons association or a local authority, which can exercise them in the name of the commons council as its agent (Defra, 2009b, draft regulation 17). The latter is important in preserving the balance between statutory management through the council at county level and local control of livestock management within the farming community on each individual common.

The draft Cumbrian land management regulation would also introduce close control over the leasing and licensing of rights without the land to which the rights attach. Even if the period of the proposed lease is within that laid down by law (two years in England), the approval of the commons council will be required if it exceeds a (shorter) minimum period to be specified in the order. The council's decision on approval 'will have particular regard to the views of the local association if existing for that area and any guidance on the leasing of rights produced by the Council' (Defra, 2009b, draft regulation 3).

The Cumbrian model is an interesting example of the regulatory framework that could be introduced where commons councils are established for large 'farmed' commons where the exercise of rights has a substantive economic value to appropriators. It also illustrates the potential for the creation of regulatory management powers that locate power within the local farming community and associate sustainable management of the commons with concepts of 'locality' defined in terms of rights of economic appropriation. The way in which it is proposed to exercise these powers would exclude wider societal interests, such as community groups and recreational interests, from any meaningful role in sustainable commons management even if the latter are locally based.

Research into institutional models for commons management has tended to ignore the problems for the establishment of commons councils on non-agricultural commons. The variety of land uses exercised over common land is considerable and varies from place to place. Many commons either have no – or at most marginal – agricultural value and the framework laid down in the 2006 Act for the establishment of commons councils has more limited relevance in these cases. The Norfolk case study (see Chapter 9) illustrates this problem. Of the statutory powers potentially vested in commons councils by the Commons Act 2006, those relating to the management of vegetation and the control of the exercise of common rights over the land would, in this context, have primary relevance: although Thornham common is grazed by livestock, the common grazing marshes at Brancaster are not. The primary focus of the powers conferred on a commons council for the Norfolk commons would therefore have to be the control of the exercise of common rights such as wild fowling, and of the harvesting of produce such as sea lavender, seaweed and samphire. This might permit much closer control of the exploitation of the common resource; but the role of a statutory common council would inevitably be quite different from that on 'agricultural' commons. Given the very large number of commoners with exploitation rights (e.g. over 300 in the case of Brancaster common CL 65 alone), many of whom live at considerable distances from the commons, the establishment and running of a commons council would be challenging. And given the absence of commercial exploitation of the common resource, the primary focus of any management rules introduced under the 2006 Act – for example, to restrict wildfowling – would probably have to be nature conservation.

The management problems on many lowland commons, where the primary use of common land is recreational and the number of active common rights holders is minimal, would be different again. Barrow common, in the Norfolk case study (see Chapter 9, p182) provides an exemplar of the management problems faced by lowland commons in this category.

Management powers: Potential impact upon property rights

On 'agricultural' commons, the introduction of binding rules governing the use of common grazing rights will enable a commons council to bind inactive graziers in order to prevent them from exercising previously unused common rights. This will facilitate the speedier conclusion of environmental management schemes on common land (see Rodgers, 2007). It will also remove the necessity of accommodating the property rights represented by registered (but unused) rights in environmental management agreements. This was necessary in the case of the Environmentally Sensitive Area agreements negotiated for Eskdale and Cwmdeuddwr Commons in the case studies examined in Chapter 6 and 8, for example, and proved problematic. If commons councils introduce agricultural management rules of this kind, however, a situation will arise where some commoners will have registered rights that they are not legally entitled to exercise. The rights will be 'sterilized' for the period of the restriction. This will considerably reduce their economic value, although the 'rights' themselves – being registered on the commons register – will still subsist at law.

This scenario could give rise to interesting questions, not least whether there has been a 'taking' of property without compensation. Of some importance here is the distinction between property rights theories located in the discourse of ownership and 'rights' (Honore, 1961; Harris, 1996), and more dynamic models of property that stress its central role as a mechanism for the allocation of land-based utility rights (Gray, 1994). These were examined in Chapter 4. The property entitlement of each commoner will be unaffected because his theoretical 'right' (to graze or to take peat or bracken, etc.) will still be reflected in an entry in the commons register, even if he cannot exercise it. The application of a resource allocation model of property rights, based on access to resource utility, will, however, produce a different – and arguably more accurate – interpretation indicating that a modulation of property rights will have been effected. The passing of agricultural management rules by a commons council will abrogate the property rights of commoners whose right to graze is thereby restricted or removed. The fact that they retain registered rights is irrelevant insofar as those rights will have ceased to give access to a resource (i.e. the taking of grass by grazing). The same would be true of common rights of a non-agricultural nature, such as the rights to wildfowl and samphire in the Norfolk case study (see Chapter 9), if a commons council were to pass land management rules regulating the manner in which rights are exercised. The commons register in such cases will have ceased to reflect the allocation of the agricultural resources to which registered rights notionally give access, and as it will no longer reflect the true distribution of land-based utility it cannot be said to represent the true allocation of property rights in the common.

A grazier whose rights have been restricted by the commons council will not be able to trade them in a management agreement (e.g. under the Sheep and Wildlife Enhancement Scheme (SWES) or Higher Level Stewardship (HLS)) unless they continue to confer access to an element of utility (i.e. an exercisable right of access to common grazing). Similarly, a commoner with wildfowling or other recreational rights that are potentially restricted by land management rules introduced under the 2006 Act would possess a notional property right with no economic exchange value. A 'bargaining' model of property rights would hold that, insofar as common rights in these cases have been restricted, and cannot be accommodated in an economic exchange, they could no longer be viewed as a species of property right. The Commons Act 2006 therefore represents a move to explicitly link the exercise of property rights to the promotion of sustainable management of the commons. This can only be fully understood within a dynamic property rights model. The more traditional interpretations of property based in ownership discourse fail to capture the flexible nature of the property relationship in the commons, or to capture the dynamic role of property rights in delivering environmental management of the commons.

Commons councils: Stakeholder perceptions

The model for statutory commons councils set out in Part 2 of the Commons Act 2006 was tested against the perceptions of appropriators and stakeholders by qualitative research carried out by the Contested Common Land research project. Focus groups were conducted in the Ingleton and Elan Valley case studies to investigate stakeholders' views of the advantages and disadvantages of establishing statutory commons councils. Additionally, the Eskdale case study was within the Defra pilot Shadow Commons Council for Cumbria. The focus group participants were primarily farmers and landowners, a restriction justified on the basis that the Commons Act 2006 requires that particular regard must be paid to the views of persons having legal rights over the common when establishing a commons council.

The focus groups identified a number of potential disadvantages for the setting up of commons councils. The participants found the cost of establishing and running a commons council, as well as the potential for interference by external bodies, such as government departments, especially disadvantageous. A closely related issue was the fear of losing customary management, and with it informal arrangements embedded in the principle of good neighbourliness. Given the statutory character of commons councils, having to 'bring your neighbour to court' (in the words of an Ingleton farmer interviewed) could be one of the negative effects of commons councils. The principle of good neighbourliness, a fundamental element of common pool resource (CPR) management since manorial times, still plays a role in the modern context. Finally, the increase in bureaucratic arrangements if regular meetings would have to be held was also perceived as problematic by both groups.

In the Ingleton case study, stakeholders identified other potential disadvantages of commons councils. This can be explained by looking at variable factors such as the influence (or lack of it) of agri-environmental schemes in the case study area, or the impact of differential perceptions of property rights generated by the different management systems used to regulate grazing in an historical context (in Ingleton the stinting system gave rise, for example, to a close association of stints with notions of 'property'). Many participants questioned the relevance of a commons council when the existing commons associations functioned very efficiently and managed the common in a sustainable and effective manner. Ingleborough Common does not have a single agri-environmental scheme requiring the participation and consent of all the commoners – the only management agreements in the case study area were SWES agreements with individual farmers. Ingleton commoners had not, unlike their counterparts in the Elan Valley and Eskdale, experienced the difficulty of achieving an agri-environmental scheme for the whole common using the weak, non-statutory powers of the existing commons association. By contrast, the Elan Valley focus group considered the statutory status of a commons council potentially very beneficial when negotiating future agri-environmental schemes.

The contrasting attitude of the two groups to inactive graziers was also interesting. The prospect of passing binding rules that could prevent inactive graziers from exercising dormant rights, while welcomed by the Elan Valley focus group, was considered an unjust removal of property rights by the Ingleton group. This perception could be attributable to the stinting system characterizing the management of the commons on Ingleborough and Scales Moor, which has encouraged graziers to interpret the property rights conferred by stints as a tradable commodity, to be valued independently from their exercise and from the land they are intended to benefit (i.e. to which they are appurtenant). This is a legacy of the different historical practices used to govern the commons prior to the Commons Registration Act 1965.

Other advantages often suggested for commons councils (e.g. enhanced power to enforce rules, and better representation arrangements) were not considered of great significance by either focus group. Many of these were considered to be characteristics of their existing commons associations, and informal dispute settlement between graziers was a preferred option. On the other hand, the acquisition of greater powers to ensure the proper management of the commons was considered to be the most important advantage of establishing a commons council by both the groups. An important by-product of this, for the Elan Valley group, was the perceived potential for greatly facilitating access to funding through agri-environment schemes.

Finally, both groups were asked what model of commons council they would favour. Given the flexibility offered by the Commons Act 2006 in relation to the institutional design of commons councils, this question is important if we are to predict how diverse the new institutional landscape of the commons could be in the future. Both the commoners and the landowners would strongly prefer to have separate commons councils representing each common, rather than an umbrella organization, in order to represent and reinforce local management diversity. However, the anticipated setting-up and running costs of establishing a statutory commons council constitutes a significant financial barrier to implementing institutional organization on this model, unless financial incentives are deployed (e.g. through the funding arrangements for public agri-environment schemes). Overall, the groups' perceptions of the potential advantages and disadvantages of establishing a statutory commons council were finely balanced.

Commons councils and 'sustainable' commons management

To what extent do commons councils have the potential to reconcile conflicting land uses and thereby deliver sustainable management of our common lands, as intended by the Commons Act 2006? They will be statutory bodies established by order of the secretary of state or the National Assembly for Wales, their rules will be legally binding and their powers externally recognized. Their legal status as bodies corporate will be a guarantee for the conservation bodies that the terms of collective management agreements will be complied with. Additionally, the commons councils' legal power to make binding land management rules and to regulate the exercise of common rights, where used, will guarantee the implementation of environmental management schemes on common land. Their ability to make binding agricultural management rules could also revitalize and legitimize customary arrangements. Potentially, therefore, commons councils could have the ability to address the negative impacts upon the sustainability of commons management attributable to the property rights regime established by the Commons Registration Act 1965, such as the over-registration of rights on some commons and the failure to subject registrations to a sustainability appraisal before they became final.

The Commons Act 2006 is not prescriptive as to commons councils' size and membership, and a considerable degree of freedom is left to stakeholders in the implementation of Part 2 of the Commons Act 2006. As the size of a commons council is not predetermined by the Act, it could cover a whole county (as in the model proposed in the Cumbria pilot study) or only one common land unit. As we have seen, the 2006 Act leaves it to each commons council to decide on the scope of its membership, which may vary from one common to another and reflect the different interests (agricultural, recreational, landowning and community groups) with a role in the management of the common. Commons councils could become the new collective voice for common land, where multiple perceptions could constructively work towards the building of an all-encompassing sustainability. They could also contribute to an institutional politics that recognizes the local scale, so valued by the commoners.

Nevertheless, the disadvantages of commons councils need to be overcome if they are to become the local embodiment of sustainability principles and their application. The principal constraints identified above are establishment and running costs, the loss of informal collective institutions and the potential impact upon the principle of good neighbourliness. These are not insurmountable problems. The financial burden could be minimized by securing economies of scale (e.g. by establishing an overarching council for groups of commons, as is proposed in Cumbria) so that establishment costs can be shared among different common land units. This model would retain the freedom of existing informal commoners' associations to manage their own common at local level, while securing statutory rule-making powers under the 2006 Act and giving the commons council an additional coordinating role. This model would also preserve the role of informal institutions by ensuring the survival of local commons associations. Where commons councils are established, the use of their new powers to establish 'live' registers of common land will help to minimize the problems encountered by the conservation bodies when trying to identify current rights holders. This will make it easier for the conservation bodies and groups of commoners to secure agri-environmental schemes on common land. And, finally, the power to create new common rights vested in a commons council will be useful where mixed grazing with sheep and cattle is sought, in order to promote habitat recreation, but this is constrained by the pre-existing registered rights. Overall then, commons councils have the potential to become platforms for the discussion and reconciliation of different normative orders and regulatory standards in order to develop a wider understanding and practice of sustainability.

Commons councils: A paradigm for institutional governance?

One of the key themes of this book is the need for a reappraisal of institutional and neo-institutional approaches to CPR governance (see Chapter 1 p11ff). The dynamism of common property rights is a key issue recognized by neo-institutionalist analyses of commons governance. From the above review of Part 2 of the Commons Act 2006, it is evident that in the English context, statutory commons councils would fulfil most of Ostrom's design principles (see Box 1.1 in Chapter 1). The boundaries of the CPR will, for example, be clearly identified in each case by the establishment order under the 2006 Act (principle 1); the collective choice arrangements for commons councils will permit individuals affected by operational rules to participate in modifying them (principle 3); and the land management rules that a council can adopt under the 2006 Act can provide for monitoring by appropriators or by monitors who are accountable to the appropriators (thus satisfying principle 4).

The picture is somewhat more complex than that posited by Ostrom and other institutional scholars, however, given the specific legal context in which CPR management is set. There are important external management influences at play of a kind not envisaged by Ostrom's institutional model – both in terms of the normative standards for CPR management that are applied to secure 'sustainable' management (e.g. in protected sites such as Sites of Special Scientific Interest (SSSIs)), and in the administrative and enforcement arrangements for implementing land management rules (in which the criminal law plays an important part). Commons councils therefore represent a 'hybrid' form of collective CPR management tool in which land management practices based on local custom and social practice are given collective sanction by appropriators; but in relation to which the goals and objectives to be sought by land management are defined externally to the CPR institution, and are subject to review and monitoring by external agencies and public bodies (such as Natural England).

Although most of Ostrom's design principles are satisfied, some are partially satisfied by the application of factors external to the CPR institution and supplied by state agencies or authority. So, for example, graduated sanctions will be applied under the 2006 Act for the infringement of operational rules established by a commons council, but not in the sense envisaged by Ostrom. In the institutional model posited by Ostrom it is important that appropriators who violate operational rules are likely to be assessed graduated sanctions by other appropriators or their appointees (design principle 5). Under the 2006 Act, graduated sanctions for the breach of the land management rules adopted by a commons council will be applied in the last resort through the application of the criminal law. And monitoring of appropriators will be undertaken both by officers appointed by the commons council (principle 4) and by external bodies such as Natural England. Where a common includes land within an SSSI, Natural England's powers to monitor the condition of natural habitats, and to restrict the carrying out of operations likely to damage their conservation interest, will be key factors in ensuring its 'sustainable' management. Natural England's officers are not accountable to appropriators for the manner in which these powers are exercised; indeed, in some cases they may restrict the actions of appropriators or require them to change their management practices to prevent future habitat loss. And if they refuse to do so they have a number of legal sanctions that can be applied to ultimately ensure compliance – including the use of management notices and compulsory purchase (1981 Act, section 28K) .

The limiting determinism and rigidity of Ostrom's design principles have been recognized by more recent neo-institutionalist literature, while the importance of *local* and *precise* rules for governing the commons effectively has been emphasized (see *inter alia* Gibbs and Bromley, 1989; Schlager and Ostrom, 1992; Becker and Ostrom, 1995; Keohane and Ostrom, 1995; Agrawal and Ostrom, 2001; Agrawal 2003). Collective management institutions are still, however, widely interpreted as 'the rule of the games in society', and the neo-institutionalist analysis therefore continues to concentrate on rules, law and governance (North, 1990, p3). These rules prescribe individual actions within the group, thus eliminating both the risk of free-riding and the need for members to negotiate every new transaction with each other, which would be costly and would depend upon individual bargaining power. In order to achieve sustainable resource use, locally devised CPR institutions often constrain the behavioural options of individual actors by establishing property rights which are limited in exercise and eligibility.

The hybrid governance model represented by commons councils partially fits within the neo-institutionalist representation of successful CPR institutions. As we have seen, one of the strengths of commons councils is their potential ability to make rules to bind dissenting minorities and thereby facilitate the securing and monitoring of agri-environmental agreements on common land. In doing so, the councils will be able to constrain individual appropriator's actions; but they will not be able to do so through the imposition of collectively agreed property rules as envisaged by neo-institutionalist scholars. The property rights of appropriators are determined by the terms of the commons registers established under the Commons Registration Act 1965 (and maintained under Part 1 of the 2006 Act). A commons council will be able to constrain the actions of appropriators through the use of legally enforceable powers sanctioned by the state, applied to control the *exercise* of common property rights and to target them to achieving sustainable management. In this regard the 'public interest' is a key element shaping the exercise by a commons council of these regulatory powers, and this also includes external factors – for example, the public interest in nature conservation and in landscape preservation.

Nevertheless, it remains the case that the active role of resource users is a central component for successful institutional design. This is usually subdivided conceptually into participation at constitutional choice, collective choice and operational choice level (Ostrom, 1990, 1999; Ostrom et al, 2002). If resource users have the authority to formulate and modify the general rules of the regime (constitutional choice level), devise policy-making process and resource management (collective choice level) and be responsible for controlling the appropriation of resource and the enforcement of the rules (operational choice level), the CPR is likely to be sustainably managed. This multilevel conception of CPR governance is structured in a hierarchical manner whereby the operational choice level is affected by the collective choice level, which, in turn, depends upon decisions taken at the constitutional choice level.

Given that local stakeholders will have a central role in devising the rules and structure of a commons council, it would appear that the institutional solution proposed by the Commons Act 2006 satisfies these premises for successful CPR governance. A closer examination of the hybrid nature of the model shows, however, that it not only sits uneasily within the neo-institutionalist model of CPR governance, but that it also illustrates some of the latter's shortcomings. In the case of a statutory commons council, there are interpenetrations by external normative orders at each level of the multilevel paradigm for collective choice governance:

1 At the *constitutional choice level*, appropriators have primary responsibility for formulating the general rules of each commons council. These have to be formally approved, however, by the secretary of state before a commons council can be established. And the rules themselves have to be sanctioned by an establishment order that will take the form of a statutory instrument made under the Commons Act 2006
2 At the *collective choice level*, appropriators will have the primary right to determine the rules to be applied to govern resource management. Where this is done through the use of land management rules made under the 2006 Act, however, the rules will be subject to external validation by the secretary of state, and will derive their legal authority from a statutory instrument made under the 2006 Act. It must also be remembered that if the land is within a protected area, such as a Site of Special Scientific Interest (SSSI), a Special Protection Area (SPA) or a Special Area of Conservation (SAC), some decisions on resource allocation will have already been appropriated to the public conservation bodies through the site notification, and these will take priority in law over collective choice decisions made by appropriators acting through the commons council.
3 At the *operational choice level*, the officers of a commons council will have power to control the appropriating of the land resource and oversee the enforcement of land management rules. Once again, however, an external element is introduced through the applicability of the criminal law to enforce rules passed by a commons council and sanctioned by the secretary of state under the 2006 Act. And, in the case of a protected site (such as an SSSI), the operational choices available to commoners will be restricted by the list of operations likely to damage the site's conservation interest (OLDSIs) served with the site notification, contravention of which is a criminal offence (1981 Act, section 28E).

Note

1 See the Commons (Severance of Rights) (England) Order 2006, SI 2006/2145; and the Commons (Severance of Rights) (Wales) Order 2007, SI 2007/583 (W.55).

Part II

Commons in Focus: Four Case Studies

The remaining substantive chapters of this book use a case study methodology to examine the broad themes identified in earlier chapters by focusing on four geographically distinct case studies. The underlying aim of this approach is to provide a secure evidence base from which conclusions may be drawn. The enduring role of custom and tradition has been noted earlier, and these were essentially local factors, varying according to differences in environment, society and economy. Moreover, since a central theme of this book is the interplay between local systems of governance and a national cultural context and body of legislation, it is only by unpicking this interface on the ground that it is possible to fully understand environmental governance as it applied to common land. The approach taken in the following chapters bears features in common with what has been termed 'micro-history', the guiding principle of which is that detailed analysis at the local level will uncover subtleties of meaning which may challenge more general assumptions. As one practitioner of 'micro-history' has put it, the aim is not only to 'explore the working out of wider social and cultural processes at a local level, but to use the local to challenge our view of the very nature of these processes' (Reay, 1996, p262).

The four case study areas (see Figure 1.3 in Chapter 1, p5) have been chosen to present a view of the wide diversity of environmental problems affecting common land and its management in historical and modern contexts. Three lie in upland England and Wales and illustrate the diversity of historical and contemporary experiences in the environment in which the majority of registered common land lies; the fourth, in East Anglia, includes both coastal marsh and inland heath, and thus typifies the very different types of common land found in lowland England. All of the case studies illustrate the wide range of different pressures on common land today: a legacy of overgrazing in the uplands contrasting with under-grazing of lowland commons; differential recreational pressures on upland and lowland commons; tensions between nature conservation and agricultural resource use; and tensions between nature conservation and recreational land uses. All four are subject to statutory environmental and/or landscape designations with different models of legal protection – for example, National Parks, Sites of Special Scientific Interest (SSSIs) and Areas of Outstanding Natural Beauty (AONBs). They therefore focus the discussion on the interactions between property rights and concepts of sustainable management across time, and between competing land uses and the delivery of statutory management obligations under modern legislation.

The case studies are *Eskdale, Cumbria* (Chapter 6), a large upland hill farming common with a strong tradition of local management under manorial court by-laws and (in modern times) through an active commoners' association; *Ingleborough and Scales Moor, North Yorkshire* (Chapter 7), representative of upland commons in an area with a deep-seated tradition of 'stinting', offering an opportunity to study the impact of a different property rights regime than that found in other upland areas, such as Eskdale; the *Elan Valley, Powys* (Chapter 8), comprising extensive upland commons exhibiting the distinctive management traditions found on common land in mid-Wales, but where property rights were transformed through compulsory purchase by Birmingham Corporation for water catchment; and *Brancaster and Thornham, Norfolk* (Chapter 9), where the commons comprise coastal marsh and inland heath, on which grazing is of much less significance but a range of other customary uses, including wildfowling and the gathering of samphire, take place in the context of an internationally important wetland habitat.

The specific objectives of the research into these case studies have been to trace the governance mechanisms used at local level since the 17th century and to explore how these reflected changing conceptions of sustainability; to examine rights registered under the Commons Registration Act 1965 and the governance mechanisms used since then; and to consider the local impact of legal and economic instruments within the framework of self-regulation envisaged by the Commons Act 2006. A carefully structured methodology was used to approach these questions in each case study. Archival research was carried out to locate by-laws governing the use of commons administered by manorial courts and to identify post-manorial institutions (commoners' associations, etc.) and their history. Qualitative research, using semi-structured interviews with samples of local stakeholders – typically comprising farmers, land managers/owners, representatives of voluntary groups, environmental bodies and governmental agencies – was applied to identify the contemporary environmental problems presented by each area, the management systems applied, and the present and anticipated use of environmental governance techniques and instruments. Focus groups addressed stakeholders' perceptions of the options for self-regulation by commons councils under the Commons Act 2006. And stakeholder workshops in each of the case studies at the conclusion of the project facilitated the reflective development and refinement of the research findings. Readers wishing to view more detailed qualitative research data than that cited in the following chapters can consult the working papers presenting data from each case study on the research project website at http://commons.ncl.ac.uk/casestudies.

Each of Chapters 6 to 9 is intended to present a detailed examination of the governance of the commons in the case study presented, highlighting the conjunction of historical and contemporary processes to create unique and often iconic landscapes. Only by examining the intersection of processes on the ground – for example, between tradition and modern property rights; environmental character and changing conceptions of environmental value; evolving patterns of economic use and aesthetic and recreational demands – can the governance of common land be fully understood.

6

Eskdale, Cumbria

Eskdale Common, in the heart of the English Lake District, exemplifies many of the most urgent pressures on common land, centring on the interplay between the fragile economics of hill farming and the fragility of upland ecosystems. The common consists largely of rugged rocky land, comparatively small in scale (even Scafell Pike, at 978m, the highest point in England, does not reach 1000m) but mountainous in character (see Figure 6.1). The 'fells' (the vernacular term of Scandinavian origin used to describe the uplands of Cumbria) surrounding Eskdale are quintessential Lake District sheep country. In 1839 it was said that the three valleys of Eskdale, Miterdale and Wasdale supported 20,000 'small fell sheep', many probably ancestors of the modern Herdwick, the distinctive breed of the Lake District (see Brown, 2009). The commons were extensive but the quality of grazing was poor. The commentator of 1839 wrote that 'On the lower fells 2 acres would probably summer 3 sheep, but on the debris by the side of Wastwater called "the Screes" & on the higher parts of Scawfell there are many hundred acres on which the strongest wether would scarcely & seldom venture to find its way.'[1]

At over 3000ha in extent, Eskdale Common (CL 58) represents the surviving wastes of the manor of Eskdale, Miterdale and Wasdalehead, which lie between the deeply incised valleys of Wasdale and Eskdale. Like many Lakeland commons, grazing rights in Eskdale were traditionally governed by the rule of levancy and couchancy. Grazing was regulated until the latter 20th century by an award of the manor court in 1587, the older customary framework eventually being eclipsed by statutory governance models, and the lapsed manor court replaced by an active commoners' association.

In many respects, then, Eskdale is archetypal pastoral common land. But it is also a landscape of preservation, owned by the National Trust and lying within the Lake District National Park, a region long thought of as a birthplace of tourism and landscape preservation, and symbolic of an aesthetic ideal which can be traced back to the Romantics. For Wordsworth, Eskdale was 'The Green Vale of Esk – deep and green, with its glittering serpent stream' (Wordsworth, 2004, p108). Coleridge, facing a treacherous descent into the valley from the summit of Sca Fell, thought 'the upper part of it the wildest & savagest surely of all the Vales that were ever seen from the Top of an English Mountain and the lower part the loveliest' (Coleridge, 1956, p841). Since 1951, the Lake District has been designated a National Park, and at the time of writing moves are under way to achieve inscription as a World Heritage Site. The common contains

Figure 6.1 *Eskdale Common: Peat hut on Boot Bank, with Sca Fell in distance*

Source: Angus Winchester

sites of both cultural and ecological importance, embracing parts of two large SSSIs and containing two smaller ones and falling within the Lake District Environmentally Sensitive Area (ESA). As such, Eskdale is a case study of a contested space, a traditional hill farming common in a highly valued conservation area, heavily visited for recreational purposes. It represents many of the defining characteristics and cultural shifts associated with 'contested' common land in England and Wales since 1600. It is also a richly documented case, allowing an unusual level of insight into the evolution of institutions, customary bodies and legal codes as they have applied to a single land area over time. It may therefore be thought of as a touchstone to our other three case studies, which each reveal significant departures from the 'classic' model exemplified by Eskdale.

Common rights and governance to 1965

Property rights

The origins of the manor of Eskdale, Miterdale and Wasdalehead lay in the partition of the baronial forest of Copeland between three heiresses in 1338. The valleys of Eskdale, Miterdale and Wasdale formed the southern third, allotted to Margaret, wife of Thomas de Lucy, through whose descendants it passed to the Percy family, Earls of Northumberland and their successors, the Wyndham family, latterly Barons Leconfield

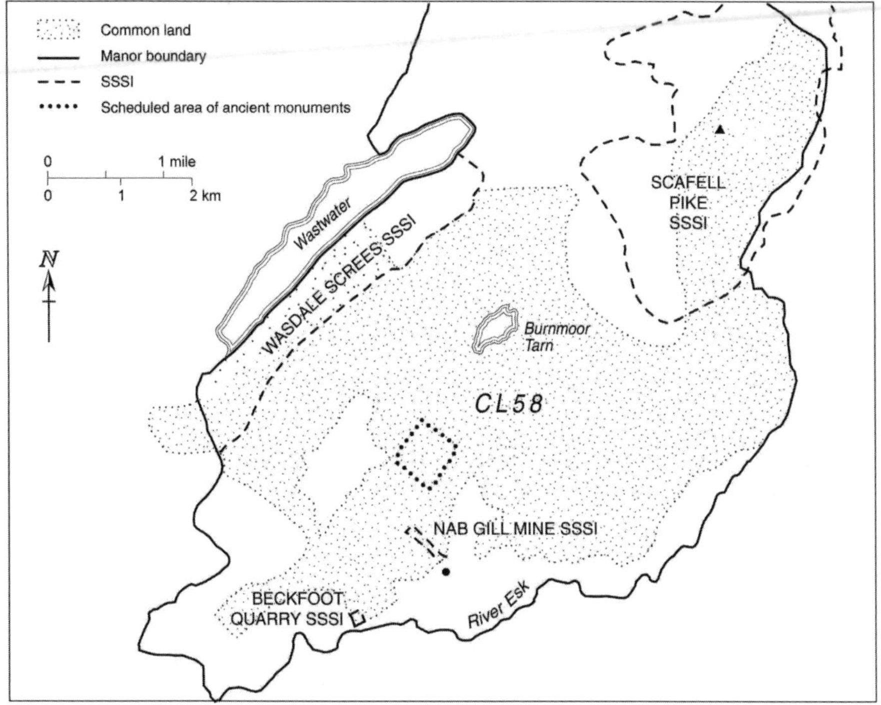

Figure 6.2 *Eskdale Common: Boundaries of common land (CL) unit and environmental designations*

Source: Cumbria County Council, Common Land Register, www.natureonthemap.org.uk/map.aspx?m=sssi

and Egremont (Liddell, 1966, pp116–117). The unity of the manor, covering Eskdale, Miterdale and Wasdale, masks striking differences in the evolution of settlement and property rights regimes on different sections of the wastes. All three valleys lay within the medieval baronial forest; but whereas Wasdalehead was the location of four demesne stock farms in the early 14th century, Eskdale and Miterdale were open to peasant colonization (Winchester, 1987, pp42–44). These contrasting histories in the medieval period probably explain significant differences in the management of the commons in the post-medieval centuries. The southern sections flanking Eskdale and Miterdale, which remain open common land to the present and form the main subject of this case study, were subject to the rule of levancy and couchancy. In contrast, the Wasdalehead commons were stinted (a legacy of the demesne stock farming regime), and were eventually enclosed by private agreement in 1808 (see Winchester and Straughton, 2010). Between these two contrasting areas of pasture there was a third category of land, the high fells in the centre of the manor (covering Sca Fell, Kettle Cove and Slightside), which had the status of lord's freehold. Although never physically separated from the rest of the wastes, this area was not common land; its separate legal status derived from the fact that it was reserved for game in the late medieval period as the lord's 'deer fence' or 'frith'(Winchester, 2007, p172) (see Figure 6.3).

In 1979, ownership of Eskdale Common was transferred to the National Trust. The lord's freehold and other sections of the high fells had been vested in the National Trust earlier in the century as a memorial to those lost in World War I. Scafell Pike and the surrounding land area above 3000 feet (914m) were given to the nation by Lord Leconfield in 1919 in memory of Lakeland men killed in the war, the plaque on the summit recording that the gift was 'subject to any commoners' rights' and a wider area of Sca Fell lying above 2000 feet (610m) was bought in 1924 and handed over to the Trust shortly afterwards. The purchasing of these summits was highly symbolic, transforming landscapes into public monuments, to be recognized and protected as part of the 'national' heritage rather than private property (Newsome, 1980, p370; Battrick, 1987, p50).

With the landowner's rights in the soil came the usual benefits of lordship, including rights to minerals and game. The exploitation of these rights, particularly in the 19th century, has left a physical legacy on the common as well as forming another dimension to contested use of the resources of the common land. The main mineral resource in Eskdale was iron ore (haematite), found in veins outcropping on the valley sides. Most mines were small, but one of the more capital-intensive was Nab Gill mine, on the common near Boot; its heyday was in the 1870s but it reopened briefly in the early 20th century (Adams, 1988, pp117–123). The survival of a number of grouse shooting butts and the 19th-century shooting lodge overlooking Burnmoor Tarn are legacies of the exploitation of game rights in the middle decades of the 19th century, when a gamekeeper was stationed on the common. Unsurprisingly, perhaps, the interaction of game and pasture rights did not always go smoothly. Heather-burning on Eskdale Moor in 1870 to 1871 led to an acrimonious dispute between the commoners and the lessee of the sporting rights, Thomas Brocklebank, a West Cumberland and Liverpool shipping magnate. The case raised questions as to whether the burning of heather was an identifiable commons 'custom'; who had a greater claim to the heather – the lord or commoners; and whether commoners could defend their burning of heather as an improvement of their pasture rights and heafs.[2]

The principal use-rights exercised by the tenants on Eskdale Common were common rights of pasture, turbary and estovers. Pasture rights were – and remain – an integral part of the local farming system. They were generally appurtenant to holdings in the valley, the size of the right governed by levancy and couchancy, and limited on the ground to distinct (but unfenced) sheep 'heafs', each associated with the flock of specific holdings. The heafing system rested on the territorial instincts of the local hill breeds, particularly the Herdwicks, which 'seem to belong to the land rather than the farmer' (Nicholson, 1991, p121). Although in strict legal terms the valley holdings had no direct property rights to 'their' heaf – common rights were to the whole common rather than any particular area of it – the recognition of distinct sections of the common as heafs was of longstanding, being stated explicitly in the manor court award of 1587 (discussed below). The tradition of transferring a core 'landlord's flock' with the tenancy of the farm provided the continuity to keep the heafing instinct alive, and was also found in mid-Wales, where there was a comparable division of common land into 'sheepwalks' (see Chapter 8, pp141–144).

While the majority of pasture rights in Eskdale and Miterdale were unstinted rights appurtenant to tenements, there were exceptions, hinting at a more complex legacy of property rights relationships. During the 16th century a group of farms at the head of the valley (Birdhow and Taw House) paid separate rent for pasture rights on 'Green Cove', probably that part of the lord's freehold on the south-eastern slopes of Slightside and Sca Fell,[3] while rights in gross on the wastes in the manor were held by some individuals from lowland communities in west Cumberland.[4] Most complex of all was the relationship between the neighbouring settlements within the manor. The tenants of Eskdale and Miterdale had no rights on the stinted commons attached to Wasdalehead, whereas the tenants of Wasdalehead had rights on all the commons in the manor.[5]

Common of turbary was of vital importance to the local community, as peat was the principal fuel in the area until the 20th century: indeed, peat-cutting continued until the 1940s. As elsewhere in the Lake District, the need to store and dry freshly cut peat led to the construction of numerous stone sheds ('peat scales') on the common (see Figure 6.1), each associated with a particular holding and often rebuilt or replaced over time (Winchester, 1984). They represented a blurring of the boundaries between the lord's rights and those of commoners: in another context, the peat scales might have been seen as encroachments on the lord's soil, which ought to be thrown down. In Eskdale, they appear to have been viewed, much like sheepfolds, as structures which were necessary to the commoners' exercise of their use-rights. Commoners in the three valleys also had rights of estovers, the most important of which was the right to take bracken (*Pteridium aquilinum*), which continued to be cut as bedding for livestock until the mid 20th century.

Overlying these use-rights and the lord's rights in the soil from the 19th century were the 'softer' concepts of public 'ownership' and access in a landscape as highly valued and deeply loved as the Lake District. Following Coleridge's early scrambles, the fells above Eskdale and Wasdale became a popular destination for a growing body of tourists seeking the 'sublime' view and access to the fells for walking and recreation, though this was by custom and practice rather than by legal right. When the slopes of Sca Fell were bought for the nation in 1924, Lord Leconfield was reported to have told the purchasers: 'I can't think why you should want to *buy* – You can go anywhere, do anything already... Still if you have money to throw away and like to buy rights which you enjoy already, well and good!' (Newsome, 1980, p370). The gifting of the high peaks to the National Trust, followed by the Trust's acquisition of several farms in Eskdale and Wasdale and, ultimately, of Eskdale Common itself, extended the Trust's property rights both as a landowner and as a holder of common rights. The National Trust's property in Eskdale represents a public body's developing stake in the land of a much-loved area, reflecting how Eskdale Common has evolved since 1600 into a public landscape, to be 'owned' and consumed visually, recreationally and culturally, as well as by the more traditional agrarian means.

Governance

From the medieval to the modern period, the main institution charged with managing the commons was the manor court of Eskdale, Miterdale and Wasdalehead. Court records survive for two years in the 1520s and, apparently continuously, from the latter 17th century.[6] The sequence of manor court verdicts running from 1678 to 1859 shows that the court generally met once a year, usually in April or May. Manorial officers appointed regularly at these court sittings included pounders (responsible for impounding stray livestock), hedge-lookers (responsible for ensuring that field boundaries were maintained) and, from 1842, a 'peat-moss looker', perhaps indicating pressure on turbary resources at a time when the number of households was increasing, as new villas and industrial dwellings caused the hamlets of Boot and Eskdale Green to expand. In its heyday, the court was a model of manorial governance, providing active oversight of a wide range of agrarian affairs, including repairs to fences and watercourses and the policing of the full range of use-rights on the common.

The framework governing the court's oversight of the common was formed by two awards laying down detailed rules for the exercise of common rights, which treated the stinted commons of Wasdalehead separately from the unstinted commons of Eskdale and Miterdale. The Eskdale Twenty-Four Book of 1587 – discussed below – laid out by-laws for Eskdale and Miterdale; an award of 1664 spelled out the regulations governing the stinted commons around Wasdalehead (for the latter, see Winchester, 2000, pp167–171). The separate identity and management regime in Wasdalehead culminated in the enclosure of the Wasdalehead Commons in 1808, privatising rights on the northern sections of the manor's wastes and also effectively removing them from the authority of the manor court.

The Eskdale Twenty-Four Book was the award of 'the foure and twenty sworn men of the lord's tenants in Eskdale Mitredale and Wasdalehead elected and chosen throughout the said lordship for the right commodity profit and benefit of common and perpetual order and stay among all the lord's tenants' in 1587.[7] The award conceived of the common as comprising three different categories of land, reflecting relief and topography and, hence, grazing capacity. Spatially restricted use-rights were assigned to each holding, thus creating a patchwork of exploitation of some complexity. The regulations laid out in the Eskdale Twenty-Four Book continued to form the basis of the management of Eskdale Common until the 20th century, long after the manor court had faded. Its importance to the local community is indicated by the fact that it was copied into the back of the Eskdale parish vestry book in 1840,[8] and it was still in use as a reference for the community in the mid 20th century: one of the first instructions given to the secretary of the new commoners' association in 1967 was to obtain a copy of the award.[9] In view of its continuing relevance to common land management, it is worth examining the provisions of this remarkable manorial document in some detail.

The award sought to govern 'the usage of the common', focusing specifically on pasture rights (see Figure 6.3). It first defined and laid out a set of by-laws to govern the use of Burnmoor, the saddle in the hills surrounding Burnmoor Tarn, which was allocated as the common pasture for the manor's 'geld goods' (bullocks, heifers and other cattle without young, and horses) in the summer. Separate regulations governed the use of the moor by the tenants of Wasdalehead and those of Eskdale and Miterdale. The number of livestock that the tenants of Wasdalehead could graze was as many as they could overwinter (i.e. it was governed by the rule of levancy and couchancy) and they were to put them onto the moor at a specific location. They could also put one work horse on the moor for one month. If the tenants of Wasdalehead had fewer livestock 'amongst themselves' than the maximum their stints would allow, they could make up the number (presumably by agistment); but these animals were to be put on

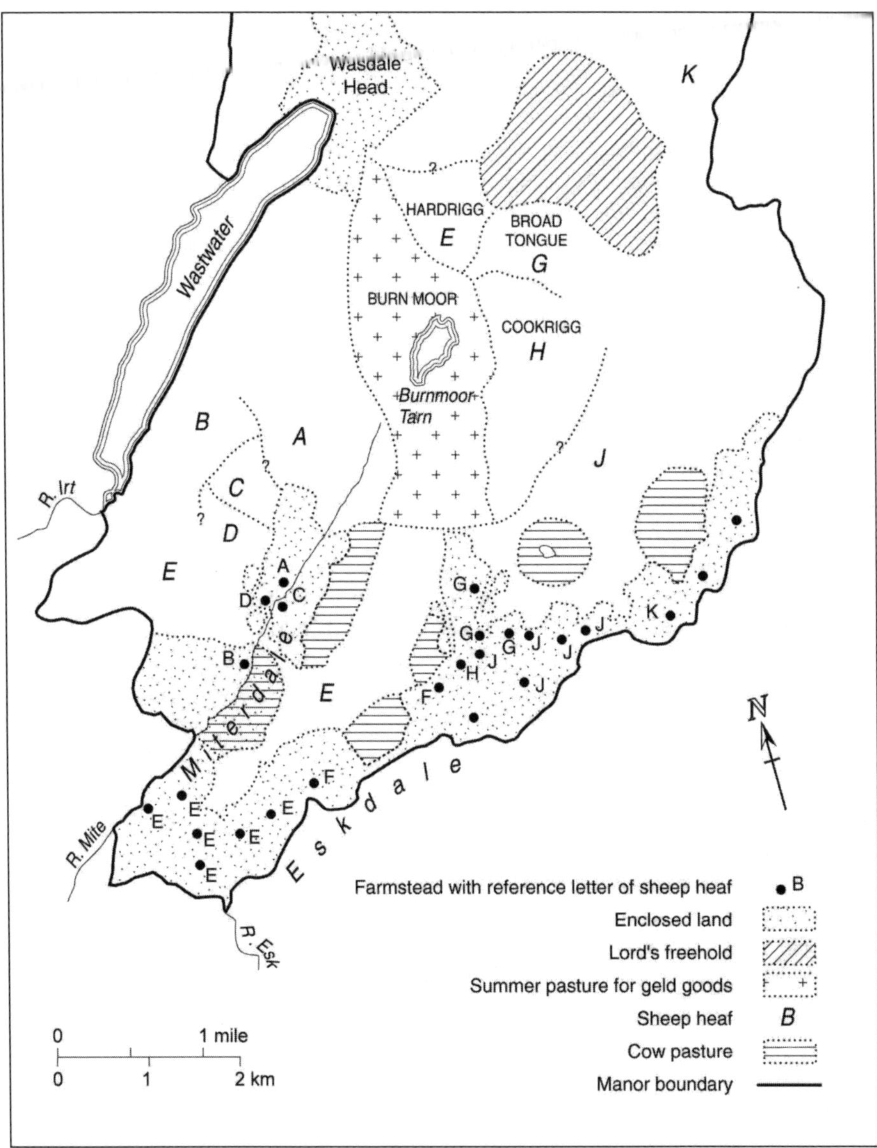

Figure 6.3 *Eskdale: Reconstruction of patterns of land use on the common laid down in the Eskdale Twenty-Four Book, a manor court award of 1587*

Source: Angus Winchester

'their own proper fell', rather than on Burnmoor. The tenants of Eskdale and Miterdale (except those at the head of the valley, 'above Blea Beck') were to put all their geld goods, cattle and horses to the moor in the spring and to take them off within a fortnight of Michaelmas (29 September).[10]

The award then specified the 'sheep drifts', the routes along which sheep were to be driven to their 'heaf', the section of the high fells assigned to the sheep of each holding. Groups of farms were to send their stock to particular heafs. For example, the award named three heafs on the western slopes of Sca Fell: Hardrigg was allocated to Spout House, Hollinhead and Borrowdale Place; Broad Tongue to Gillbank, Hows and Paddockwray; Quagrigg ('Cookrigg' in the award) to the tenants in Boot. Separate arrangements were made to settle a dispute between the tenants at the head of the valley (Wha House, Birdhow and Taw House), probably reflecting their separate grazing rights in 'Green Cove'. Their 'geld goods' were to be put 'above Eskhowfoot' and the tenants of Wha House were granted a stint of 120 sheep to graze 'above Eskcow foote' alongside those of the tenants of Taw House.[11]

The 1587 award also assigned to each holding a pasture for its milk cows, usually on the lower fellsides immediately behind the farmstead. A codicil of 1701 makes it clear that, by assigning exclusive rights to a section of the lower fells as a cow pasture, the 1587 award had led many tenants to enclose their cow pastures. Some continued to put the same number of cattle on the common, putting pressure on grazing reserves. Indeed, the award of heafs and cow pastures to individual farmers appears to have led to the perception that different sections of the common 'belonged' in a very real sense to individuals. An order of 1659 ordered a commoner whose sheep had strayed onto a section of the common assigned to someone else to drive them 'into his own common or cowpasture', reinforcing the image of the common as a mosaic of grazing grounds attached to particular farms.[12]

The regulations established in the Eskdale Twenty-Four Book were upheld and supplemented by later orders. A series of five orders made in 1659 reiterated the rule of levancy and couchancy and strengthened the rights of individuals to their sheep heafs and cow pastures.[13] Further orders made by the manor court across the 17th and 18th centuries regulated the use of drifts and heafs, reaffirmed the rule of levancy and couchancy, and controlled access to peat and bracken. Thus, for example, an order of 1705 dictated the terms of access to brackens in the Wasdalehead 'fences'; orders of 1727 and 1769 made regulations on the cutting of peat. Significantly, the court reiterated the rule of levancy and couchancy, making orders against 'wintering out' of animals or putting more animals on the common than had been maintained through the winter in 1693, 1736, 1749 and 1778, and also ordering the pounders to count each man's stock in the winter time. The rule of levancy and couchancy extended to a prohibition against buying in winter fodder (or 'vestures'), since feeding stock on hay grown elsewhere broke the principle that animals grazed on the common should be wintered on the produce of the dominant tenement. For example, in 1736 the court ordered that 'no tennant nor ocupier shal put on no Catel nether great nor smal upon the Common but those that the[y] winter upon there own Estate Neither Take any Vesters to feed them with in Winter Upon the pain of Twenty one Shilling', adding as an afterthought, 'Excepting five shiling worth', suggesting that some flexibility was allowed. Similarly, in 1778, the order stated that graziers would be fined for 'wintering out any goods above the Sum of five Shillings per year'.[14]

These regulations were policed by the pounders, whose key role appears to have been to count the number of animals on each holding in the winter time – vital information for enforcing the rule of levancy and couchancy. In 1679 the pounders were required to check the stock twice each winter, an order reinforced in 1694 and again in 1749 by specifying the dates on which every commoner's beasts were to be inspected: 24 January (or within two days) and 1 March. In 1701 the date had been modified to within six days either side of Candlemas (2 February). It appears that counting each holding's livestock was a longstanding practice; the years in which they were specifically instructed to undertake the task may indicate a need to reaffirm the practice after a lapse or hint at pressure on grazing and a concern to re-establish the rule of levancy and couchancy.

The penalties imposed upon those breaking the court's regulations shed light on the seriousness with which different aspects of the use of the common were viewed. Individuals were regularly presented to the court for offences such as overstocking, hounding, driving sheep on or off the common at the wrong time of year, and so on. Financial penalties (or 'amercements') of between 1s and 6s 8d were the norm for most offences across this period, with 6s 8d (half of a mark, the medieval unit of currency) being a standard sum, as was common elsewhere. However, certain orders – particularly those made in relation to stocking numbers – set the penalty noticeably higher and rose over time, probably reflecting increasing concern about overstocking the common. Thus, an order of 1736 preventing graziers from stocking more animals on the common in summer than kept in winter carried a fine of 21s; similar orders made in 1749 and 1778 carried the higher penalties of £1 19s 10d and £1 19s 10½d, respectively (sums which fell just below the customary upper limit of 40s for amercements in manor courts), underlining the importance of the orders, and probably suggesting that overgrazing was becoming a problem. By the early 19th century the commons around Eskdale were said to be seriously overstocked.[15] While the levels of penalty tell us something of the court's intentions with regard to enforcement and punishment, we cannot be sure from verdict sheets alone that the offenders complied in paying them. The practice of 'affearing' (mitigating) penalties after the sitting of the court gives rise to further uncertainty. It is likely that the court was sometimes unable to force a payment, particularly in its later years.

The 18th and early 19th centuries saw the manor court's increasing withdrawal from common land management (Straughton, 2008, pp134–142). The order of 1778 was the last written statement of the rule of levancy and couchancy, though the court also recorded disputes over grazing rights in 1785. But such intervention in common land matters was now rare, and it is apparent from these records that suitors and jurymen were failing to attend, and some were looking for higher or external legal arenas in which to resolve their disputes, as, for example, in a lawsuit of 1795, which involved a claim that an individual had made a large intake on the common, thereby infringing on a neighbour's sheep drift and encouraging the encloser to overstock the common.[16] The last significant order relating to the management of stock came in 1841 and concerned the perennial problem of diseased livestock on the common. It should, however, be noted that the manor court continued to meet on an almost annual basis until 1859 (the end date in the run of surviving verdicts), and was continuing to appoint constables, pounders, hedge-lookers, peat-moss lookers and a grieve at these sittings. It seems probable that officers continued to operate some form of policing on the common, though seemingly reluctant to bring offenders before the court and steward. Courts were still called from time to time after 1859, as shown by the survival of a handful of precepts and jury lists for the late 19th century, though no verdict sheets survive.[17]

Quite how the commons were regulated in the century 1840 to 1940 is therefore unclear. The parish council for Eskdale and Wasdale, formed in 1895, was largely silent on the subject of common land until the 1930s and 1940s, when questions arose over footpaths and rights of way – reflecting the increasing importance of tourism in the parish. During World War II, the parish council was also concerned by the compulsory purchase of a piece of common land by the Ministry of Supply and by trespasses on the common by a grazier without right. These cases prompted the council to explore the feasibility of setting up a commoners' committee for Eskdale; a surviving list of all commoners in 1943 was probably drawn up as part of these proceedings.[18]

The formation of a commoners' committee in Eskdale in 1945 is of especial interest because of the role played by the clerk to the parish council, the Reverend H. H. Symonds, a conservationist and preservation campaigner, who was also secretary of the Friends of the Lake District – the foremost preservation 'pressure group' in the region – and closely connected to amenity bodies such as the Ramblers' Association and the Standing Committee on National Parks (Cousins, 2009, pp43–45). It is apparent that Symonds was the driving force behind the creation of the commoners' committee for Eskdale, corresponding with Lawrence Chubb (of the Commons, Open Spaces and Footpaths Preservation Society), negotiating terms with Lord Leconfield's agent and drafting the constitution; Symonds also became the committee's first secretary.[19] However, the committee must have been relatively short lived. In its evidence to the Royal Commission on Common Land 1955–1958, which included a copy of the Eskdale constitution, the Ramblers' Association suggested that the committee had fallen into disuse after the first secretary (Symonds) had moved away.[20] There is perhaps an intimation here that the committee lacked the grassroots support necessary to make it a lasting, sustainable authority on the common (Straughton, 2008, pp174–183). Although Symonds's organization lapsed, the void would later be filled by a new and more successful body, the Eskdale Commoners' Association, established in 1967.

Records of the short-lived commoners' committee shed light on problems of governance and management in the post-manorial era. In 1944, there was uncertainty over whether the traditional rule of levancy and couchany still applied, and hints that breaches of the rule were taking place. One of the commoners asked Symonds: 'Can a Commoner or tenant take in cattle from outside the parish, to summer'?[21] The constitution of the 1945 committee gives some idea of the priorities for governance and management at this time. It did not tackle levancy and couchancy, but rather focused on 'proper observance of traditional heafs' – that is, keeping graziers to their designated grazing areas. The committee was perhaps more interested in protecting the 'private' nature of the heafs and preventing flocks from impinging upon each other than they were in controlling actual stocking numbers. Other matters that the committee was expected to oversee included the condition of walls, fences and gates; proper observance of the limiting dates for putting stock to the common; the illegal exercise of grazing and other rights by non-commoners; encroachments; and 'general maintenance of the custom of the common'.[22]

The transition from manorial to post-manorial governance in Eskdale illustrates at a local level many of the issues relating to the management of common land nationally in the modern period: enclosure (the private enclosure agreement for the Wasdalehead Commons); collapses in traditional governance mechanisms and the use of alternative strategies (such as lawsuits); the struggle to create sustainable management bodies; and modern themes of landscape preservation and access. There are also continuities. It is remarkable that a document of 1587 held sway for such a considerable length of time and, though it eventually lost its primacy, the principles behind it (such as the maintenance of the heafing system) are still relevant in Eskdale in the early 21st century.

The commons today

Commons registration and the 1965 Act

The starting point for a discussion of the governance of Eskdale Common must be its registration as a single block of common land (Cumberland Register, CL 58) on 15 May 1968. The registration became final following a commons commissioners' decision on 28 January 1981. Mirroring past agricultural practices, the rights section of the register discloses rights of pasture (sheep, cattle and horses), turbary, estovers and, in two cases, rights to take water for cattle from brooks on the common.

There are 12,330 registered rights to pasture sheep, cattle and horses, the majority of which are rights for sheep – of which 10,757 are rights appurtenant to land and 873 are rights in gross. The rights in gross are contained in just 2 entries: 1 for 600 sheep or cattle at a conversion rate of 20 sheep/1 cow[23] and one for 227 sheep or cattle at a conversion rate of 10 sheep/1 cow, or 20 sheep/1 horse.[24] These rights have subsequently been transferred to tenants of the National Trust, and added to rights held by the latter as appurtenant to their tenanted farms.

Eskdale provides a good example of the problematic outcomes of the registration process initiated by the Commons Registration Act 1965, and the anomalies to which it gave rise. Four of the register entries that record pasturage rights have rights to graze cattle in addition to sheep. Twenty-eight registered entries have cattle pasturage rights expressed *as an alternative* to sheep. In 14 of these cases the register applies a conversion rate of 10 ewes and followers/1 cow, and in the other 14 a conversion rate of 20 ewes and followers/1 cow. This discrepancy does not appear to have a basis in customary practice on the common, or in agronomic requirements. The commons association initially agreed at a meeting on 8 May 1968 that its members would register their rights using a ratio of 20 sheep/1 cow.[25] A number of the original entries in the rights section of the register were registered on 29 June 1968, and these all apply the agreed 20/1 conversion rate. At a further meeting on 12 August 1970, the association agreed that the stocking rate to be used for registering rights should be an average of 2 sheep per acre of the common, or 6 per enclosed acre of each farm with common rights. It was agreed that the conversion rate of 20 sheep/1 cow was excessive, and a substituted ratio of 10 sheep/1 cow or 20 sheep/1 horse was agreed upon.[26] Members who had not yet done so agreed to register their rights on this basis before completion of the registration process under the 1965 Act. A number of applications for registration made from August 1970 onwards therefore apply the 10/1 conversion rate. The secretary was asked to enquire of the commons registration officer whether pre-existing provisional registrations could be revisited; but it was agreed at a further meeting of the association on 26 August 1970 that the numbers registered would be accepted without requesting any reduction.[27]

To add to the complexity of the picture painted by the commons registers, it must be noted that some graziers were not members of the commons association and were therefore not party to its decisions on prospective registrations. As a result, several applications to register common rights made after August 1970 still reflected the original 20/1 conversion rate, and some applied a wholly different formula to registered rights. Some of the registered rights are also difficult to interpret meaningfully – for example, 'the right to graze 5 sheep or cattle (20 sheep = 1 cow and follower)'.[28] Several other entries use a numerical conversion rate that does not give a workable figure for cattle grazing rights.[29] One entry reserves a right to graze geese, although this right has not been exercised for many years.[30]

Most entries give a right to graze sheep and followers without time limit; several entries, however, specify that lambs less than one year old can only be grazed on the common from 1 May to 31 October in any year, and several reserve rights to graze cattle to 1 November in any year (but without stating when the cattle may initially be put to the hill in any given year). The dates reflected longstanding custom: both 1 May (under the ancient name of 'Beltane') and 31 October are stipulated in the Eskdale Twenty-Four Book of 1587 as the times at which livestock were to be put to and taken from the common, respectively. This reflects the importance that customary practice – as reflected in the Eskdale Twenty-Four Book – has retained down to the present day. It is also illustrative of the fact that customary practice was not uniformly captured in the registered rights established under the 1965 Act, most of which do not restrict grazing by cattle or sheep by reference to the annual calendar.

Registered rights of turbary and estovers are more limited: there are 14 entries recording registered rights to take peat or turves on the common (turbary) and five registered rights to estovers. The latter is sometimes expressed as the right to take bracken[31] and sometimes generically as a right to 'estovers'. It will be recalled that common of estovers, broadly defined, includes not only bracken but a right to take gorse, heather, ferns and similar growths (see Chapter 1 pp6–7). It can also include house bote (the right to take timber to repair houses or buildings or as fuel) or hay bote (the right to lop timber to repair fences). It is not clear whether the registered rights on Eskdale Common for generic 'estovers' should be construed in this wider sense, or whether the intention was to record a right to take only bracken – the presence of entries limited to the latter would indicate that this was intended in all cases and reflected the historic practice on the common. This is another example, therefore, where it would be necessary to go behind the registers to establish the full extent of the rights they record. There are also two entries recording a right to take water from brooks for animals grazing the common.

Commons governance

Contemporary commons governance in this case study focuses on the role of two bodies: the Eskdale Commoners' Association, and the National Trust. The Eskdale Commoners' Association was founded by a group of Eskdale commoners in 1967, primarily to prepare for the registration of rights under the Commons Registration Act 1965. Membership was voluntary and open to anyone claiming rights 'on the Fells and other land' in Eskdale, Miterdale and Wasdalehead, within the parish of Eskdale.[32] Observers with interests in the land or farms in the valley also attended meetings from time to time, including representatives of the Leconfield Estates (which still owned the soil at this time), the National Trust, the Forestry Commission and the National Farmers Union

(NFU). The difficult and protracted process of registering rights formed the main task of the organization in its first months, and was well documented in the association minute book. As has already been noted, the registration of rights in Eskdale resulted in a legacy of problematic registrations.

Following the conclusion of commons registration, the association has continued to be the main management institution for the common. It has sought to look after both the fabric and use of the common, ensuring that boundary walls, fences or gates are in good repair, dealing with unlawful activities on the common, and designing and enforcing rules regarding the proper stocking and maintenance of heafs.[33] It remains an instrument for collective action today, dealing with issues as varied as heather loss, protection of heafs, unlawful fencing and vehicles, trespasses by animals from neighbouring commons, and the implementation of agri-environment agreements on the common (the Eskdale Environmentally Sensitive Areas agreement is discussed below). A new set of management rules was adopted in 1980 regulating heafing and the pasturing of fell-bred/purchased animals, shepherding, marking of sheep, and prohibiting the leasing of rights. The association's constitution was also revised in 1982.[34] The association is therefore an active and effective local management body which has continued to evolve, with members regularly refining and adapting its function to accommodate change.

The National Trust is today the principal landowner, owning not only the soil of the common itself, but also all but two of the farms with a turnout of livestock onto the common grazing. As a charitable landowner, the National Trust's policies are constrained by the National Trust Acts of 1907 to 1971 and focus on balancing the needs of recreational access to its land with a strong focus on environmental protection and the maintenance of a sustainable rural community. Land owned by the Trust must be used to promote its statutory purposes: 'promoting the permanent preservation for the benefit of the nation of lands and tenements (including buildings) of beauty or historic interest and as regards lands for the preservation (so far as practicable) of their natural aspect features and animal and plant life' (National Trust Act 1907, section 4). Common land owned by the Trust must be maintained unenclosed and un-built upon as open spaces for recreation and enjoyment by the public, although the Trust does have statutory power to improve common land and to carry out minor works, such as the erection of sheds for storage of materials and the provision of footpaths and roads (1907 Act, section 27). These powers were extended by the National Trust Act 1971 to include power to provide recreational facilities and to erect buildings, subject to the proviso that the consent of the secretary of state is required for any works that will impede public access to the land. The 1971 Act also confers the power to make by-laws to prevent nuisances, including the power to prevent the digging of turves, soil or other substances (such as peat) and the cutting of vegetation on National Trust land (1971 Act, sections 23, 24).

The Trust is actively involved in monitoring and shaping the agricultural management of the common. Its role in this case study therefore presents a stark contrast to the inactive and/or absentee landowners found in the Ingleton and Elan Valley case studies (see Chapters 7 and 8). The Trust exercises a major influence on the agricultural management of the common through the terms of the farm tenancy agreements of those farms it owns that have a turnout of livestock onto the common. It uses long fixed-term farm business tenancies to confer security of tenure on its tenants, and these include special clauses requiring the observance of management requirements to promote nature conservation. The emphasis is on the achievement of balance between economic production and environmental protection. A key variable to attain this balance is the diversification of each farm business –for example, through 'green tourism' and bed-and-breakfast accommodation.

Despite its role as the principal landowner, the National Trust plays only an informal role in arbitrating disputes between tenants. Although it is a conservation landlord, the Trust plays a limited role in relation to key aspects of the environmental governance of the common. It is not involved in the scientific assessment of the conservation status of the land that is within the SSSIs on the common, neither is it involved in the negotiations between Natural England and its individual tenants for the conclusion of management agreements (such as Sheep and Wildlife Enhancement Scheme (SWES) agreements; see below). In general terms, the Trust would prefer a more balanced and less technocratic approach to the conservation of natural features on the common; rather than focusing on a numerical reduction of sheep through the SWES, for example, the Trust would prefer 'managed change' in the management of the common, giving conservation a more human face.[35] The formation of a statutory commons council would potentially give the Trust a greater role in decisions affecting the implementation of nature conservation policy on the common.

The role of the commons register in relation to the management of contemporary grazing practice is marginal. Most commoners do not have a copy of the register, and few of them have ever consulted it. Significantly, some graziers are also unaware whether they have rights to convert sheep grazing rights into cattle. Interestingly, although most acknowledge that this is a 'grey area', they tend to associate this not with the inconsistencies in the registrations captured in the commons register, but with the land management requirements of Natural England's environmental policies for the common. The registers also fail to reflect current practice in relation to rights of turbary and estover, for bracken is no longer taken for animal bedding, and neither is peat dug by any of the graziers who actively use the resources of the common. The irrelevance of the commons registers to most farmers when calculating their rights, and to identifying the types of land-use right they possess over the common, illustrates the secondary role that property law structures have on environmental management in the case study. This is, in part, a consequence of the inherent flaws of the 1965 Act, especially the lack of a 'live' grazing register. The graziers welcomed the reforms to commons registers that will be brought about by Part 1 of the Commons Act 2006. Updating the register would be instrumental to understanding the current property rights situation on the common and thereby foster the sustainable management of the common in the future.

Finally, the commoners' attitudes to questions of 'locality' and their interrelationship with property rights are markedly different from those of stakeholders in some of the other case studies – notably, Ingleton and Norfolk. All commoners in the Eskdale research sample expressed strong support for the legislative policy of the Commons Act 2006 in prohibiting the severance of common rights from the land they are intended to benefit (2006 Act, section 9; see also Chapter 4, p60). Some articulated this view in terms of local governance and sustainability, associating appurtenant rights with a strong sense of 'place' and 'locality'. Noticeably, however, the majority did not try to justify their antagonism towards severance in these terms, and assumed that the appurtenant character of common rights – as rights attached to dominant land – was simply an essential attribute of their character as rights in or over land. There are two principal reasons for this perception. There have been very few transfers of common rights in Eskdale, and where this has occurred they have been acquired as a consequence of the purchaser acquiring the dominant tenement to which they attach; and the historical management of the common grazing by the system of levancy and couchancy has also strongly contributed to a cultural perception of common pasture rights as rights attached to land, and therefore incapable of severance and sale independently of the dominant tenement. This is very different from the perception of stint holders in, for example, Ingleton, where common grazing rights are perceived of as commodified personal property rights that can be traded independently of land (see Chapter 7, p127).

Environmental governance

The sub-alpine heath land of Eskdale is a habitat of national and international environmental importance. This is demonstrated by the fact that the common hosts four SSSIs, it lies within the Lake District National Park and partially within the Lake District High Fells Special Area of Conservation (SAC).

Statutory environmental designations

The Lake District High Fells Special Area of Conservation (SAC)

The Lake District High Fells was designated an SAC in 2005 and hosts many upland tarns of European-level conservation significance. The Annex I habitats in this case study that are the primary reasons for the designation under the EC Habitats and Species Directive are northern Atlantic wet heaths with *Erica tetralix,* European dry heaths, Alpine and Boreal heaths with *Calluna vulgaris,* locally bilberry *Vaccinium myrtillus,* siliceous slopes and siliceous scree of the montane to snow levels.[36] The principal threat to these habitats is overgrazing, especially on unfenced common land where control of grazing is difficult to achieve, but recreational interests also potentially contribute to their vulnerability (JNCC, 2006). As in the other case studies, the farmers' appreciation of the legal significance of the SAC designation is limited. There are no immediate constraints imposed upon agricultural practice by the designation of the SAC, whereas land-use controls in the SSSIs are more immediate and relevant to the management of the common.

Sites of Special Scientific Interest (SSSIs)

There are four SSSIs notified under the Wildlife and Countryside Act 1981 within the case study: the Scafell Pikes SSSI, Wasdale Screes SSSI, Nab Gill Mine SSSI and Beckfoot Quarry SSSI (see Figure 6.2). Two of these – Nab Gill Mine and Beckfoot Quarry – are geological SSSIs and of marginal significance to the management of the common pool resource represented by Eskdale Common itself. The notification of the Scafell Pikes SSSI and the Wasdale Screes SSSI has, on the other hand, very important significance to the environmental governance of the common and its natural features.

Scafell Pikes SSSI was notified in 1988, and provides an important example of a summit boulder field with lichen heaths and a series of gills. The slopes below the summit plateau are characterized by scree, mat grass and bilberry heath. According to Natural England's management statement for the site,[37] the montane heaths are self-sustaining; grazing should be limited to the summer period and should be light in intensity (Natural

England, 2005a). Stock numbers and patterns of livestock movement are also key factors for the preservation of scree and dry upland heath. The list of operations likely to damage the special conservation interest of the site (OLDSIs) is standardized and very similar to that in the Wasdale Screes SSSI and the other case studies (see pp129, 153). It does not offer specific land management advice targeted at the special characteristics of each SSSI, with the result that different habitats which have been differently managed in the past may be subject to the same consultation requirements as notified OLDSIs. As in the other case studies, the list of OLDSIs for the Scafell Pikes SSSI ignores the inherent limitations of the common graziers property rights as *profits à prendre*. So, for example, the supplementary feeding of livestock, and the release of any wild, feral or domestic animal, plant or seed, are prohibited as OLDSIs. These are activities that commoners have no legal competence to carry out by reason of their registered grazing rights.

According to a recent condition assessment of the area, it is in 100 per cent unfavourable recovering condition (Natural England, 2009). This assessment is founded on the argument that the renewal of the ESA agreement covering the common in 2004 (as to which, see below), together with the use of Sheep and Wildlife Enhancement Scheme (SWES) agreements, will lead to the long-term recovery of the common as well as of the freehold fell at the summit of Sca Fell. However, the recovery of the habitats could potentially be undermined by stock encroachment from nearby non-SSSI heafs if effective monitoring of livestock grazing patterns is not maintained. It is perhaps also noteworthy that the potential impact of recreational pressures – for example, climbing and hill walking – is, in practice, downplayed by Natural England's condition assessments of the SSSI, which stress the importance of the conclusion of land management agreements with graziers targeted at reducing grazing pressure.

The Wasdale Screes SSSI was designated in 1987. It runs along the southern shore of Wast Water and forms a classic geomorphological example of one of the best screes in Britain, with cliffs in the higher areas and unstable screes at lower levels. These are principally formed of resistant acid rocks of the Borrowdale Volcanic Series. In addition to its geomorphological interest, the site has important mountain flora habitats, which include nationally rare species such as alpine lady's mantle, alpine clubmoss and mountain saxifrage. The Wasdale Screes SSSI is in unfavourable recovering condition according to Natural England (Natural England, 2010c). There have been substantial improvements in the protected habitats since 2007, when a site assessment found 70 per cent of the area to be in an unfavourable condition with no improvement. The principal reason for the improvement since 2007 is attributable to the impact of the sustainable grazing achieved following renewal of the ESA and SWES agreements in 2004. As for the Scafell Pikes SSSI (see above), Natural England considers that the control of stocking density is the key to achieving a full recovery of the SSSI (Natural England, 2005b).[38]

Many of the farmers were unaware of the precise nature of the notified OLDSIs in either the Scafell Pikes or Wasdale Screes SSSIs and had little appreciation of the nature of the land-use restrictions that flowed from the notification of the sites as SSSIs. Unsurprisingly, none of the Eskdale graziers had served written notice seeking operational consent from Natural England (or its predecessors) to carry out OLDSIs (1981 Act, section 28(5)). The preferred management instruments have instead been agri-environmental management agreements (principally ESA). Natural England would like to see a move towards more positive management, especially for restoring the gill woodland in the case study and promoting shrub regeneration. Nevertheless, although SWES is itself a scheme based on the use of 'positive' management agreements, the primary focus has hitherto been on imposing restrictions on the graziers' activity – restricting livestock levels and prohibiting supplementary feeding and the burning of heather. This is a strategy that is likely to continue in the future under, for example, the Higher Level Stewardship (HLS) scheme.

Management agreements

Environmentally Sensitive Area (ESA) and Sheep and Wildlife Enhancement Scheme (SWES)

Eskdale common is within the Lake District ESA, having been designated in 1993 (by the Environmentally Sensitive Areas (Lake District) Designation Order 1993). The whole common was entered into a ten-year Tier 1 (heather fell) ESA management agreement negotiated by the Eskdale Commoners' Association in 1995. This required commoners to remove 40 per cent of their stock in order to promote heather regeneration, and reduced summer grazing by sheep to 5139 and winter grazing to a maximum of 3852. Unlike the ESA agreement management on Cwmdeuddwr Common (see Chapter 8, p154ff), the Eskdale ESA agreement targeted the reduction of livestock grazing in a standardized manner by fixing the average grazing density sought to a maximum of 1.5 sheep per hectare in the summer and 1.125 in winter.

The small number of active graziers (eight in total) is a significant variable accounting for the success of the ESA. Concluding the agreement was not straightforward, and English Nature had to make payments to 11 commoners to 'buy out' 1275 sheep grazing rights that were not being used. Having secured an agreement, however, the commoners' association has been able to administer the agreement very effectively, rendering free-riders' behaviour and internal disputes unlikely. Another significant variable is the impact of the National Trust's farm business tenancy agreements. These require the Trust's tenants (all but two of the active graziers) to 'use all reasonable endeavours to enter into the (ESA) Scheme Agreement' (National Trust, Standard Farm Business Tenancy Agreement, Schedule 4, para 5.2).

The ESA agreement was renewed for a further ten years in 2004, and coupled with individual five-year SWES agreements with the active graziers on those parts of the common within the Wasdale Screes SSSI and Scafell Pikes SSSI. These brought about a further 40 per cent reduction in livestock grazing numbers as part of a combined strategy linked to the renewal of the ESA agreement under the Sustainable Grazing Initiative for Cumbria (Johnston et al, 2006). The average annual grazing density sought under the SWES is 0.8 ewes per hectare. Unlike the Eskdale ESA agreement, SWES agreements are individually negotiated agreements between Natural England and each active grazier. Because they provide for further stock reductions on the portions of the common within the SSSIs, and not elsewhere, the impact of the SWES has been to create a differentiated environment on the common. Additionally, although all of the active graziers have participated in the SWES, they did so on a different basis. Two removed all their stock from the common under five-year SWES agreements, whereas the others reduced stocking numbers to meet the overall target set by Natural England. The effect of this has been to create 'vacuums' in the grazing available on the common where their hefted sheep flocks used to graze and to destabilize the pattern of the hefting system on the common. The remaining flocks have begun to move into the vacuums to take up the additional grazing, and this, in turn, has increased the difficulty of gathering sheep and increased the time that has to be devoted to shepherding. The impact of the reductions in sheep grazing pressures on the vegetation (including heather) has also been questioned (see Butler, 2007).

Prospective Higher Level Stewardship (HLS)

The future environmental governance of Eskdale Common will depend upon it being entered into a Higher Level Stewardship (HLS) agreement following expiry of the current ESA agreement in 2014. The approach sought by Natural England under HLS will combine the approaches seen in the ESA and the SWES agreements into a single comprehensive and collective agreement, but will also go further by including provision for mixed grazing with cattle and sheep to encourage heather regeneration. Although reductions in sheep grazing densities have, according to Natural England, been beneficial, this is not considered sufficient in itself to return the heather habitats to favourable conservation condition. Mixed grazing will be prioritized by the HLS because cows have a less selective grazing pattern than sheep, grazing the taller grasses and trampling bracken infestations, enabling sheep to follow and graze down the shorter grasses thus exposed. The utility of mixed grazing to promote the environmental sustainability of the common is also recognized by most of the commoners interviewed, and is reflected in customary agricultural practices – for instance, those evident in the *Eskdale Twenty-Four Book*.

The realization of mixed grazing may, however, be hindered by the property rights regime reflected in (and the inconsistencies of) the commons register. Many graziers do not have rights to graze cattle, and the conversion rates for calculating cattle grazing are also inconsistent, as outlined above. Two solutions to this problem may be posited. One would be the creation of new common rights using the powers granted by the Commons Act 2006; the other would be the licensing of 'surplus' grazing by the owner of the soil to graziers seeking to graze cattle in addition to sheep.

Both are likely to be problematic. Before new rights can be registered, a sustainability appraisal will have to be undertaken by Natural England, and this must consider the cumulative impact of the exercise of the new rights with those already extant upon the register. The full exercise of all rights currently registered would be unsustainable in itself, so it is difficult to see how the addition of 'new' rights could, viewed cumulatively, be justified. And there is probably no notional 'surplus' grazing available to the landowner (the National Trust), even though they may be willing to licence additional rights to their tenants for the purposes of introducing mixed grazing with cattle. The Rural Payments Agency calculate the extent or otherwise of the surplus grazing available to the owner using a formula based upon a stocking rate of 0.25 livestock units (LU) per hectare for Severely Disadvantaged Area (SDA) moorland. This will be multiplied by the area of the common to arrive at a notional maximum stocking figure. Comparison with the number of registered grazing rights in the commons register for that common land unit will then disclose whether there is any surplus grazing ('headroom') available to the owner (Defra, 2005, p4). Eskdale Common extends to 3071.5ha, giving a notional maximum stocking figure of 767.875 livestock units. As a ewe is 0.15 livestock unit, this gives a maximum grazing capacity much lower than the registered total of 12,330 grazing rights (notionally, the maximum stocking capacity would be 5119 ewes).

Future governance

Cumbria was one of three trial 'shadow' common councils examined in research sponsored by Defra in 2008 (Aglionby, 2009). The research resulted in a proposal to establish an umbrella council for the whole of Cumbria. The position in Cumbria is perhaps atypical of that elsewhere. The Federation of Cumbria Commoners is a very active organization and Cumbria commoners are already accustomed to a wider (county) level of interaction. Under the Cumbria model individual common land units would be given the freedom to decide whether to join the commons council, maintaining the principles of voluntarism and local control promoted by the Commons Act 2006. Nevertheless, Eskdale commoners expressed concerns about the loss of local control of agricultural management that this might entail.

Under the Cumbria model, participation in HLS and other agri-environmental schemes will only be possible for each common if a consensus of 75 per cent of active graziers is in favour. The membership of the Cumbria commons council would be limited to 15 voting members, of whom 10 will be 'active' graziers (one from each region of Cumbria), 2 inactive graziers, 3 representatives of landowners, and up to 4 co-opted members. Each stakeholder group would elect its own representatives. It is not currently proposed that other interest groups – such as environmental organizations, local authorities or recreational groups – would be members of the statutory commons council. Recreational interests will, to some extent, be represented by the three landowners, who are also likely to have sporting and agricultural interests in the commons. The emphasis will be on resolving potential internal conflicts within an individual commoners' association without resorting to the legal enforcement powers available to a statutory commons council.

On 9 June 2009, the Committee of the Federation of Cumbria Commoners voted in favour of setting up an umbrella commons council on this model. There are, however, outstanding issues concerning the funding of set-up and running costs for the council, and further discussions between Natural England and the Federation of Cumbria Commoners will be required to resolve these. Although the prospect of extensive devolution of management power to local associations under the Cumbrian model goes some way to assuaging the concerns of many commoners, other concerns relating to its funding, duration and the role of the landowners remain to be resolved. It has been proposed that the council should initially be established for five years.

Conclusions

Eskdale differs from the other case studies in displaying a history of strong manorial governance. Contemporary governance is also being reshaped under the influence of strong institutional governance structures: the Eskdale Commoners' Association plays an important role in managing the common, and the establishment of the Federation of Cumbria Commoners has made it possible to consider the establishment of a commons council under the 2006 Act (potentially one of the first in England and Wales). Institutional governance structures have made – and continue to make – a stronger impact here than in Ingleton or the Elan Valley, for example.

Eskdale is a typical open upland common, with livestock management governed prior to 1965 by the principle of levancy and couchancy, mediated by strong manorial court regulation and a tradition of hefting. The modern representation of property rights in the commons registers is, however, indicative of the flaws in the registration process undertaken during the late 1960s. Even here, on a common with a strong history of manorial governance and customary practice – recorded, moreover, in the *Eskdale Twenty-Four Book* – customary management practices have not been accurately reflected in the registers compiled under the 1965 Act. The inconsistencies in the registration of grazing rights is, in part, attributable to the influence of informal arrangements made by the Eskdale Commoners' Association without consultation with external public or private bodies – in other words, to the absence of any external audit of provisional registrations unless they were challenged and referred to a commons commissioner.

The organization of commons grazing management shows strong similarities with that of the other large open upland case study: the Elan Valley (see Chapter 8). The use of heafs has a similar effect to the 'sheepwalks' in the Welsh context, redefining the boundaries of the common in the farmers' collective conceptualization of it as a shared and common 'space' – the individualization of sheepwalks and heafs to specific parts of CL 58 render the common 'uncommon' as far as its use as a common pool resource is concerned. The use of a complex heafing system for agricultural management has also ensured equitable access to the common resource and helped to prevent free-rider behaviour by appropriators, although the integrity of the heafing system is under threat as stocking levels have reduced under agri-environmental schemes.

Eskdale has a 'loved' landscape with wide, and iconic, public appeal. It is subject to heavy recreational use (especially hill walking); but this rarely conflicts with farming on the common. It is part of the Lake District National Park and largely owned by the National Trust, which actively seeks to promote a sustainable future for both its landscape and rural communities. Environmental objectives centre on heather regeneration – by reducing the over-wintering of livestock, reducing overall grazing levels and potentially reintroducing mixed grazing with cattle. This poses a challenge to traditional management systems, not least because the heavy reduction in grazing results in flock sizes which are too small to maintain the boundaries of heafs. As the principal landowner, the National Trust aims to promote sustainable management 'with a human face', and acts as a bridge between the scientific approach to conservation issues adopted by Natural England and the more pragmatic attitude to sustainability demonstrated by the commoners themselves.

As in the other case studies, environmental governance mechanisms flowing from the legal status of much of the common as SSSI have little practical impact on its management. The list of OLDSIs served on commoners with the SSSI notifications has little impact upon their farming activities and is poorly understood. The OLDSIs, as elsewhere, are poorly integrated with the property rights represented in the common registers. Elsewhere (e.g. in the Ingleton case study: see Chapter 7) the notification as OLDSIs of operations that graziers have no legal competence to carry out (supplementary feeding, etc.) provides an additional enforcement mechanism – potentially available to Natural England where there is an absentee landowner. In Eskdale, however, the National Trust takes an active interest in the common's management. Legal governance mechanisms – such as the lists of OLDSIs – therefore have even less potential relevance than elsewhere. In practice, Natural England has, as elsewhere, favoured a consensual approach to nature conservation based on the use of agri-environment agreements such as ESA and HLS.

Diversification of the rural economy is central to the National Trust's conception of rural sustainability. In addition to participation in agri-environmental schemes such as the ESA, 'green tourism' is key to the economic viability of most farm businesses and is integral to the business planning undertaken when Farm Business Tenancies are offered by the Trust to potential tenants. In Eskdale, therefore, farm diversification may reshape the concept of 'farming' in an upland area. Whether it will also reshape the self-conceptualization of commoners into providers of multifaceted rural services less directly linked to agricultural production is less clear. Hill farming culture (of which the traditional commons management is a key feature) remains strong in the Lake District and, indeed, is seen as an element in the region's 'outstanding universal value' in current proposals for World Heritage Site inscription.

Notes

1 PRO, IR 18/716, question 11.
2 CRO, D/Lec, SL 14/7, Saul and Lightfoot papers related to common rights, 1870–1871.
3 The minor place-name Greencove Wyke survives at NY 211 060.
4 CRO, D/Lec, box 301, Percy Survey, f. 134; D/Lec, box 94, Senhouse verdict, 1579.
5 CRO, D/Lec, box 94, draft case, Robert Grave agt. Isaac Fletcher [c. 1800].
6 CRO, D/Lec, box 299/18, 20; D/Lec, box 94, manor of Eskdale, Miterdale & Wasdalehead; estreats of fines, 1668–93; jury verdicts, 1678–1859.
7 No contemporary copy is known. The text survives in two recensions: a copy incorporated into a revised award of 1659, itself copied in 1794 and again in 1840: CRO, YPR 4/18; and a copy dated 1692, with an additional verdict of 1701, which survives in a late 18th-century copy: CRO, D/Ben/3/761.
8 CRO, YPR 4/18, Eskdale Select Vestry Book 1826–1903.
9 Eskdale Commoners' Association Papers (private): minute book, 1967–1980, 8 March 1967.
10 In 1659 the date was amended to 1 November: CRO, YPR 4/8, p[3].
11 'Eskhow'/'Eskcow' foot has not been identified: 'the heaf for the Wha House stint' is described as 'at doucragg [Dow Crag, NY 221 065] to the ffould at threaptongue foot'. The size of the stint of sheep is given as 'three score sheep' for each of the two tenants of Wha House; subsequent references to 'those hundred sheep' use the number in the sense of the 'long hundred' of 120.
12 CRO, YPR 4/8, p[3].
13 CRO, YPR 4/8, pp[1–4].
14 CRO, D/Lec box 94, Eskdale Jury Verdicts, 1678–1859.
15 CRO, D/Lec, box 94, draft brief in case of *R. Grave v. I. Fletcher*, c. 1800; TNA, IR 18/716, question 11 (tithe file, 1839).
16 CRO, D/Ben/3/752.
17 CRO, D/Lec box 94, Eskdale Jury Verdicts, 1678–1859; CRO, D/Ben/3/752; D/Lec Box 94, Precepts and Jury Lists, 1678–1896.
18 CRO, YSPC 7/2, Eskdale and Wasdale Parish Council minute book 1895–1963; CRO D/Lec 94, Eskdale Commoners' List, 1943.
19 CRO, WDSO/117/B/vi/6/1/2: FLD Files.
20 The Ramblers' Association, *Save Our Commons*, pp30–32.
21 CRO, WDSO/117/B/vi/6/4: FLD Files, legal papers, letter from Armstrong to Symonds, 7 June 1944.
22 CRO, WDSO/117/B/vi/6/4: FLD Files, legal papers, Eskdale Commoners' Committee constitution, 1945.

23 Register of Common Land, Register Unit Cumberland CL 58, Rights Section entry 62.
24 Register of Common Land, Register Unit Cumberland CL 58, Rights Section entry 65.
25 Eskdale Commoners' Association Minute Book, 1967–1980 (in private hands), 8 May 1968.
26 Eskdale Commoners' Association Minute Book, 1967–1980 (in private hands), 12 August 1970.
27 Eskdale Commoners' Association Minute Book, 1967–1980 (in private hands), 26 August 1970.
28 Register of Common Land, Register Unit Cumberland CL 58, Rights Section, entry 67.
29 Register of Common Land, Register Unit Cumberland CL 58, Rights Section – for example, entries 70 and 71.
30 Register of Common Land, Register Unit Cumberland CL 58, Rights Section, entry 30.
31 Register of Common Land, Register Unit Cumberland CL 58, Rights Section, entry 20.
32 Eskdale Commoners' Association Minute Book, 1967–1980, 14 February 1967.
33 See, for example, the rules agreed on 3 June 1980, recorded in Eskdale Commoners' Association Minute Book, 1980–1995.
34 Eskdale Commoners' Association Minute Book, 1980–1995, 3 June 1980 and 23 March 1982.
35 Semi-structured interview, 2007
36 Other Annex I habitat that are a primary reason for the designation of the site are *Juniperus communis*, siliceous alpine and boreal grasslands, hydrophilous tall herb fringe communities, blanket bogs and old sessile oak. Annex I habitats that are a qualifying feature are species-rich nardus grassland (priority feature), alkaline fens and calcareous rocky slopes with chasmophtic vegetation. There are no Annex II species that are a primary reason for the selection of the site and slender green feather-moss is the only Annex II species that is a qualifying feature for the site selection (see www.jncc.gov.uk/ProtectedSites/SACselection/sac.asp?EUCode=UK0012960).
37 See 'A statement of English Nature's views about the management of Scafell Pikes Site of Special Scientific Interest (SSSI)' (Countryside and Rights of Way Act 2000, Schedule 11(6), 16 September 2005, www.sssi.naturalengland.org.uk/Special/sssi/sitedocuments.cfm?type=vam&sssi_id=1001922).
38 See 'A statement of English Nature's views about the management of Wasdale Screes Site of Special Scientific Interest (SSSI)' (Countryside and Rights of Way Act 2000, Schedule 11(6), 27 April 2005, www.sssi.naturalengland.org.uk/Special/sssi/sssi_details.cfm?sssi_id=1002125).

7

Ingleborough and Scales Moor, North Yorkshire

Like Eskdale, the parish of Ingleton is a hill farming area, although it differs markedly in its geology and topography, lying in the heart of the dramatic karst limestone scenery of Craven district in North Yorkshire. It contains several tracts of common land, two of which – Ingleborough Fell and Scales Moor – form the focus of this case study. The summit of Ingleborough (723m) is famed as a hill walkers' destination (one of the 'three peaks' of the Yorkshire Dales) and an iconic landmark, visible from a wide district and immediately recognizable because of its distinctive flat-topped profile (see Figure 7.1). Equally as famous is the invisible landscape that lies beneath: the extensive cave systems which have drawn visitors to experience the 'natural curiosities' of the area for over 200 years (Johnson, 2008, pp1–11). Today, the limestone pavements, heaths and blanket bogs of the Ingleton area are recognized as being among the most highly valued conservation landscapes in England and Wales, while also supporting upland pastoral farming and a range of intensive recreational uses. The area lies within the Yorkshire Dales National Park and has a number of protective designations, including the Ingleborough Complex Special Area of Conservation (SAC), Ingleborough Site of Special Scientific Interest (SSSI) and Whernside SSSI (covering Scales Moor).

The common land under study comprises three registered commons (see Figure 7.2). Ingleborough itself contains two separate registered commons lying open to one another: Ingleborough Common (CL 134, covering circa 760ha), and Clapham Bents, Newby Moss and Simon Fell (CL 208, 741.82ha). Together they form one of the larger commons in the area and embrace a variety of land types, rising from acid peat moorland and sparsely vegetated limestone pavement to the steep mountain slopes of Ingleborough itself. The other common under study is Scales Moor (CL 272, covering 413.74ha), also known as Twisleton Fell, which lies to the north-west of Ingleborough, on the opposite side of the Chapel-le-Dale valley in the manor of Twisleton-and-Ellerbeck. It consists largely of a plateau containing expanses of limestone pavement but rises to the slopes of Whernside (736m).

The particular historical interest of these commons lies in the development of systems of stinting, whereby pasture rights on the commons are limited by number, rather than by the rule of levancy and couchancy – in marked contrast to the unstinted

Figure 7.1 *Ingleborough from Scales Moor: The section of dry stone wall in the foreground is a 'bield', to provide shelter for sheep*

Source: Angus Winchester

commons of our Eskdale and Elan Valley case studies. The transition from common *sans nombre* to a stinted regime was a comparatively recent development on both Ingleborough and Scales Moor, showing how landowners and commoners adapted their property rights to changing socio-ecological conditions in the modern period. But the stinting of lower moorland pastures around Ingleton can be traced back to the 16th century, pointing to a deep-seated tradition of stinting which eventually extended upwards onto the higher manorial wastes. The definition and development of pasture rights are therefore especially dynamic in this case study area, affecting rights to the soil and the legal status of communal pastures. Another particular feature of the case study is the landowners' use and management of upland pastures as grouse moors, resulting in a sometimes difficult balance between sporting and agrarian interests. Both Ingleborough and Scales Moor also exhibit a long tradition of collective management strategies at grassroots level, from traditional regulation by manor courts, to the stinting agreements and annual meetings of graziers and landowners recorded in 19th- and 20th-century minute books.

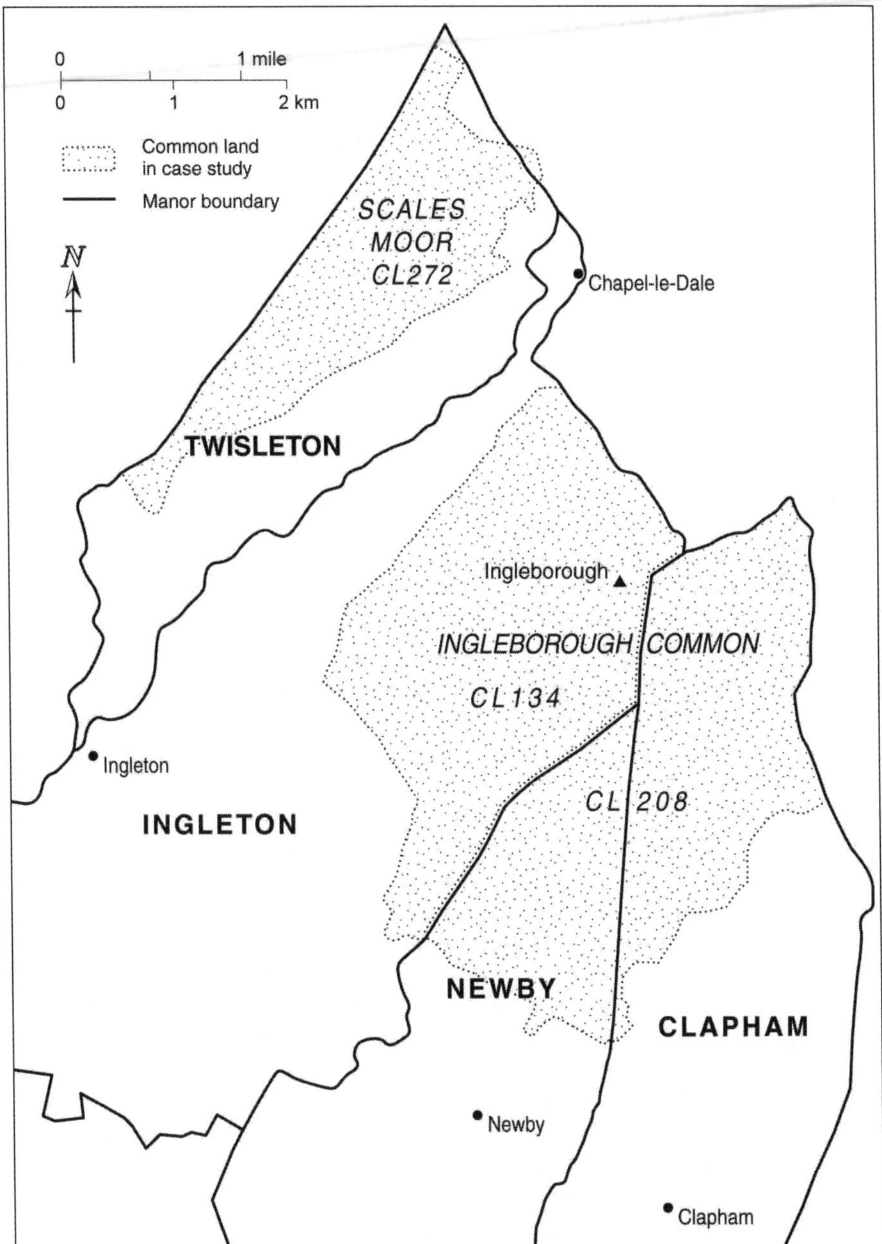

Figure 7.2 *Ingleborough and Scales Moor: Common land (CL) units and manorial boundaries*

Source: North Yorkshire County Council, Common Land Register. Manorial boundaries reconstructed from perambulations in NYCRO, ZUC 1/3/1 (Ingleton, 1754), WYRO, WYL 524/143 (Newby 1683).

Common rights and governance to 1965

Property rights

The commons under study fell within the territories attached to settlements along the foot of the Pennine scarp. Four separate manors were involved. Ingleborough Common was shared by the manors of Ingleton, the village at the foot of the Chapel-le-Dale valley, and Newby and Clapham, settlements on the southern skirts of the mountain. Manorial boundaries took the form of sight lines across the open common, converging on the peak of Little Ingleborough, giving each manor a section of the waste. The manors of Clapham and Newby came into the same ownership in the 19th century, with the result that the boundary between them has ceased to have any significance. As noted above, at registration, two common land (CL) units were registered: one for the Ingleton side of the common, the other for the Clapham and Newby side. Scales Moor, by contrast, forms a single unit, belonging to the manor of Twisleton with Ellerbeck, a small estate focusing on inbye land between the two valleys which converge at Ingleton.

Several manorial boundaries were disputed in the 16th and 17th centuries, the causes including both enclosure of waste and pressure on common rights. Disputes over the boundary between the manors of Newby and Ingleton are implied when the lord of Ingleton was presented at Newby court in 1568 and 1570 for encroaching and enclosing land,[1] and probably lie behind the need to erect a boundary stone on Ingleborough Common: a squared sandstone boundary marker of 17th- or early 18th-century date, inscribed 'I' and 'N', marks the dividing line between Ingleton and Newby at Grey Scars. The boundary between Twisleton and Ellerbeck and the neighbouring manor of Thornton was disputed in 1575, access to turbary apparently being one of the points of contention.[2] Some intercommoning is recorded in the early modern period, the tenants in some parts of Newby manor paying annual 'overshot' rents to lords of neighbouring manors, so that their cattle could stray onto those lords' common lands.[3]

In the early-modern period the extent of common land within these manorial territories would have been considerably greater than is currently the case. Environmental factors limited the area of productive inbye land to comparatively small areas surrounding the farmsteads, leaving large tracts of open waste beyond. By the 17th century much of the lower moorland, at around 300m, had been physically separated from the remaining waste and shared by groups of farms, leaving only the higher reaches as unenclosed waste. In the Southerscales area of the Chapel-le-Dale valley this process was recalled in the early 19th century: 'the lower part of [the commons] being Grass land of a better quality they walled off from the out Commons or Mountainous part, using the Lower Commons for Cows & Cattle & the Higher or Heath for the Sheep'.[4]

These 'lower commons' typically took the form of stinted pastures, shares in which were expressed in terms of a numerical grazing right. The Ingleton area shared with other parts of the central Pennines a deep-rooted history of stinting on such shared pastures. Stinting is recorded from the earliest court rolls in the area: in 1543, men were presented for not keeping 'le stynt' with their animals on Sleights Pasture, a stretch of lower moorland near Ribblehead. Later 16th-century presentments for 'le overstinte' and for putting animals on the common pasture *supra le stand* (i.e. 'above the stint') suggest that stinting was widespread. Most of these stinted pastures had probably been physically separated from the waste by 1600: from its name, Scar Close, recorded in 1543, was clearly physically separate, as was Fell Close, on the slopes of Ingleborough, which is shown as an enclosure on a map of 1619.[5] The presence of an 'oulde close' and a 'Newe close' at Winterscales in 1591 suggests continuing enclosure at that period.[6]

Manorial interest in the grazing or soil seems to have been conspicuously absent for long periods, and a legacy of weak manorial control allowed a high degree of autonomy in the exercise of common rights, the separation of stinted pastures and their eventual subdivision. A survey of the upper division of Newby manor (covering the head of the Chapel-le-Dale valley and Ribblesdale) in 1683 went so far as to claim that no manorial waste remained and suggested that these stinted lands were owned and controlled by the tenants:

> *We find that there are no wasts Moors or Comons within the said Manor but such as are all Instinted pastures and do belong to the said Customary Tenants & Tenements aforesaid & are not reputed, nor ever were wast grounds, but the said Customary rents (are and have been) paid for the same together with the said Customary Tenements & as well for the one as for the Other, And the same are now & always have been Stinted by the Tenants of this Lordship as they from time to time do think & have thought fit & Convenient. And the said Customary Tenants by their by-laws or agreement amongst themselves do for some years Stint the same to fewer or more Cattle gates as their occasions require which they have often done, & by the Custome of the said Manor may doe without the consent of the Lords or any of his Officers.*[7]

Unsurprisingly, this process of appropriation by groups of tenants led to confusion over the legal status of land and rights, which came to a head in Newby manor when a new lord of the manor, James Farrer, took over in 1810. In 1812, Farrer sought legal opinion over whether he retained rights to soil and minerals within the stinted pastures. It was implied that by allowing tenants to enjoy the pastures for some considerable time without interference or exercise of the lord's privileges, successive lords had weakened their own title in the land. Once separated from the waste, stinted pastures were often subdivided between stintholders, a process of enclosure which took place without the lord of the manor's knowledge or consent. It was claimed that as much as 1500 or 2000 acres had been lost in a process whereby tenants 'entered into an agreement appointing arbitrators or Commissioners who set out the allotments as they thought right ... without any application to the Lord of the Manor who was ignorant thereof'.[8]

The process of appropriation and stinting – attenuated and informal though it was – resulted in a major change in the legal status of these stinted pastures. On some – perhaps all – of them the graziers enjoyed a right of sole or several pasture, since the lord's interests in the grazing had been granted away, lost or negated. It could be argued that the loss of a community of use between lord and tenants meant that such pastures ceased to be true common land (see Gadsden, 1988, § 1.27–1.28, 1.60–1.61). In practice, the exact legal status of those stinted pastures which remained undivided was ambiguous (and perhaps largely irrelevant to the users), until the Commons Registration Act 1965 demanded that a decision be made. Some of the lower stinted pastures of the area were registered as common land: Winterscales Pasture (CL 368) on the slopes of Whernside,

Littledale (CL 473), Blea Moor (CL 194) and Cam End (CL 103) fall into this category. Other rough grazing lands which might formerly have had the status of stinted pastures, but which had been converted into severalty or had come into sole occupancy, were not registered as common. For example, Gayle Moor, originally used by the group of four tenements at Gayle, was already in the hands of a single occupier by 1839 and was not registered as common land under the Commons Registration Act.[9]

In the cases of Ingleborough and Scales Moor, formal stinting regimes emerged at a relatively late date, but the treatment of the surrounding lower pastures shows that the discourse and practice of stinting was already familiar to the grazing community. Thus the transition to stinting on the manorial waste can be viewed as the extension of a system developed on sections of the lower moorland to the higher commons. The historical processes which lay behind the stinting of Ingleborough and Scales Moor differed significantly. On Ingleborough, there is some ambiguity. The grazing rights of customary tenants in Ingleton manor were said in 1592 to be 'without stint, Rate or Number' (Balderston, undated, p272), though the rights on Ingleborough held by tenants of the neighbouring manor of Twisleton were described in 1625 as:

> *... so much common of pasture on and throughout all the commons on Ingleborough within the Lordship of Ingleton formerly agreed upon ... as doth or ought to belong unto three oxgange and a-half to any of the tenants of Ingleton aforesaid without any rent paying for the same.* (Balderston, undated, p287)

The implication is that not only were the rights of tenants in the neighbouring manor governed by stint, but it was also possible to conceive of the grazing rights of Ingleton tenants in similar terms. It is therefore possible that at certain junctures, the pasture rights of some groups of graziers were limited by number. Nevertheless, Ingleborough Common appears to have continued without a comprehensive and durable stinting regime until the later 20th century. Unsuccessful attempts to introduce stinting as a measure to control overgrazing were made in 1848 and again in a protracted campaign between 1877 and 1889. Reflecting on these attempts in 1896, one commentator claimed that 'the ancient custom of unlimited rights on commons is a gross injustice to the farming community and a source of wanton cruelty to moorland sheep and cattle' (Carr, 1896).[10] Although the common was not formally stinted until after registration of rights under the Commons Registration Act 1965, the minute book of the Ingleborough Fell Commoners (running from 1927) shows that a numerical system predated formal stinting. Each member had to inform the meeting of the number of animals that they intended to graze on the common that year, so that the shepherd's wages could be apportioned fairly between the graziers. The meeting's membership did not cover all commoners on the fell, and it is not clear whether graziers were working within the confines of a notional upper limit for flock sizes (the numbers vary from year to year); but this annual proposal of numbers suggests that an individual's flock size had to be deemed reasonable by fellow graziers.[11]

On Scales Moor the transition to stinting was effected by the commoners themselves in the early 19th century. In 1810 the graziers of Scales Moor agreed to impose a stint and to appoint a herdsman. The common was to be stinted at the rate of 'One Beast Gate for every Shilling Land tax with which we are respectively assessed' and the formula by which the beastgate was converted into grazing numbers for sheep, horses and young beasts was to be such 'as is usual and accustomed'.[12] It was an informal grassroots agreement that failed in the face of 'disputes and differences' which arose 'as to the number of sheep and cattle which each owner and occupier is entitled to turn upon the said Common'.[13] A more formal stinting agreement was drawn up in 1842, based not on land tax assessment but on an attempt to measure the carrying capacity of the common. Scales Moor was computed to contain 1000 acres and to be capable of supporting a maximum of 800 sheep. The number and value of cattlegates were adjusted accordingly. It was decided that each cattlegate would enable a commoner to graze 5 black-faced Scotch sheep or 4 white-faced sheep, and that the total number of cattlegates attached to the common should be 160. Any person found overstocking the common could expect legal proceedings to be taken, funded by the stintholders in proportion to their stints. Whereas the role of the lord of the manor in the 1810 agreement is unclear, the new agreement explicitly stated that stinting would not affect the lord's rights.[14]

One overriding question is: what was the benefit of introducing stinting on the commons and pastures of the Ingleton area, and why might stints be preferred over grazing rights *sans nombre*? Stinted grazing rights were expressed in terms of 'gates', each 'gate' giving the right to graze a certain number of animals. In the early-modern period most stints were expressed as 'cattlegates'; but there are also references to 'beaste gates', 'sheepe gates' and 'ewesgates'.[15] As elsewhere, a formula was used to convert a stint expressed in cattlegates or beastgates into a pasture right for other species, four sheep to one cattlegate being the modern norm on a number of the commons and pastures in the case study area. This provided a number of possible advantages (see Winchester and Straughton, 2010). As the 1842 agreement for Scales Moor shows, stocking numbers could be assessed and apportioned to reflect the carrying capacity of the common as a whole, rather than the inbye belonging to individual commoners (the measure of levancy and couchancy). Moreover, the stinting formula could be adjusted to allow fewer or more animals to be grazed should the carrying capacity of the common ever change. Stints also allowed for closer definition of who had grazing rights and how many animals they were permitted to graze, allowing for greater control over the exercise of rights. Finally, a stint or gate became a flexible and potentially profitable commodity in its own right once it was severed from the inbye land or holding. In some cases stints had come to be treated as rights in gross and conveyed separately from holdings of land in the Ingleton area by the 17th century, showing a longstanding tradition of treating pasture rights as personal heritable property. Several surrenders of land in Newby manor in 1609 consisted solely of stints in shared pastures and when the manor was surveyed in 1683, holdings consisting solely of stints were recorded. The principal holding of at least one of the tenants of these stints was outside the manor.[16] The legality of transferring beastgates did not go without question: in 1812, the Lord of Newby asked whether his court should refuse to allow the admittance of tenants to beastgates separately from holdings in order to emphasize that stints were appurtenant common pasture rights and thus safeguarding the lord's claims to the soil.[17] Despite this, stints have continued to be sold or let by private agreement or at auction, and the power to transfer stints is seen as an important facet of the common right (Tyler, 2002, p9).

Grazing was only one of an array of uses of common land in this area. Other common rights recorded in the local sources include turbary (perhaps particularly for cutting sods rather than peat, since mineral coal was mined at Ingleton) and rights to gather rushes for animal bedding and to take stone. The property rights of the lords of the manors included game and mineral rights, the exercise of which added further layers of activity (and potential conflict) on the commons. Ingleborough landowners were particularly interested in using their common lands as grouse moors, a process that intensified after the manors of Newby and Clapham were purchased by the Farrer family in the 19th century (Johnson, 2008, pp218–225). The *Ingleborough Fell Commoners' Minute Book, 1927–2007* records that the shepherd occasionally also performed the role of 'game watcher' for the Ingleborough Estate; but relations between graziers and game interests could sometimes be difficult, with disagreements over appropriate stocking levels. Shooting activity had reduced on Ingleborough by the late 20th century as a result of heather loss and reductions in grouse numbers, and a lack of profitability in the sport; but on both Ingleborough and Scales Moor the landscape still retains tangible reminders of the exercise of game rights in the form of stone grouse butts and shooting cabins on the common. The landscapes of both Ingleborough and Scales Moor also reveal extensive evidence of surface quarrying. In the case of Scales Moor, one phase of this can be related to the quarrying of limestone pavement for garden rockeries in the early 1950s.[18] Such remains point to the exploitation of mineral rights, probably over a long period of time, either by the lords themselves, through leases to second parties, or by commoners as part of their extraction of resources for walls and buildings (Johnson, 2008, pp198–199).

Governance

Surviving manor court records – a few from the 16th and 17th centuries, more from the 18th to early 20th centuries – confirm that the courts of all four manors oversaw the exercise of common rights.[19] However, there is a general paucity of by-laws or presentments concerning pasture rights, suggesting that, as a result of the separation of stinted pastures from the manorial waste and the frequency of non-resident lords, those exercising grazing rights operated with a degree of autonomy from the manor court. This may also reflect the existence of local hamlet meetings or 'byrlaws' (*birelagii*), at which regulations for day-to-day farming practice were drawn up, comparable to those recorded elsewhere in the Pennines (for which, see Winchester, 2000, pp42–45). This is the implication of the reference to 'by-laws or agreement' about stints made among the tenants themselves in Newby manor in 1683 (cited above). Although manor courts continued to be held, most pasture rights were, in effect, managed outside the courts. Consequently, it is probably a mistake to view the watershed between manorial and post-manorial governance in quite the same light as elsewhere. Since there seems to have been autonomy in management from a relatively early stage, it is likely that there was underlying continuity in governance and management strategies, outside and irrespective of the manor courts. Indeed, some 18th-century courts appear to have been perfunctory affairs: it was said of Newby manor that non-resident stewards, who rarely set foot in the manor, held courts at which 'they hurried through as much as possible'.[20] Although manor courts continued to be held in Clapham, Ingleton and Newby until the early 20th century, some were little more than shams: at Clapham the jury was occasionally reduced to one member or even none at all by the late 19th century, implying that the lord and steward were now holding courts as a mere formality.[21]

The fading or collapse of manor courts did not leave an institutional vacuum, as communities of graziers were already accustomed to taking collective action on stinted pastures. By the 20th century day-to-day management of several commons was in the hands of commoners' meetings. The earliest for which records are known was the Scales Moor stintholders' (or 'gateholders') meeting, for which minute books survive covering 1884–1898 and 1901–1991 (see Figure 7.3).[22] The emergence of the new management institution was presumably a consequence of the more formal stinting agreement on Scales Moor, drawn up in 1842 after the false start in 1810. The new agreement contributed towards a more stable period of management, with annual stintholders' meetings, which took place in a barn beside the road linking the groups of farms at each end of the common, typically involving the appointment of a salaried shepherd, reviewing the accounts, letting the 'mole gate' (a stint let to raise the fee paid to the mole catcher), and dealing with repairs to infrastructure, such as the wash dub and closure periods. The meeting depended on mutual accountability and oversight: in a list of rules contained in the first volume of minutes, it was ordered that if any of the committee had a 'just and reasonable suspicion' that a person was overstocking, it was their duty to call on the committee to investigate with a general count of the stock. As with other stinted pastures in this case study area, the role of the herdsman was also critical to management and governance, and he had immediate authority over the pasture: stintholders were not permitted to move livestock on the common without giving the herdsman notice. The list of rules detailed the herd's duties and the conditions of his employment. It was reputedly the custom for candidates for the post of shepherd to assemble on the Moor; the gait holders would then vote on who should be employed for the ensuing year (Tyler, 2002, p9). During the 20th century, the system of appointing herds seems to have become more problematic: in the 1920s, for example, stintholders could not agree on a wage, nor could all graziers be persuaded to pay their share. After 1938 few meetings were recorded (the book contains minutes of 1968, 1990 and 1991 only); but it is known that shepherds were still appointed from time to time. Collective activity was a strong tradition on Scales Moor: a washfold at the north-east end of the common was a focus of communal events until the 1940s. Each year on 16 June the stintholders gathered all the sheep from the Moor; the male lambs were castrated and the hoggs (the previous year's lambs) were washed before clipping. At the end of a hot, strenuous day the community gathered on the moor near the fold for pillow fights and wrestling competitions.[23]

Comparable commoners' meetings are recorded from the Farrer family's Ingleborough Estate, although the estate as landlord took a more prominent role, compared to the grassroots character of the meetings on Scales Moor. Under the influence of the estate, new policies and practices spread from pasture to pasture: in 1934 the gaitholders of Littledale asked that the Ingleborough Estate's agent should 'draw up Rules for Littledale Pasture on similar lines to those which are now in force on Bleamoor and Camm End Stinted Pastures'.[24] On the Ingleborough Estate's commons the development of post-manorial governance bodies must be seen in the context of the landowners' interest in grouse shooting. The estate's interest in facilitating new

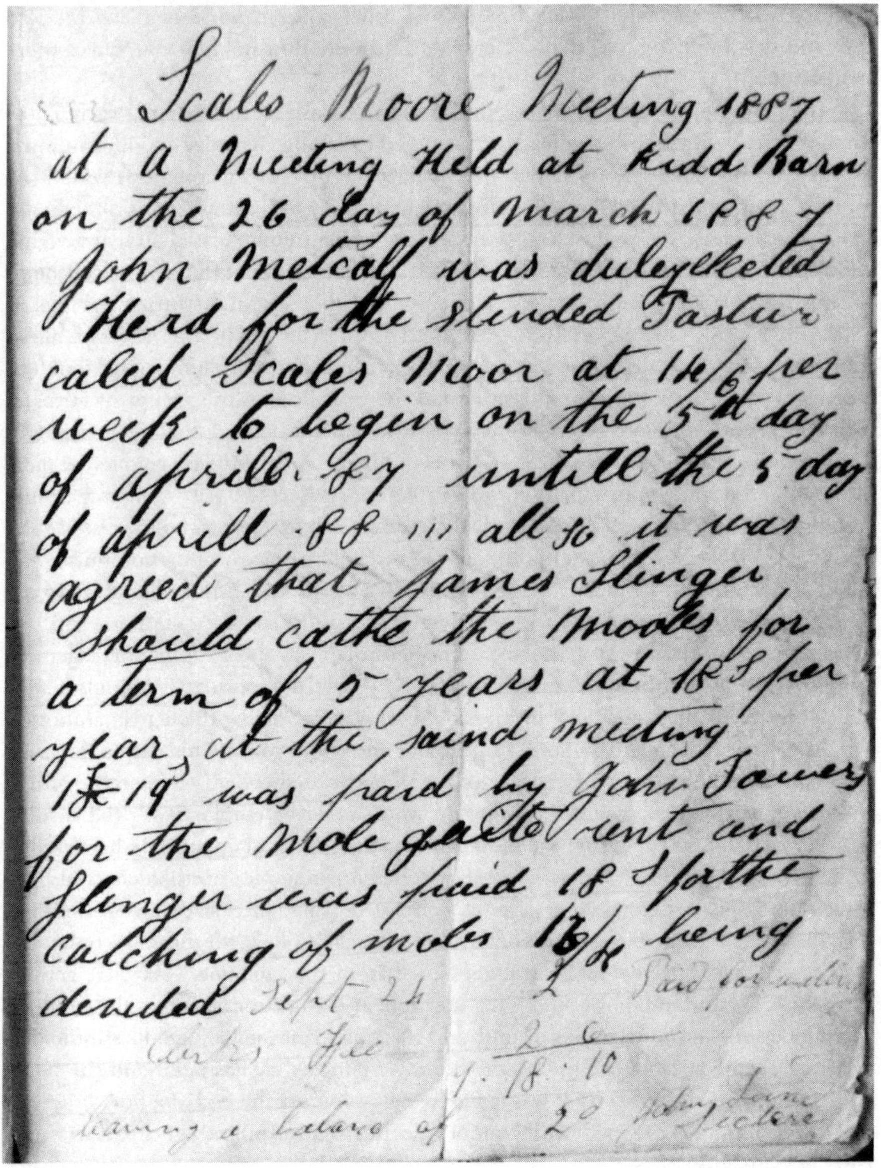

Scales Moore Meeting 1887
at a Meeting Held at Kidd Barn
on the 26 day of March 1887
John Metcalf was duleyelected
Herd for the Stinted Pasture
caled Scales Moor at 14/6 per
week to begin on the 5th day
of aprill. 87 untill the 5 day
of aprill. 88 ... all so it was
agreed that James Slinger
shauld cathe the mooles for
a term of 5 years at 18s per
year at the saind meeting
1£ 19d was paid by John Tower
for the mole gaite rent and
Slinger was paid 18s for the
catching of moles 17/4 being
devided Sept 24 2 Paid for moles
Clerks Fee 2 0
1 . 18 . 10
leaving a balance of 2d John Towers Sectare

Figure 7.3 *Scales Moor stintholders' meeting: Entry in the minute book recording the annual meeting of rights holders in 1887*

Note: Business consisted of electing a shepherd, appointing a mole catcher and letting the 'molegate', a stint from which the rent was used to pay the mole catcher and the costs of the meeting.

Source: reproduced by permission of Mr J. Metcalfe

institutions, fostering shepherding, formalizing grazing rules and stint rates in the 19th and 20th centuries stemmed, in part, from a desire to protect or create the appropriate conditions for grouse, and these institutions provided a vehicle by which competing interests could be negotiated. Although the purpose was not directly stated, in 1932 the estate compensated gaitholders on Littledale at the rate of 3 shillings per head for reducing stocking numbers: it seems likely that graziers had been asked to reduce numbers in order to provide the necessary environment for grouse.[25]

Grouse shooting was also one element of the mix on Ingleborough, for which a minute book survives, recording meetings of the 'Ingleborough Fell Commoners' since 1927.[26] The commoners, again under the authority of the Ingleborough Estate, met annually to appoint a shepherd; regulate and agree stocking numbers; set the dates for sheep gatherings and for 'boon' days (for collective maintenance work); and deal with the repair of sheep folds, walls, fences, gates and drains. Latterly, the commoners performed the role of shepherd themselves on a rota system. This body had responsibility for the south-eastern side of Ingleborough Fell (CL 208), in the manors of Newby and Clapham. However, membership of the meeting did not necessarily include *all* those with grazing rights on the Newby and Clapham side of Ingleborough Fell. The meeting was initially described as a meeting of 'the Commoners of Ingleborough Fell who have contributed towards the wages of a Shepherd', and centred on those commoners who were tenants of the Ingleborough Estate: in 1931 it was reported that shepherding had been introduced '24 years ago' (i.e. circa 1907) by tenants of the estate following 'difficulties and friction' over herding by commoners. Later meetings strove to widen participation. In 1966 one member of the meeting was given the task of going to see 'all graziers up to Ingleton Parish Boundary and to ask them if they would join in and contribute to the Fell Commoners Shepherd'. At the next meeting newcomers were formally welcomed, with the chairman emphasizing the 'need to try and maintain co-operation between all commoners of those who grazed on this side of Ingleborough Fell'. These post-manorial governance institutions operated in a context of complex historical boundaries, which, in theory, dictated membership and the areas covered, but were not necessarily immutable.

These collective management bodies ensured proactive policing of grazing rights at grassroots level well into the 20th century. A long tradition of policing illegal grazing by impounding foreign or stray animals can be traced through the manorial and post-manorial documents. In 1704 the court at Clapham appointed the manorial bailiff to be 'keeper and supervisor' of all the wastes in the manor, requiring him to impound foreigners' cattle and to take a payment of 2d for each horse or 'made beast' and 1d for each heifer, calf or sheep.[27] By the early 19th century the courts at Clapham and the neighbouring manors were appointing 'pinders' to perform this role. At Ingleton they were appointed on a fairly regular basis at courts held between 1821 and 1840 and in the 1880s; at Newby, a scale of penalties to be charged by the pinder was laid down in 1826 and appointments of a pinder are recorded in 1845, and then almost annually between 1852 and 1868.[28] It is possible that pinders were sometimes dealing with the impact of large-scale stock movements through the area, as well as local stocking issues, since major drove roads passed through Ingleton parish and a cattle fair was held in the parish at Gearstones, near Ribblehead, until 1872. Cattle were grazed overnight on open pasture or land let by local farmers (Johnson, 2008, pp158–162).

It seems likely that the role of the pinder in policing stray animals would have been subsumed within the role of the shepherd, once salaried shepherds came to be appointed to manage individual commons. As noted above, shepherds were a key element of the post-manorial management bodies, and might have almost complete authority over the common during the months of their employment, with commoners prohibited from going onto the common to move their own stock without the shepherd's permission or attendance.[29] Their role and abilities were sometimes contested, with graziers sometimes requesting to herd their own animals.[30] In 1889, the Scales Moor meeting recorded a case of assault on the herd by one of the stintholders, dealt with by the Ingleton Petty Sessions.[31] There also seems to have been some concern that shepherds appointed by the Ingleborough Estate would be viewed as unofficial gamekeepers by graziers: in 1934 the estate took over the payment of the shepherd employed on both Littledale and Winterscales, and the agent sought to reassure graziers that their interests would not be sidelined (the agent impressed upon the Littledale stintholders that 'the shepherd was there to look after their sheep and for their benefit as well as that of the Estate generally').[32] Elsewhere, however, the distinction between game-keeping and shepherding was less clear. In 1927, the man elected as shepherd by the Ingleborough Fell commoners was also the 'Game Watcher' on the moor; it was decided that his new role as shepherd would not prevent him from performing his duties as 'Watcher' and, indeed, a later entry suggests that the shepherd's job description had developed to include game watching and driving grouse across the fell. In 1934, the agent reported that there was no longer a need for the shepherd's services as game watcher or for driving grouse across the fell because there were not enough grouse to warrant the payment and there had been no grouse shooting of late.[33] The significance and purpose of shepherding in post-manorial governance is perhaps more complex than at first appears.

Other common rights also required management. To judge by the frequency of orders and presentments in the manor courts, the most contentious areas of resource exploitation on the commons were the removal of peat, turf, heather, soil and stones. Orders requiring peat diggings to be drained and the vegetated sod to be replaced are suggestive of the environmental problems to which 'unneighbourly' exercise of turbary rights was prone.[34] Stripping turf and sods destroyed pasture and increased vulnerability to soil erosion. One driver behind this was the construction of limekilns (see Johnson, 2008, pp201–203); another was land improvement: in 1774 Newby court noted that 'several persons of late years have digged Delved and graven up great quantities of the Comons or Waste Grounds ... to burn into Ashes and mix the Soil with Lime and sometimes lead the Soil into their inclosed Grounds for the Improvement thereof'.[35] Removal of sods appears to have reached a crescendo in the later 18th century, though the problem persisted: in 1822 the lords of Newby complained that the tenants had 'openly & grossly violated all custom & right' in taking turf out of the manor, destroying the surface of parts of Newby Moor and by burning turf into ashes there.[36]

In these contests over resources, it is far from clear how successful the manor courts were as governance bodies. Perhaps they tell of a period of weak governance in the century from circa 1750 to circa 1850, before the rise of commoners' meetings in the later 19th and 20th centuries. By then the pressures on the commons had changed, as small-scale lime-burning was replaced by industrial-scale production elsewhere, local landowners sought to exploit their game rights by managing commons as grouse moor, and graziers sought closer management of grazing by using hired shepherds. A further change in management regimes took place in the mid-20th century in the context of a decline in grouse numbers and organized shoots from the 1930s (Johnson, 2008, pp222–223), and the concentration of grazing rights in fewer hands as holdings were amalgamated. The aggregation of gaits into fewer hands simplified management of stock, perhaps reducing the need for salaried shepherds and formal meetings of management bodies.

The commons today

Commons registration and the 1965 Act

Custom, practice and the registration process

The documentary evidence for the collective organization of agricultural management (see earlier), both before and after the introduction of commons registration, enables us to study the manner in which practices derived from collective decision-making within the local farming community were transmitted into property rights under the 1965 Act. The influence of the history of stinting on these commons can be seen both in the nature of the rights registered under the 1965 Act and the manner in which they are expressed in the commons registers. Many (but not all) are recorded as sheep gaits, and many of the registered pasturage rights are specific as to the numbers of sheep and followers permitted on the moor by registered sheep gaits. For example, entry 5 on the Scales Moor Register (CL 272) confers a right to graze 91 7/8 black-faced sheep or 73 ½ white-faced sheep with or without lambs, expressed to represent 91 sheep gaits or 18 6/18 cattle gaits (with 1 cattle gait being equal to 5 black-faced sheep and 4 white-faced sheep). Another example is provided by entry 8 on the register for CL 272 which confers 104.375 sheep gaits. This level of precision is entirely absent in the common registers for the other upland case studies – Eskdale and Cwmdeuddwr – where grazing management had been, prior to 1965, notionally organized around the levancy and couchancy system.

Nevertheless, the relationship in the Ingleton case study between collective organization, local practice and the commons registers is a complex one. It was noted above that the stinting of these commons did not take place in a systematic or uniform manner, and a stinting regime was not formally adopted on Ingleborough Common until after the registration of rights under the Commons Registration Act 1965. The Ingleborough Fell Commoners' Association covered only the south-eastern portion of Ingleborough (CL 208), and its membership did not necessarily include all those with grazing rights on the Newby and Clapham side of the moor. This may explain the discrepancies in the manner in which rights were registered under the 1965 Act. At a meeting on 21 February 1967, the commoners minuted that 'There was quite a discussion regarding the coming commons registrations. It was agreed that the stocking rate for Ingleborough Fell should be 1½ acres per sheep',[37] implying that rights were calculated on the acreage of the common (rather than the carrying capacity of the inbye land). The Ingleborough Fell Commoners' Minute Book shows, furthermore, that the commoners discussed proposals from English Nature and the Ministry of Agriculture, Fisheries and Food (MAFF) (now the Department for Environment, Food and Rural Affairs, or Defra) to address stocking levels on Ingleborough in 1994 and 1995.[38]

By 2004 there were approximately 4000 gaits registered to Ingleborough Common, showing its importance as a pastoral resource and the potential for grazing pressures to impact upon the ecological management of its highly sensitive environmental features – indeed, English Nature wanted sheep numbers reduced by 882 under the Sheep and Wildlife Enhancement Scheme (SWES) in 2004.[39]

It is also unclear whether graziers on Ingleborough regarded the annual grazing figures collectively agreed[40] as a definitive figure or merely as a notional upper limit for flock sizes. The figures registered under the 1965 Act would, in this context, reflect the legally permissible maximum number of stock that each grazier could put to the common in any one year – indeed, this interpretation of local practice on Ingleborough common would accord with the terminology of the 1965 Act itself, which refers to registered rights of pasturage giving a right to graze that is exercisable 'in relation to animals not exceeding the number registered' (1965 Act, section 15 (3)).

The registration of sheep gaits on Scales Moor reflects a different historical and organizational context, and presents a more straightforward example of customary practice being formalized in property rights through the registration process under the 1965 Act. The terms of the 1842 agreement (discussed above) clearly survived largely intact in local custom and usage, and both informed and structured the registration of rights undertaken in the late 1960s pursuant to the 1965 Act. The need to register rights under the Commons Registration Act 1965 seems to have precipitated the brief revival of the formal Scales Moor stintholders' meeting in 1968. Graziers recorded an adjustment of the stint rate, which underlined their concentration on sheep: it was determined that one gait or stint would equal one black-faced sheep, or four-fifths of a 'Lowland' sheep, and that no cattle or horses would be grazed on the moor. In 1990, it was recorded in the stintholders' meeting minutes that there were then 809 registered sheep gaits on the Moor (though with only two-thirds of this stocking level permitted from December to early April), which was then estimated to comprise 1022.33 acres – a figure roughly comparable with the total acreage and maximum stocking density (800 sheep gaits) recorded in the 1842 agreement.[41] The conversion rates for black- and white-faced sheep in the 1842 agreement are clearly reflected in several of the registered entries in the commons register, as are the very precise calculations of conversion rates for cattle, black- and white-faced sheep. On the other hand, the number of rights does not tally exactly with the 1842 agreement (the commons register for CL 272 has registered rights to graze 827 black-faced sheep in total).

Registered common rights

A study of the commons registers for the three CL units that make up the common land in this case study (CL 134, 208 and 272) reveals an overwhelming preponderance of registered sheep pasturage rights. There are very few registered rights of turbary or estovers, or of pasturage rights for cattle, notwithstanding that all were exercised in the past:

- *Cattle:* only six entries in the register for CL 134 record a right to graze cattle on Ingleborough common.[42] All registered rights are otherwise for sheep and followers, hoggs or wethers. Similarly, only one entry for CL 208 mentions the conversion of sheep gaits to cattle (4 sheep gaits = 1 cattle gait; 6 sheep gaits = 1 horse gait).[43] Three of the entries for CL 272 (Scales Moor) record cattle gaits in addition to sheep gaits, in one case restating the very precise conversion rate of the 1842 stinting agreement.[44]

- *Turbary:* there are only two entries conferring rights of turbary on the Clapham side of Ingleborough Common (CL 208) and none on the Ingleton side (CL 134). There are two registered rights of turbary on Scales Moor (CL 272).
- *Estovers:* there is one right of estovers registered on the Clapham side of Ingleborough Common (CL 208), expressed as a right to take rushes, bracken and heather,[45] and none on the Ingleton side (CL 134). Both entries giving rights of turbary on Scales Moor also give rights to estovers, expressed as the right to cut rushes.[46]

The paucity of registered rights for cattle illustrates a wider problem generated by the registration process under the 1965 Act. The 1842 stinting agreement on Scales Moor calculated grazing densities primarily by reference to cattle gaits (fixed at 160), and gave precise conversion rates to give equivalent grazing figures for sheep. Clearly, the primary concern was the sustainable use of the grazing resource – the nature of the animals grazing the common was not in itself the primary issue. The registration of rights under the 1965 Act has effectively removed this flexibility and constrains potential management choices for the future grazing regime on the common. It could, for example, present major difficulties for the introduction of a mixed grazing regime with sheep and cattle under future agri-environment management schemes (such as Higher Level Stewardship, discussed further below). Although much local practice and custom has been reflected in the registers, therefore, this has certainly not uniformly been the case – the registration process has also suppressed some agricultural management practices that were prevalent in earlier centuries.

Stints as commodified property rights

It was noted above that the ability to transfer stints is perceived as an important facet of the common rights in this case study. Examined in the context of the legal rules governing common rights, a perception of stints as freely transferable property rights might suggest that they are regarded as being held 'in gross' (see Chapter 4, p55). Paradoxically, however, most of the sheep and cattle gaits on both Ingleborough Common and Scales Moor were registered under the 1965 Act as appurtenant (and therefore attached) to specified agricultural holdings or parcels of land, and not as rights in gross. Despite registration in this form, nevertheless, the registers reveal numerous transfers of rights without land after registration in the late 1960s, and their subsequent conversion and re-registration as rights in gross. The evidence, therefore, reveals a curious situation where the legal categorization of rights upon their initial registration failed to reflect cultural perceptions among local stakeholders as to their key attributes as property rights (their perceived transferability as a distinct species of property right separate from appurtenant land). The mismatch between cultural and legal perceptions as to the nature of the registered rights has now assumed considerable significance under the Commons Act 2006, which prohibits the future severance of appurtenant rights and prevents their sale separately from the dominant tenement (see below).

Ingleborough On CL 134 (Ingleton) there are currently 28 registered entries of common rights expressed as appurtenant to specified holdings or parcels of land. All common rights were initially registered under the 1965 Act as appurtenant rights. However, between April 1982[47] and May 2000[48] there was a succession of applications to re-register common rights that had formerly been rights appurtenant to land as rights held in gross. There are now 19 entries of grazing rights expressed as held in gross, in addition to the 28 entries for appurtenant rights. With the exception of one entry (of rights acquired by the Nature Conservancy Council),[49] these all represent cases where the common rights were severed from the holding to which they were formerly attached (i.e. appurtenant) and converted into rights in gross.

The other portion of Ingleborough common (CL 208: Clapham and Newby) presents a similar picture. All rights were initially registered as appurtenant to specified holdings or parcels of land. Starting on 11 September 1989, a number of applications were made to re-register severed rights as rights in gross.[50] There are now six entries of rights held in gross – one of which is held by the Nature Conservancy Council.[51] All appear to be cases where the rights have been acquired with or without the land to which they were formerly attached, and on acquisition then converted into rights in gross personal to the holder of the rights.

Scales Moor The evidence for the survival of the notion of stints as commodified property rights is also ambivalent in the case of Scales Moor (CL 272). One of the entries made under the Commons Registration Act 1965 was a registration of rights in gross. All others (originally nine in total) were expressed as being appurtenant to holdings or land. One of these[52] was severed and re-registered as a right in gross in 1985. There are two additional entries of rights in gross – both of grazing rights purchased by the Nature Conservancy Council.[53]

'Closed' grazing periods A characteristic feature of the collective organization of the grazing regime on Ingleborough Common and Scales Moor was the adoption of 'closed' periods each year during which livestock were not permitted on the commons. This practice is reflected in the registers, but is not uniformly recorded.

On *Ingleborough Common* the closure period on CL 134 is most commonly referred to as 5 November to 9 December, annually. Most entries record a right to graze sheep and followers until 5 November, and sheep or hoggs from 10 December. Some variation in the closure dates is reflected in the commons registers, however, with some entries giving a right to graze sheep and hoggs from 6 December, and the majority from 10 December. Some entries permit grazing only to 28/29 February, others until April. On CL 208 (Clapham and Newby), by contrast, the registered rights present a uniform closed period from 1 to 30 November, inclusive. Curiously, it is not the same closed period as on the Ingleton section of the common (see above). Clearly, customary practice has not been uniformly recorded in the entries made under the 1965 Act. Additionally, in the case of both CL 134 and CL 208, some entries do not record a closed period at all, and claim grazing rights throughout the year.[54]

On *Scales Moor* a similar picture emerges – the rights registered here reflect historic practice, but with some slight variation in the nature of the rights registered and of the practices they record. The closed period on Scales Moor runs from 10 November to 10 December each year, and is reflected in the majority of registrations under the 1965 Act. Some entries record the closed period as running from 16 November,[55] and some have no registered restrictions on grazing that reflect the closed period.[56] As with Ingleborough Common, customary practice is not, therefore, uniformly represented by the entries made under the 1965 Act.

Adaptation of property rights

Property structures have been adapted to the needs of contemporary commons management in a manner not seen in the other case studies presented in this work. In some respects this reflects a continuation of historical practice, and in others a break with traditional practice. We saw above that weak manorial control was a feature of this case study in the 18th and 19th centuries, and the lack of active ownership interests remains a feature today. The only active landowner is the Clapham Estate, which owns the soil of the Clapham and Newby portion of Ingleborough Common (CL 208). Both Scales Moor (CL 272) and the Ingleton side of Ingleborough Common (Cl 134) have absentee landowners. The Ingleton Commoners' Association has taken the legal form of a limited company, and the lord of the manor of Ingleton has given it power of attorney to manage the common and carry out the functions and powers of the owner of the soil. This is an unusual arrangement, not commonly encountered elsewhere, and has very important implications for the future management of the common and its ability to enter agri-environment schemes such as Higher Level Stewardship (HLS). On Scales Moor, the identity of the absentee landowner is currently unknown, a factor that does not impinge upon collective management of the grazing *per se*, but could have important consequences for future management if the consent of the landowner is required to alter existing management strategies – including entry to schemes such as HLS.

The tradition of stinting these commons has, as we have seen, affected the cultural understanding of property rights as tradable commodities, and the commoners consider their rights to be personal tradable assets. This perception runs counter to the legislative policy of the Commons Act 2006, which is premised upon the prohibition of severance being a key element in perpetuating local management and control (2006 Act, section 9; see also Chapter 4 p60). Nevertheless, the advocacy by commoners of a right of severance in this case did not diminish the importance that they attached to local control of agricultural management. The prohibition on severing appurtenant rights from the land was simply not considered to be an essential requirement for fostering local control.

The number of grazing rights exercised today is considerably less than the numbers reflected in the registers. Unlike the position in the Elan Valley and Eskdale case studies (see Chapters 6 and 8), this reduction is only partially to be attributed to the impact upon property rights of land management agreements promoting nature conservation. There are very few agreements on either Scales Moor or Ingleborough – only a couple of Sheep and Wildlife Enhancement Scheme (SWES) agreements negotiated with individual farmers. Natural England has, instead, adopted a more direct strategy to reduce the pressure of livestock grazing on the common and its habitats: purchasing and/or renting sheep gaits in their own name and then leaving them unexercised. The registered rights of turbary and estovers are not exercised in a modern context, but (as in Eskdale) they have been exercised in living memory. Two commoners recall their fathers cutting peat on the common in June until the 1970s.

Commons governance

The contemporary governance of Ingleborough Common is bifurcated in a manner that reflects the manorial history of landownership in the case study (as explained above) and the division of the common into two separate registered blocks of common land – CL 208 and CL 134. The Ingleborough Fell Commoners' Association covers the Clapham and Newby side of Ingleborough Common (CL 208). The Ingleton side of the common (CL 134) has a separate, and much more recent, committee, set up in 1990 and now constituted as a limited company. Before 1990 there seems to have been a lack of governance structures for Ingleton.[57] The two commons associations therefore display a quite different institutional evolution, even though the common is unfenced and the two areas of common land are open to each other and experience many of the same land management issues. It is nevertheless clear from the *Ingleborough Fell Commoners' Minute Book* that the two committees sometimes work together to coordinate closed grazing periods and gathering days.

Environmental governance

The Ingleborough case study differs from the other two upland case studies in that modern environmental governance is not dominated by agri-environmental agreements. The only land management agreements with Natural England are specific to the environmental designation of the land as a Site of Special Scientific Interest (SSSI). And these are not, in themselves, of fundamental importance to the current management of the common for nature conservation. As noted above, Natural England has pursued a different strategy to preserve the environmental quality of the commons by purchasing rights in gross.

Statutory environmental designations

The Ingleborough Special Area of Conservation (SAC)

The Ingleborough Complex SAC extends to 5769.29ha and hosts several Annex I habitats, including *Juniperus communis* formations on heath, calcareous grassland, blanket bogs and limestone pavements. The key difference between this habitat type and that found in the other case studies is the need for flexible grazing management on different parts of the site, and at different times of the year, rather than a simple overall reduction in grazing pressures. Natural England emphasizes that the 'diversity of interests of the limestone pavements, juniper and limestone rock habitats is dependent on there being a range of grazing intensities, from moderate to light to areas with no livestock grazing. Heavy livestock or rabbit grazing has been damaging' (JNNC, 2006c, at 4.3). Although all the commons in the case study are within the SAC, none of the farmers considered that it impacted upon the land management they practised. Because the site is also an SSSI, most of the land-use controls that have practical relevance have been introduced under the Wildlife and Countryside Act 1981 (as amended).

Sites of Special Scientific Interest (SSSIs)

The case study includes two large SSSIs: Ingleborough SSSI (5230ha) and the Whernside SSSI (2600ha). The former encompasses both CL 208 and CL 134, while the latter covers all of CL 272. They were both re-notified in 1986 under section 28 of the Wildlife and Countryside Act 1981, as amended.

Both Ingleborough and Scales Moor are karst areas, characterized by limestone pavements produced under glacial conditions, and Scales Moor has one of the most extensive unbroken horizontal limestone pavements in Britain. Both SSSIs support similar vegetation, including blanket mires, calcareous grassland, dwarf shrub heath and sub-montane acid grassland. Scales Moor has been assessed by Natural England as in unfavourable recovering conservation condition (Natural England, 2010a). The condition of vegetation on Ingleborough SSSI was reassessed by Natural England in 2010 (Natural England, 2010b). While the majority of the SSSI units within the site were assessed as unfavourable but recovering with appropriate management (83 per cent of the overall area of the SSSI), several units remain in unfavourable conservation condition with no change, and the site therefore presents a major challenge for future conservation management.

The list of operations likely to damage the special conservation interest (OLDSIs) for each SSSI is lengthy, extending to 28 activities that require the consent of Natural England before they can be lawfully carried out. The OLDSIs of most practical importance for the preservation of the habitats on Ingleborough Common and Scales Moor are the introduction of stock feeding and changes in stock feeding practice, the killing or removal of wild animals, and the extraction of minerals, including peat, shingle, sand and gravel, topsoil, subsoil, lime, limestone pavement and spoil. As in the other case studies, the list of OLDSIs is poorly integrated with the property rights subsisting over the common. The latter are *profits à prendre* – the right to take grass (by the mouth of the sheep or cattle), peat, turf and rushes from the former manorial waste. Those OLDSIs prohibiting cultivation, mowing, and the supplementary feeding of livestock or the release of materials or animals are therefore notionally redundant as they identify operations that commoners have no legal capacity to undertake on the common. Nevertheless, notifying these operations as OLDSIs offers an additional state-mediated mode for ensuring adherence in practice to the limitations on common property rights. This can be significant where – as in Ingleton and on Scales Moor – there is an absentee owner of the soil, and no one with *locus standi* to ensure compliance at common law with the land use restrictions inherent in common rights.

The practical impact in the case study of the service of the list of OLDSIs under the 1981 Act is limited. The majority of graziers believed the principal restriction imposed by the SSSI notification was a restriction against supplementary feeding and had no knowledge of the other OLDSIs. And some confused the notified OLDSIs with the 'closed' grazing period (see above). Clearly, the graziers' perception of the OLDSIs is limited to what tends to affect their daily farming practice, and does not extend to all 28 OLDSIs in the SSSI notification. It should be added that the list of OLDSIs served by Natural England is standardized and of general application, as in the other case studies, and does not capture the distinctive habitat management needs of specific sites. As in the other case studies, the list of OLDSIs prohibits the removal of peat in the SSSI, thereby negating the registered rights to turbary in all three CL units in the case study. Given the graziers' ignorance of the nature and implications of the OLDSIs served with the SSSI notification, it is not surprising that none have used the statutory consultation mechanism in the 1981 Act to seek operational consent for OLDSIs, or sought a management agreement on refusal of permission to carry them out (1981 Act, section 28; Defra, 2001).This reflects the position in the other case studies.

Sheep and Wildlife Enhancement Scheme (SWES)

There have been eight Sheep and Wildlife Enhancement Scheme (SWES) agreements on Ingleborough Common covering approximately 880 grazing rights, but none on Scales Moor. The SWES agreements in this case study were individual five-year 'positive' agreements running from 1 November 2003 to 31 May 2009, and required a capitalized five-year stock reduction for a specific number of sheep gaits.

Each SWES agreement included a management plan describing the nature conservation importance of the land, Natural England's objectives and the positive management measures to be undertaken by the grazier to achieve the return to favourable conservation condition of the habitat. The requirements of the three principal habitat types (limestone pavement, limestone grassland and blanket bog) dictated the positive management objectives in each agreement. The focus was on the preservation of limestone pavement, the limestone grass that occurs among the fragmented limestone pavements to the west of the common and the mosaic of acid grassland and mire habitats that extend to the remaining parts of the common. The agreements gave scientifically defined guidance on what will be considered as 'favourable condition' for the habitat in each case – for example, by reference to the approximate percentages in which specified types of plant species should be present. In relation to the blanket bog habitats, for instance, the agreements indicated that favourable conservation condition requires that bog mosses should be abundant and prohibit the extraction of peat. This replicates the prohibition in the list of OLDSIs and reiterates the prohibition on the exercise of turbary rights. Finally, each agreement had a series of clauses headed 'positive management', the most important of which prohibited the exercise of grazing rights 'bought out' by the agreement, prohibited the transfer or leasing of rights, and insisted upon the observance of the closed period during which no grazing was to take place (i.e. from 5 November to 5 December each year). The agreements also prohibited foddering on the moor (other than in severe weather), and prohibited the application of fertilizers, pesticides, drainage works and burning. It will be apparent from the above that the terms of the SWES agreements further demonstrate the poor integration of environmental governance mechanisms with common property rights, in that many of the activities regulated (and paid for) under the SWES are matters which commoners have no legal competence to carry out by virtue of the nature of their rights as *profits à prendre*.

Alternative strategies: The purchase of rights in gross

The use of SWES agreements to target sustainable grazing management has been complemented by the strategic purchase by Natural England (and its predecessors, the Nature Conservancy Council and English Nature) of grazing rights on both Ingleborough Common and Scales Moor. Following purchase, the rights remain unused and are effectively 'sterilized'. This is viewed by Natural England as a cost-effective mechanism to reduce grazing pressures on the common. Ingleborough graziers have divergent views as to the ecological impacts of this strategy. Some thought that the resultant reduction in grazing pressures had encouraged heather regeneration, while others pointed out that many of the rights now held by Natural England had been bought from inactive graziers, and their neutralization had therefore had a minimal impact upon the common. On Scales Moor, Natural England holds rights purchased from a grazier who previously grazed his stock in the centre of the moor, with the consequence that (according to other graziers) a grazing vacuum has been created that has interfered with the pattern of heafs (settlement of flocks) on the common. It is perhaps noteworthy that this phenomenon was also a feature of the impact of the use of SWES agreements to manage grazing levels in the Eskdale case study (see Chapter 6, pp105–106).

Impact of the Single Payment Scheme

All of the active graziers in the Ingleborough case study receive the single farm payment, but its impact upon sustainable management has been much more limited than in the Elan Valley case study (see Chapter 8, p156). In Ingleborough, its influence has been felt more at a cultural level than at a practical agricultural one. The cross-compliance requirement for claimants to keep the land in good agricultural and environmental condition (GAEC) was closely identified with the farmers' own perception of, and attachment to, the common's environment. The GAEC condition was, in other words, seen more as a set of values reflecting and governing their existing practices than as a set of legally prescriptive conditions.

The rules used to calculate single payment entitlements were not regarded as unfair simply because they include the rights of inactive graziers and thereby 'dilute' the entitlements of active common graziers. Most of the Ingleborough graziers believed that every person holding rights of common should be entitled to the single farm payment. This was justified on two grounds: on the one hand, it was argued that retired graziers fall within the category of 'inactive' graziers and should not be excluded; on the other, it was claimed that ownership of a common right should in itself guarantee payments. The commoners' perceptions in this regard are closely linked to the cultural history of stinting in this case study. The numerical expression of common rights as sheep gaits has generated a perception of property rights as commodified personal entitlements, and this perception extends to subsidy payments within the common agricultural policy that are linked to rights in the manner of the single farm payment.

Environmental governance: The future

The SWES agreements on Ingleborough Common came to an end in 2009. Ingleborough is in the Yorkshire Dales Target Area of the Higher Level Stewardship (HLS) scheme.[58] Land management agreements under HLS are for ten years, with a break clause in the fifth year. In the case of common land, the agreement must normally be negotiated between Natural England and a body representing all farmers with common rights. This is a problematic requirement in relation to Ingleborough given the difficulty of achieving unanimity and securing compliance by all commoners with the terms of the agreement.

Unsurprisingly, Natural England is primarily focused on the ecological restoration of the common, whereas the graziers view the sustainability of the common primarily in financial terms. Nevertheless, their views sometime converge – for example, both recognized the difficulty of achieving unanimity to secure and then enforce the terms of an agreement. This reflects the lack of a cohesive cultural identity for the commons within the case study. This problem is hidden behind the discourse in Natural England's HLS handbook itself, where centrality is assigned to the potential economic gains for participants, although express mention is made of the potential for disputes between farmers in relation to common land.

A problem, from the perspective of Natural England, is the lack of a cohesive representative body for the graziers on CL 208 (the Clapham portion of Ingleborough Common). Since there is no physical boundary between the two blocks of common land that comprise Ingleborough Common, and both present the same ecological problems, an ideal solution would be a single and comprehensive HLS agreement for the whole common encompassing both CL 134 and CL 208. The management of CL 134 is viewed as unproblematic, as it has a representative association that is (as a limited company) legally capable of binding its members. But the management structure on CL 208 does not permit the same level of legal certainty guaranteeing performance of a prospective HLS agreement.

The pressing need for a resolution to these problems was highlighted by the adverse SSSI condition assessment undertaken by Natural England in 2010, which recorded portions of the common as continuing in unfavourable conservation condition (Natural England, 2010b). As a result of this, Natural England has indicated its intention to offer two separate HLS agreements to commoners managing CL 208 and CL 134. In the case of CL 134, the agreement will be offered to the limited company formed by the commoners in 1990 to manage the common. The membership of the company does not currently encompass all those with registered common rights over CL 134, however, and a separate partnership agreement between the latter and the company will be required. On CL 208, the HLS agreement will be offered to the Ingleborough Fell Commoners' Association; but (as with CL 134) the latter does not currently represent all commoners, and a separate partnership agreement will be required guaranteeing the compliance of non-members with the terms of the HLS agreement. The agreements sought by Natural England will include management option HL10 (restoration of moorland) with a supplement in the first year for preparation of legal agreements. It is also proposed to fence off up to 10ha of limestone pavement (management option HK16).[59]

The management structures on Scales Moor are less complex, and an HLS agreement was concluded with the Scales Moor stintholders early in 2010 on similar terms as those proposed for Ingleborough (see above) – including a partnership agreement with registered commoners who are not active graziers or members of the association. The HLS management option here is moorland restoration (HL10 with supplements in year one for legal and other costs). Scales Moor has an absentee landowner, and the stintholders' association has carried out extensive searches to identify ownership without success. An option in these circumstances would have been for the Yorkshire Dales National Park Authority to countersign the agreement on behalf of the owner of the soil (see Commons Act 1899; Open Spaces Act 1906, section 9). In the event, this was not insisted upon by Natural England and the agreement was concluded without the landowner's participation.[60] The position of Natural England as a 'grazier' holding sheep gaits on both Ingleborough and Scales Moor has required special accommodation within the terms of both the Scales Moor HLS agreement and the prospective HLS agreements for Ingleborough Common. Natural England will, under the terms of the agreements, undertake not to utilize the common grazing rights that they themselves own.

This complex legal resolution to the ecological management regime for Ingleborough Common and Scales Moor has been necessitated by the unique property rights to which they are subject, and (in the case of Ingleborough) the organization of the common into separate blocks of registered common land reflecting the former manorial boundaries. A statutory commons council established under Part 2 of the Commons Act 2006 would provide a neat solution to most of these problems; but as noted in Chapter 5, this is not regarded as an attractive option by stakeholders in the context of Scales Moor or Ingleborough Common.

Both groups of stakeholders shared a similar understanding of the environmental management issues. Natural England's prime objective through HLS is to achieve localized and flexible grazing control at different times of the year, as some areas of the common are overgrazed while others are under-grazed. The majority of the farmers recognized that if the HLS required them to reduce general grazing pressures, the commons might be at risk of under-grazing. This worry is informed by the experience of overall sheep reductions under the SWES agreements. Some of the farmers stressed that the common had in the past suffered intense grazing in localized areas, and almost no grazing elsewhere – the challenge of a livestock grazing regime that allowed for movement of stock from one area of the common to another at specific times of the year is recognized as the primary issue by both the graziers and Natural England, and not overgrazing *per se*. These problems are also reflected in the 2010 condition assessment by Natural England, which recorded under-grazing as a problem on some parts of the common, and overgrazing on others (Natural England 2010b: see, for example, unit numbers 39 and 42).

Conclusions

In conclusion, what can the history of commons governance and its contemporary challenges in this case study tell us about changing perceptions of 'sustainable' commons management? This case study exhibits a number of unique features in sharp contrast to the other upland case studies in this work. Its dominant features lie in the development of stinting as a management tool for organizing access to the principal common resource (grazing), and a history of weak manorial governance, with absentee landowners on large parts of the commons – and a local resident landlord solely on the Clapham side of Ingleborough Common. Informal enclosure by appropriators was a historical feature of land management in the early modern period. There are also few farm tenants, and the pattern of contemporary land tenure is mostly of owner occupancy (with the exception of the Clapham Estate on CL 208). Ingleborough Common is itself subject to heavy recreational use (principally caving and walking), and caving, in particular, sometimes conflicts with farming in a manner not seen in the other case studies.

The historical development, and contemporary organization, of property rights has had a fundamental impact upon perceptions of 'sustainable' governance and the manner in which it should be pursued. The legacy of stinting has influenced the legal categorization of property rights and the form in which they are expressed in the modern commons registers. But, as pointed out above, local custom and practice have not been uniformly reflected in the contemporary property rights captured in the commons registers established under the 1965 Act. Stinting has unquestionably contributed to a strong sense of property rights as personal assets, detached from land and freely transferable, but in a context where the maintenance of firm links between notions of 'locality' and property rights is nevertheless seen as fundamentally important for the 'sustainable' management of the common resource.

The Ingleton case study also manifests environmental governance issues quite different from those in the other case studies. Many of these are specific to the particular problems presented by the conservation of limestone pavement habitats. This requires the adoption of a flexible regime for managing livestock grazing, rather than the approach seen in Eskdale and Cwmdeuddwr where off-wintering of stock to promote heather regeneration is a key issue. In Ingleton the timing of grazing and movement of stock to different parts of the common at different times of the year are key objectives, and not just the prevention of over-wintering on the common. Grouse shooting has also been an important consideration shaping land management in the past, whereas it has had less of an impact in the other case studies.

The environmental management challenges presented by the case study have led the conservation bodies to adopt an innovative and targeted approach to governance. The use by Natural England of its powers to purchase common grazing rights is a feature of environmental governance in this case study that is absent elsewhere. Their ability to acquire rights and then hold them as rights in gross (unattached to land) is recognized in the Commons Act 2006 (2006 Act, section 9(2) and schedule 1, para 1 (1)(b)). But the 2006 Act will put an end to the transfer of rights without land within the local farming community, other than by the temporary leasing of rights permitted by the legislation (2006 Act, section 9(1); see also Chapter 4, p60). It will not, in future, be possible to transfer rights independently of land and convert them into rights in gross in the manner formerly practised by stakeholders in this case study, and reflected in entries on the Ingleton registers between 1982 and 2000. The 2006 Act will therefore impose a quite different perception of 'locality' and community – one that relies upon fixing rights to the land they are intended to benefit – than that currently evidenced among local stakeholders.

Notes

1 WYRO, WYL 524/142, 19 July 1568; 31 August 1570.
2 PRO, E134/17 Eliz/East 7.
3 WYRO, WYL 524/143; PRO, E134/17 Eliz/East 7.
4 WYRO, WYL 524/209: 'First Draft Explanation of the Plan of the Higher Division', undated (early 19th century).
5 PRO, MPC 235.
6 WYRO, WYL 524/142, 13 April 1543; 31 August 1570; '33/34 Eliz'.
7 WYRO, WYL 524/143.
8 WYRO WYL 524/209: 'First Draft Explanation of the Plan of the Higher Division', undated (early 19th century).
9 Gayle Moor was said (early 19th century) to have been shared by High Gale, Low Gale, Raise Gale and Gate Cote: WYRO, WYL 524/209.
10 We should like to thank Alan King for drawing this source to our attention.
11 Ingleborough Estate Office, Clapham: Ingleborough Fell Commoners' Minute Book, *1927–2007*.
12 WYRO, WYL 524/209, agreement to stint Scales Moor, 16 January 1810.
13 Scales Moor papers (penes Mr J. Metcalfe): typescript of the 1842 stinting agreement, pp2–4.
14 Scales Moor papers (penes Mr J. Metcalfe): typescript of the 1842 stinting agreement, pp2–4.

15 WYRO, WYL 524/142, 33/34 Eliz; 10 July 1609.

16 WYRO, WYL 524/142, 10 July 1609; WYL 524/145.

17 WYRO, WYL 524/209, copy of opinion related to rights, in Newby, 1812.

18 Information from Messrs H. C. Bargh, Chapel-le-Dale, and J. S. Metcalfe, Ingleton, 2009.

19 *Ingleton*: court roll, 1505-6 (PRO, SC 2/211/68); presentment, undated, 18th century (NYCRO, ZXF/3/3/4); presentment, 1718 (NYCRO ZXF/3/3/2); court rolls, 1749–1835 (Yorkshire Archaeological Society (Leeds) [hereafter YAS], MD335, box 12); court book, 1771 (YAS, MD335, box 27); verdict, 1795 (NYCRO, ZXF/3/3/3); court books, 1820–1934 (NYCRO, ZUC/1/3/2-5). *Twisleton & Ellerbeck*: court books, 1772–1928 (CRO, Acc 18 WD/PP, box 3). *Newby*: court rolls, 1543–1620 (WYRO, WYL 524/142); verdicts, 1771–1896 (WYRO, WYL 524/177, 524/237, 524/239, 524/249; 524/253); court books, 1801–1934 (NYCRO, ZUC/1/4/1–4). *Clapham*: court rolls, 1699–1710 (WYRO, WYL/179, 181); verdicts, 1699–1709 (WYL/184); court book, circa 1700–1750 (WYL/178); verdicts, 1725–1730 (WYL/187); court roll, 1722 (WYL/180); court roll, 1727–1757 (WYL/192); verdicts, 1758–1901 (WYL/174, 236); court book, 1758–1925 (YAS, MD335, box 19); court roll extracts, 1783–1833 (NYCRO, ZTW/11/2/3); court book, 1833–1925 (NYCRO, ZUC/1/2/1).

20 WYRO, WYL 524/209, 'First Draft Explanation of the Plan of the Higher Division', undated (early 19th century).

21 WYRO, WYL 524/236, Clapham verdicts 1872–1901.

22 Scales Moor papers: minute books, 1884–1898, 1901–1991, on which the following paragraph is based.

23 Information from Messrs Andrew Humphries (2008) and J. S. Metcalfe (2009). The washfold was at SD 732 782.

24 Ingleborough Estate Office, Clapham: Littledale Stinted Pasture Minute Book, 1930–1939, 6 April 1933. The rules for Blea Moor and Cam End have not, however, been traced.

25 Ingleborough Estate Office, Clapham: Littledale Stinted Pasture Minute Book, 1930–1939, 25 January 1932.

26 Ingleborough Estate Office: Ingleborough Fell Commoners' Minute Book, 1927–2007, on which the following paragraph is based.

27 WYRO, WYL 524/179, Clapham court roll 1699–1710, m. 6v.

28 NYCRO, ZUC 1/3/2-3: Ingleton court books 1820–1854, 1831–1895; ZUC 1/4/1: Newby court book, 1801–1925, 31 March 1826.

29 Scales Moor rules, 1865 (copy in Scales Moor Minute Book, 1901–1991).

30 Ingleborough Fell Commoners' Minute Book, 1927–2007, 6 March 1931.

31 Scales Moor Minute Book, 1884–1898, statement dated 1889.

32 Littledale Stinted Pasture Minute Book, 1 March 1934.

33 Ingleborough Fell Commoners' Minute Book, 1927–2007, 27 April 1927, 2 February 1934.

34 WYRO, WYL 524/179, Clapham court roll 1699–1710, m. 6v.; NYCRO, Ingleborough Estate provisional list: Box 16/6, Newby court roll, 1739–1810, 21 April 1741.

35 WYRO, WYL 524/249: Newby verdicts, 1771–1810, 7 April 1774.

36 NYCRO, Ingleborough Estate provisional list: Box 16/6, Newby court roll, 1739–1810 and WYRO, WYL 524/249: Newby verdicts, 1771–1810; NYCRO, ZUC 1/4/1: Newby court book, 1801–1925, 4 April 1823.

37 Ingleborough Fell Commoners' Minute Book, 1927–2007, 21 February 1967.

38 Ingleborough Fell Commoners' Minute Book, 1927–2007, 12 August 1994, 16 February 1995.

39 Natural England, *Condition of SSSI Units: Ingleborough*, tabular data from Natural England staff member Philip Eckersley (accessible via Natural England SSSI, www.english-nature.org.uk/Special/sssi, compiled 1 August 2007).

40 And recorded in Ingleborough Fell Commoners' Minute Book, 1927–2007.
41 Scales Moor Minute Book, 1901–1991.
42 North Yorkshire County Council, Register of Common Land [hereafter NYRCL], CL 134, rights section, entries 16, 18, 31, 32, 33 and 52.
43 NYRCL, CL 208, rights section, entry 86.
44 NYRCL, CL 272, rights section, entry 5 (presumably because black-faced Scottish sheep are generally smaller than English breeds).
45 NYRCL, CL 208, rights section, entry 87.
46 NYRCL, CL 272, rights section, entries 11 and 15.
47 NYRCL, CL 134, rights section, entry 47.
48 NYRCL: entry 93 was the last application (made on May 4 2000) to register former appurtenant rights as severed and held as rights in gross.
49 NYRCL, entry 65 (13 sheep gaits).
50 NYRCL, CL 208, rights section, starting with entry 74.
51 NYRCL, entry 84 (7 sheep gaits).
52 NYRCL, CL 272, rights section, entry 10, replaced by entry 14 (16 May 1985).
53 NYRCL, entries 21 and 23.
54 For example, NYRCL, CL 134, rights section, entry 6, records a right 'to graze 62 sheep with followers throughout the year over the whole of the land comprised in this register unit'.
55 NYRCL, CL 272, rights section, entries 6 and 7.
56 For example, NYRCL, CL 272, rights section, entry 8.
57 In 1995, the Ingleborough Fell Commoners noted that 'the Ingleton area has only had meetings for a few years': Ingleborough Fell Commoners' Minute Book, 1927–2007, 16 February 1995.
58 For the specific objective of this target area, see http://www.naturalengland.org.uk/planning/grants-funding/es/hls/targeting/docs/Yorkshire_Dales.pdf.
59 Natural England, pers comm, 2010.
60 Natural England, pers comm, 2010.

8

Elan Valley, Powys

The third upland case study is in the heart of mid-Wales, in the Radnorshire Hills to the west of the Wye Valley. It lies in the parish of Llansantffraed Cwmdeuddwr, a territory of considerable antiquity, taking its name from Cwmdeuddwr, 'the commote between the two waters' (the Rivers Elan and Wye). The bulk of the parish consists of unenclosed hills, which, being contiguous to other hill commons, form part of the 'green desert' of the heart of Wales, or, in the more prosaic language of local shepherds, 'miles and miles of bugger all' (Howells, 2005, p6). The land forms a rolling plateau at circa 500m above sea level, cut by the narrow, steep-sided valleys of the Rivers Elan, Claerwen and Wye, in which almost all the farmsteads and inbye land are found. Since at least the 18th century it has been sheep country. The common land within the bounds of the parish comprises two contiguous blocks, the registered common land of Cwmdeuddwr Common (RCL 36) and a larger area of deregistered hill grazing (RCL 66), within the catchment of the Claerwen and Elan rivers, which forms part of Welsh Water's Elan Valley Estate. It is an area of particular environmental value, containing a number of important environmental designations, including three Sites of Special Scientific Interest (SSSIs), a Special Protection Area (SPA) and two Special Areas of Conservation (SACs) (see Figure 8.1). It lies in the Cambrian Mountains Environmentally Sensitive Area (ESA), and a central focus for modern land management is an ESA management agreement for Cwmdeuddwr Common concluded in 2001.

The central themes in common land management illustrated by this case study centre on the deep-seated patterns of customary use that give the upland commons of Wales a distinctive history through the longstanding division of the open hill grazings into sheepwalks over which individual farms had exclusive grazing rights. Paradoxically, this continuity in patterns of use is set against a backdrop of the wholesale reworking of property rights in the area as a result of the compulsory purchase of the Elan Valley watershed by Birmingham Corporation in the 1890s to supply water to the conurbation. The construction of the Caban-coch, Garreg-ddu, Penygarreg and Craig Goch reservoirs between 1893 and 1906 (and, later, the Claerwen Reservoir, opened in 1952) led to the flooding of inbye land and the extinguishing of common rights over much – but not all – of the surrounding area, transforming both the landscape and the property rights regime. Studying the contrasting histories of the two contiguous areas of Cwmdeuddwr Common and the Elan Valley Estate thus allows us to explore issues of property rights,

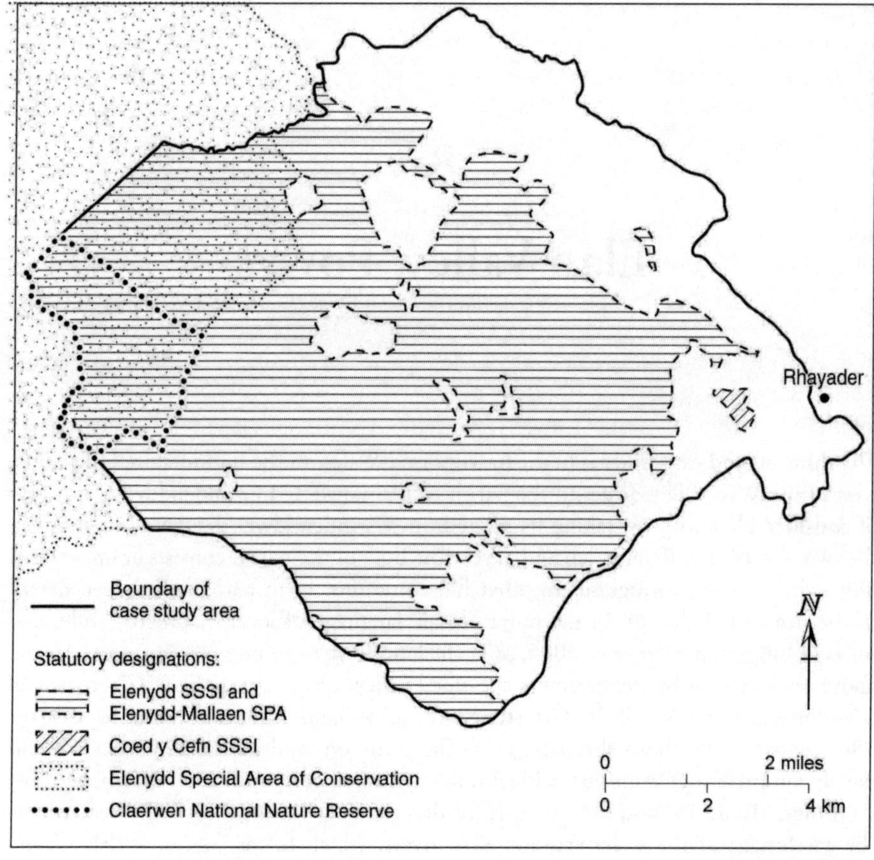

Figure 8.1 *Elan Valley: Boundary of case study area and environmental designations*

Source: www.ccw.gov.uk/landscape--wildlife/protecting-our-landscape/protected-sites-map.aspx

boundaries, use and management across two different areas of hill grazing, one of which is no longer legally defined as 'common land'.

Common rights and governance to 1965

Property rights

The history of landownership which lay behind the registration of commons was complex, the boundaries of the Elan Valley Estate, created as a result of Birmingham Corporation's purchases in the 1890s, cutting across older patterns of lordship. The parish of Llansantffraed Cwmdeuddwr comprised the two manors or lordships of Grange of Cwmdeuddwr and Cwmdeuddwr, which came into single ownership in 1825 but retained distinct identities thereafter. The manor of Grange of Cwmdeuddwr originated in a grant of the 'pasture' of Cwmdeuddwr to Strata Florida Abbey in 1184 by Rhys ap Gruffudd. Exactly what the monastic grange constituted is unclear. By the time of the Dissolution, it contained several distinct holdings (nine were listed in 1539); but whether any of these had previously been demesne stock farms (the implication of 'grange' in an upland context) is not known. After the Dissolution, the former monastic lands came to be known as the manor of Grange, though there is no evidence that it had the status of a manor during monastic times – indeed, as late as 1892 at the time of Birmingham Corporation's purchases, doubt was expressed as to whether Cwmdeuddwr Grange could be considered a true manor.[1] Between 1578 and 1585 the new owners, Sir James Croft of Croft Castle and his step-son Thomas Wigmore of Shobdon, Herefordshire, sold a number of the farms, reserving an annual rent, and establishing rights, dues and services (including suit of court) tantamount to manorial lordship (Banks, 1880, pp35–39). The second manor, known simply as Cwmdeuddwr, was a smaller estate, focused on the castle of Rhayader, and consisting of the eastern corner of the case study area. Its boundary with the manor of Grange ran across the open hill wastes, using the cairn of Crugyn y Gwyddel and a striking white quartzite boulder, Maengwyngweddw ('the widow's white stone'), as boundary markers.[2] Both manors came into the same hands in 1825 and subsequently descended together.[3]

The Elan Valley Estate, created under the Birmingham Corporation Water Act of 1892 (55 and 56 Vict, c. clxxiii), embraced not only the bulk of the manor of Grange but also portions of the manor of Builth (on the Brecknockshire side of the Rivers Claerwen and Elan) and parts of several manors in Ceredigion.[4] The boundaries of the land purchased by Birmingham Corporation were determined by considerations of water abstraction and ignored the manorial boundaries, creating a new ownership unit and adding a layer of complexity to the pattern of property boundaries across the common land. As a result, the eastern perimeter of the estate ignored the manorial boundary between the manors of Cwmdeuddwr and Cwmdeuddwr Grange, cutting through a series of sheepwalks which straddled the watershed. Across the open, unfenced hill grazings, the outer limit of the Elan Estate was marked by a series of concrete marker posts, apparently erected in 1913.[5]

The legacy of this complex history is visible in the registrations made under the Commons Registration Act 1965 (see Figure 8.2). In 1969 Llansantffraed Cwmdeuddwr parish council attempted to register 16,478 acres (6668ha) of unenclosed hill within the Elan watershed as 'manorial waste of the ancient manor of Grange of Cwmteuddwr, no longer subject to rights of common'. The area was assigned the common land unit number RCL 66. Objections were registered in 1972 by Birmingham Corporation (on the grounds that the land was not common land) and by the owners of a property in Cwmystwyth (on the grounds that part of it was 'private agricultural mountain land' belonging to them). RCL 66 was deregistered in 1981, the clinching argument being that Birmingham Corporation had purchased all rights of common in order to control the numbers and types of livestock grazing within the water catchment area.[6]

The residual area of unenclosed hill grazing east of the Birmingham Corporation boundary was treated as a single common land unit at registration – RCL 36 Cwmdeuddwr Common – though in reality it comprised remnants of the wastes of both the historic manors of Cwmdeuddwr and Cwmdeuddwr Grange. The distinction between the two manors was acknowledged in the land section of the register and on the registration maps, which distinguished between the wastes of each.[7] Ownership of the common is complicated by two small tracts of land lying close to the watershed boundary, deemed to belong to the Elan Estate, and by several other pockets of land

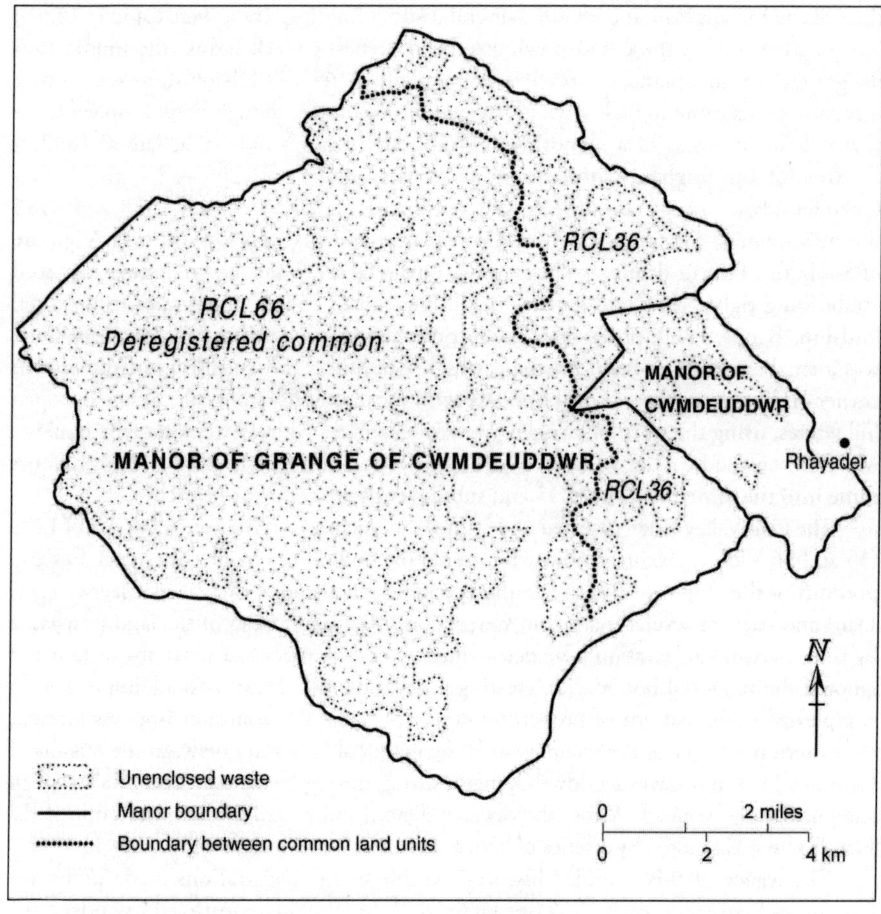

Figure 8.2 *Elan Valley Commons: Relationship between common land (CL) units and manorial boundaries*

Source: Powys County Council, Common Land Register

identified as being areas where Birmingham Corporation had purchased rights 'to the exclusion of all others'.[8] Thus the boundary of Cwmdeuddwr Common today is in some respects a modern creation, the result of the union of the two Cwmdeuddwr manors in 1825, the severances and reorganization caused by Birmingham Corporation Act 1892, and the effects of registration under the 1965 Act.

Evidence for the nature of common rights and grazing regimes before the 18th century is sparse and fragmentary. When John Leland toured the Cwmdeuddwr district between 1536 and 1539, the exercise of grazing appeared to him unlimited. He described the mountain land between the Elan Valley and Strata Florida as being 'almoste for wilde pastures and breding grounde, in so much that everi man there about puttith on bestes as many as they wylle without paiyng of mony' (Leland, 1964, pp122–123). The only explicit statement of the nature of grazing rights in the early-modern period is in a brief survey of property in Cwmdeuddwr circa 1725, which describes a holding as 'a Dayrie house & Common of pasture for Cattle & Sheep without number', implying that they were limited by the rule of levancy and couchancy.[9]

Cwmdeuddwr shared with other parts of the heart of mid-Wales a role as a reserve of upland pasture for communities in the neighbouring lowlands. As late as the end of the 18th century, there are hints that the upland pastures were under-stocked: in 1794 one commentator stated that many of the commons in Brecknockshire were 'sufficient to keep in summer three times more stock than the parishioners can send there' (Clark, 1794, p39). Agistment ('tack') allowed graziers to maximize use of lands which were poor in winter and rich in summer and, from the 16th century, there is substantial evidence for a system of 'share cropping', whereby hill farmers hired livestock from lowland farmers, taking a share in the offspring. Surviving agreements, which include some from Cwmdeuddwr, show that both cattle and sheep were involved, confirming that the early-modern hill-farming economy was based less exclusively on sheep than was the case by the 19th century (Suggett, 2005, pp182–183). Agistment remained a feature of the area into the modern period, as did the wintering-away of upland stock in the lowlands (Howells, 2005, pp116–167). In strict terms such exchanges broke the rule of levancy and couchancy; yet seasonal movement of stock was a reality, echoing older systems of transhumance, whereby a seasonal dwelling (*hafod*) on the summer pastures was linked to a permanent settlement (*hendre*) in the lowlands (Davies, 1980; Ward, 1997).

Another distinctive feature of the Welsh uplands was the division of common land into sheepwalks, restricting the pasture rights of an individual holding to a defined section of the common. It was said in 1744 that in the Cardiganshire manor of Perfedd the common had been divided 'time out of mind' into 'particular districts or liberties next adjoining to the freeholds and cottages which all the shepherds through boldness or ignorance claime as their own right and sometimes chase other people's cattle away' (Davies, 1980, p11). A distinction needs to be drawn between the area over which a holding claimed exclusive rights and the patterns of use within a sheepwalk. Many sheepwalks embraced the grazing grounds of more than one flock, each of which was a recognized functional unit, akin to the heafs of northern England. The Welsh term for the grazing ground of a particular flock was *arhosfa* (literally, 'staying place'), whereas the wider sheepwalk belonging to a holding was termed a *libert* (a term borrowed from the English 'liberty') (Wmffre, 2009, pp278–279).

A pattern of use-rights akin to those elsewhere in mid-Wales had developed in Cwmdeuddwr by the 19th century, a farm's sheepwalk usually taking the form of an area of rough grazing with clearly recognized, yet unfenced, boundaries on the common immediately above the holding and its inbye land (see Figure 8.3). As one commentator put it in 1880: 'the practice has been for each tenant to secure a distinct sheep walk, and maintain his rights on it by keeping a strong flock' (Banks, 1880, p38). Individual sheepwalks can be traced back to the latter 18th century: that belonging to Treheslog Farm is shown on estate plans of circa 1800, its extent coinciding almost exactly with that of the modern sheepwalk (Suggett, 2005, p255); that belonging to Llanerchy is mentioned in a tenancy agreement of 1796.[10] A similar antiquity is suggested for other sheepwalks, which were described as longstanding arrangements in witness statements

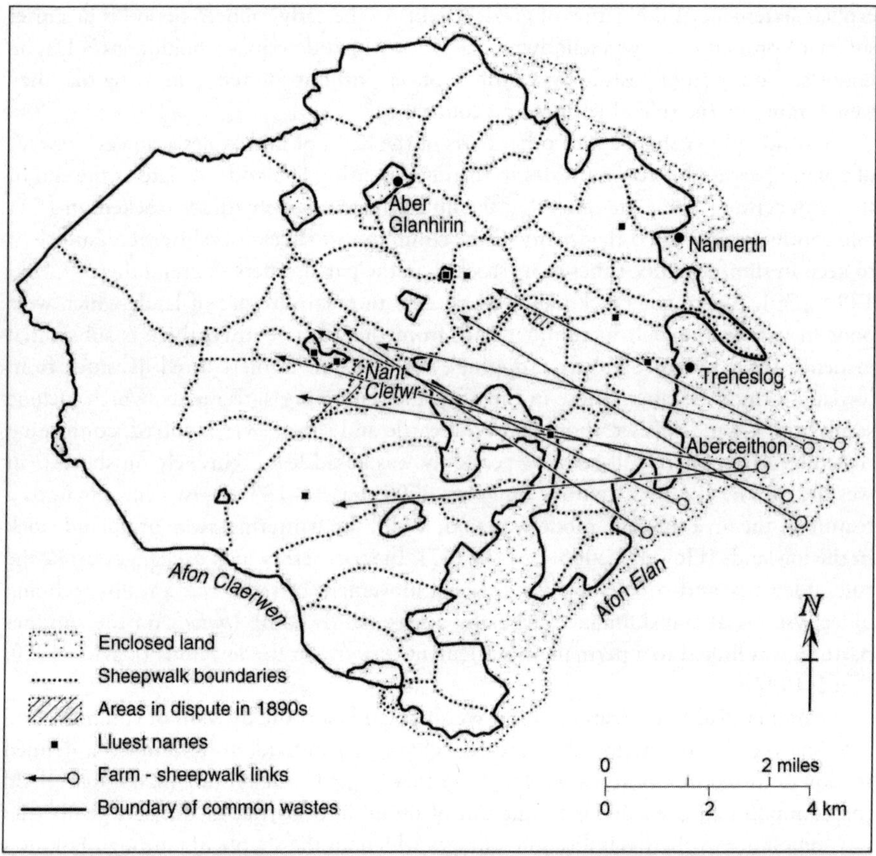

Figure 8.3 *Elan Valley: Sheepwalks circa 1900, as recorded on the Elan Estate plans*

Note: Only linkages between sheepwalks and farms in the lower Elan Valley are shown. Places named are referred to in the text.

of the early 19th century.[11] As in neighbouring areas, many sheepwalks contained two or more distinct flocks, a pattern of use which survived well into the 20th century.[12]

The link between particular sections of the wastes and individual holdings was reinforced by the practice of building seasonal dwellings known as *lluestau* (shepherds' huts) on the summer pastures (see Figure 8.4). The use of such huts as upland stations of parent farms in a neighbouring valley is widely attested throughout Wales, paralleling the summer shielings of northern England and Scotland (Davies, 1980; Ward, 1997). In Cwmdeuddwr, *lluestau* are recorded by the later 16th century, suggesting that the appropriation of sections of the common to particular holdings had begun by then. The earliest references are in two deeds of 1585, each granting a holding and its associated 'summer house'. One at Brithgwm in the upper Elan Valley was sold with its summer house called '*y Cletture mawre*' in the neighbouring valley of Nant Cletwr, 3km to the north-west.[13] During the same year, one of the holdings at Nannerth in the Wye Valley

Figure 8.4 *Cwmdeuddwr Common: The remains of Lluest Treheslog, a shepherd's cottage on Treheslog sheepwalk*

Source: Angus Winchester

was sold with the cottage or summer house called '*Llyest Pen y Rhiw*', the remains of which survive on the hill grazings above the precipitous valley side behind the farm (Davies, 1980, p9; Suggett, 2005, pp249–251). One of the deeds from 1585 also appears to chart the transition from a seasonal hut to a permanent farm surrounded by its own enclosed inbye land. The grant to Nannerth included Aber Glanhirin, described as a 'messuage or summer house', along with a bounded block of 80 acres of the common waste with licence to enclose it and annex it to the summer house: the island of enclosure at Aber Glanhirin is probably the result of that grant in 1585 (Suggett, 2005, p185, citing Banks, 1884, pp38, 40).

Although most sheepwalks and their associated *lluestau* were on the common comparatively close to the farm, the sheepwalks belonging to farms in the lower Elan Valley immediately west of Rhayader lay on distant pastures around the Nant Cletwr in the remote western side of the study area. The pattern of use seems to have been established by the 1820s; but there are hints that it represented a radical reorganization of rights in the area. The case of Lluest Abercaethon is particularly suggestive. The name, linking the *lluest* to the farm of Aberceithon more than 8km away in the lower Elan Valley, is recorded by 1886; but it replaced an earlier name, Clettwr Mawr, identifying the place as the summer house belonging to the nearby holding of Brithgwm, recorded in 1585.[14] When exactly Aberceithon and neighbouring farms acquired sheepwalks in this area has not been established.

By the late 19th century, the division of the hill grazings into unfenced but clearly recognized sheep walks can be reconstructed in detail. Birmingham Corporation's purchases involved a complex process of purchasing holdings, manorial rights to the soil, common rights to sheepwalks, and the 'settled' flocks which grazed them. As a result, every sheepwalk was mapped and measured. Despite the absence of physical enclosures, the acreages and boundaries of sheepwalks could be accurately plotted, although some small strips of land were recorded as being in dispute, or as being shared between holdings (see Figure 8.3).[15]

The legal status of Welsh sheepwalks was tested in 1875, in a case in which it was argued that certain sheepwalks in the manor of Llandewi brefi (Cardiganshire) were the graziers' own freehold mountain land. After hearing evidence of manor court presentments regulating common grazing, the jury found in favour of the lords of the manor and decided that the sheepwalks in question were manorial waste.[16] Nevertheless, the sense that sheepwalks were tantamount to private or exclusive property was evidently deep rooted within hill-farming communities. There is evidence from Cardiganshire of sheepwalks being sold or let separately in the 19th century, a practice which could result in the transfer of sheepwalks from one holding to another (Wmffre, 2009, p278); this may explain the apparent transfer of rights in the Nant Cletwr area, discussed above. In their petition against the Birmingham conveyances in the Elan and Claerwen valleys, the counsel for Edward Thomas (Llanfadog-issa Farm) and his brother, David Thomas (Treheslog Farm), argued: 'These sheepwalks are for all practical purposes treated as the private property of the Petitioners no one else exercising any right over the land and this has been the custom from time immemorial.'[17]

The status of the sheepwalks is of some importance, as the transfers between Elan landowners and Birmingham Corporation rested on the assumption that common rights could be limited to discrete areas (negating the commoners' rights over the rest of the common), and that rights to sheepwalks could be sold independently of the holding to which they were attached. In strict modern law, common rights are presumed to pertain to the whole common and not merely a designated heaf or sheepwalk (which is considered a practical means of managing pasture rights rather than a legal fixture in the landscape) (Gadsden, 1988, §3.105–3.112). The severance of sheepwalks from the holdings to which they were attached also sat uneasily with legal principles. Only ' rights in gross' or stints could be severed from a dominant tenement in this manner and it is far from clear that rights to sheepwalks would be defined in law as 'rights in gross', even if to all intents and purposes they were treated as such by graziers. By purchasing both the manorial rights and the grazing rights, Birmingham Corporation effectively extinguished the status of the sheepwalks as common land and the hill grazings within the corporation's boundary were henceforth treated as integral parts of tenanted farms, run under the terms of leases. It is perhaps an irony that a longstanding belief in the exclusivity of sheepwalks probably facilitated the expropriation of commoners' rights in this case. Yet it is a tradition that has allowed for continuities in land use and culture, despite dramatic changes in the property rights regime. The sheepwalk is still the key unit of land management in the area today.

As elsewhere, the common land of Cwmdeuddwr was also subject to other use-rights. Rights of turbary and estovers gave the local community access to vital resources – notably peat, which was the only fuel available for many of the more remote farms and shepherds' huts in the Elan and Claerwen valleys. In 1902, when faced with the threat of extinguishments of turbary rights, Edward Thomas of Llanfadog argued that: 'This is a valuable right to me, and my tenants at Nantmadoc and Gledryd and also the Shepherd who has a house on the Llyest, where he would be entirely dependent on turf for fuel. A considerable amount of turf is now used by myself and my tenants at the 4 Farmhouses.'[18] Turf-digging had a long history: there were 'old turf pits' near Aber Glanhirin in 1585 and at least two turbaries on the boundary between the manors of Grange and Cwmdeuddwr in 1797.[19] As in other upland areas, bracken was the principal species exploited under the right of estovers; the cutting of bracken for litter continued until well within living memory.[20] Some farmers cut molinia hay on the hills, known locally as *gwair cwta*, or 'rhos hay', as a source of fodder. This was probably not strictly a right of estovers, but simply another facet of pasture rights. Molinia hay was still being cut at Hirnant in the 1970s (Howells, 2005, pp64–65).

In addition, there is limited evidence of a common right of piscary. The Birmingham Corporation Water Act 1892 reserved for the inhabitants of Rhayader pre-existing rights of fishing in the Rivers Elan and Claerwen, above the reservoirs, as well as rights of turbary and cutting of 'fern and rushes'.[21] The status of the fishing rights had been debated during the Act's passage through parliament, speakers questioning whether it was a right, a privilege or merely 'immemorial custom'.[22] In the wake of the 1965 Act, Rhayader Parish Council attempted to register a right of piscary; but these rights must have been deemed to have been extinguished, or to not be categorized as 'common' rights, since the land units concerned were deregistered.[23]

Governance

Only limited evidence survives to reconstruct past systems for regulating common use-rights in the case study area. Manorial governance of common land in Cwmdeuddwr appears to have been weak. In part, this may reflect the longstanding recognition of sheepwalks as quasi-private property; in part, ineffectual manorial administration. A limited number of manor court records survive for Cwmdeuddwr Grange, all falling within the period of 1722 to 1879. The court sometimes met twice a year in the 18th century; but by the 19th century sittings appear to have been highly infrequent. An attempt to reassert the court's authority, perhaps at a time when pressures on the resources of the common were increasing, is suggested by the imposition of heavy penalties of 39s 11d in 1811 on outsiders found grazing livestock, cutting turf or digging soil.[24] Surviving records for the smaller manor of Cwmdeuddwr include only a small number of court rolls and presentments.[25] The union of the two manors after 1825 eventually resulted in the merging of jury and court officers, though they were still nominally held as separate courts.[26]

Manor court sittings became less frequent in the 19th century, the last surviving verdict sheet dating from 1878. A clean break in management systems occurred as a result of the major dislocation caused by the Birmingham Corporation Water Act 1892. The act made provision for management should the lands remain common, giving the corporation powers to make by-laws under the 1876 Commons Act to regulate the cutting of turf, heather, bracken and gorse; to regulate fishing and recreation; and to prevent nuisances and any act which might cause pollution to the water catchment. The relevant county councils had power to object to a scheme of by-laws and request an inquiry. However, common rights were extinguished and there is no record of any such by-laws having been introduced.[27] After compulsory purchase, there is no evidence for formal collective management institutions, other than through the central direction of the estate managers. Nor is it clear how the surviving common land outside the boundary of the Corporation's Elan Valley Estate was managed for much of the 20th century.

Some light on manorial governance of the commons is shed by a presentment book, covering the period of 1722 to 1817, and two later court rolls (from 1873 and 1878), for Cwmdeuddwr Grange.[28] The focus of the courts' attention was on the exclusion of trespassers rather than on close management of those exercising legitimate rights, the offences mentioned most frequently being trespasses by those cutting turf or grazing cattle unlawfully. Control of 'foreign' livestock was a recurring concern. Presentments of ten men in 1741 for putting 'Strange catels' on the common and seven men in 1745 for grazing 'forren Cattles' in the manor, 'having no right Title thereto', may refer to trespass by outsiders or to landholders from within the manor bringing in cattle from outside by way of agistment. The occurrence of persistent offenders perhaps suggests that the amercements were, in reality, a licensing system for livestock from outside the manor rather than attempts to enforce exclusion. Regular presentments against named individuals may well obscure a tacit acceptance of 'tack', provided that those involved paid for the privilege.

Despite their obvious importance to land use and management, sheepwalks are only rarely mentioned in orders and presentments. Occasionally there is explicit reference to trespass on a sheepwalk, as in 1807, when two men from Cardiganshire were amerced for 'turning sheep upon Glanhirin sheep walk having no right so to do'. A long section of Glanhirin's sheepwalk boundary marched with Cardiganshire and the presentment presumably reflects the difficulty of policing manorial boundaries in the remote wastes along the upland watershed. But this is an isolated case. It is possible that holdings were thought to effectively 'own' their sheepwalks on the common, and that the court had little authority over their management, except when outsiders tried to trespass on them.

Turbary rights were also closely guarded from intruders, orders against illegal turf-cutting being a regular element of the manor court's business. In 1734 some 23 people from outside the lordship were named and fined for cutting turf, and the importance of turbary is implied by the high penalty of 39s 11d imposed in 1811 on outsiders who cut turf in the manor. Despite the court's efforts to control access to turbary, the repeated references to intrusions perhaps suggest that its attempts were failing. The proximity of the town of Rhayader and its non-agricultural population with limited access to fuel rights may explain the persistence of illegal peat-cutting. A presentment against an inhabitant of Rhayader in 1745 'for drawing or pulling of Brand or the unburnt part of heath within the said Lordship having no right title thereto' not only suggests demand for fuel from the neighbouring town but also that heath-burning was being practised on the sheepwalks. Continuing problems with outsiders entering the common to gather materials are suggested by a blanket order of 1878 prohibiting 'all foreigners … from cutting Turf Fern and Rushes'.

A second theme visible in the manor court records from the 18th and, particularly, the 19th centuries is a concern to uphold the rights of the lord of the manor in the face of encroachments on the common. During the 1830s the manors of Radnorshire were said to contain 'numerous Encroachments on the Waste – some made by Owners or Occupiers of adjoining Property or farms, but most of them by poor labouring People, many of whom had erected and occupied cottages'.[29] In Cwmdeuddwr a series of presentments from the 18th century were followed by a more general order in 1804, suggesting that encroachments had been numerous. It ordered that 'all Incroachments and common nuisances and erected upon the said common and waste' were to be 'taken out and removed'.[30] Most of these encroachments were probably small 'intakes' from the common adjacent to existing holdings or *lluestau*, but cottage building on the wastes is also recorded. Some new cottages were in extremely remote locations, such as those built near Nant Garw and Nant Bryn-y-ieier, both on the extreme north-west limits of the manor, in 1797 and 1811.[31] Whether these are to be classed as *lluestau* or as squatters' cottages, hastily erected overnight in the tradition of the Welsh *ty-un-nos* ('one-night house'), is unclear (compare Silvester, 2007). The fact that some may have fallen into the latter category is hinted at by the presence of 'pillow mounds' (usually interpreted as rabbit warrens) in Cwm Nant-y-ffald (SN 89 72): elsewhere in Radnorshire, pillow mounds are associated with 'one-night houses', suggesting that cottagers attempted to scrape a living by answering the growing demand for rabbit skins and meat (Silvester, 2004, p64). The manor court's repeated orders to remove unlawful cottages and encroachments may well have proved impossible to enforce since as late as 1878, the jury recorded their decision to 'Continue the presentments made and Continued at former Courts of the Several Encroachments made from the wastes of this Manor'.[32]

If manorial regulation of the commons in Cwmdeuddwr was comparatively weak and ineffectual, a change to a much more vigorous and proactive governance regime occurred in the aftermath of the Birmingham Water Acts of 1892, 1896 and 1902. Thenceforth, the overriding goal was clean water; but graziers' legal interests were to be accommodated where possible. The Act also reserved rights of access to the public for exercise and recreation on the water gathering grounds, an acknowledgement that the landscape had a value beyond utility and agriculture.[33] Rules contained in early tenancy agreements show how the watershed was regulated and protected, upholding many of the terms and conditions contained in the Acts. Thus, for example, the early tenancy agreements of 1902 contain standard clauses designed to prevent pollution or damage to the land surface within the watershed. Tenants were also not permitted to 'pare bett or burn' any land, gorse, heather or coarse grasses, nor to cut any peat or turves, or alter the levels of land or contours of the land, without consent.[34] The 1892 Act empowered the corporation to prohibit the washing of sheep and use of watering places for sheep, cattle, and horses in any place where these activities might cause pollution.[35] Hence, the leases required tenants to wash their sheep at locations stipulated by the corporation, where new washfolds were built. The latest of these new folds, apparently built by the Elan Estate after the construction of the Claerwen dam in 1952, was a concrete structure in the Nant Gwynllyn Valley, outside the water catchment area, which remained in use until electric shearing replaced hand shearing in the 1970s.[36]

The leases also imposed regulations on the management of sheep and the sheepwalks. Each tenant was instructed to 'carefully maintain and use his best endeavours in keeping and maintaining the present boundaries of the unenclosed sheepwalks so as to prevent encroachments'. They were prohibited from taking in sheep, cattle or ponies by way of 'tack', either in summer or in winter, or subletting their own flocks or cattle. However, the leases accepted that young sheep could be sent away elsewhere for winter tack, 'as is customary in the district', returning in April. In return for maintaining the corporation's standing flock, the tenant was entitled to the produce of wool and sales of surplus animals, adhering to the 'custom of good shepherding' in the parish – namely, that no wethers under four years' old were to be sold (reflecting the role traditionally played by wether sheep in defending sheepwalk boundaries), and that ewes which were no longer fit for breeding were to be sold and removed from the sheepwalk.[37] The corporation's leases thus epitomize a central theme in the history of common land in the case study area, the combination of elements of traditional management systems on the common with the particular requirements aimed at preserving water quality which have dominated land management since the 1890s.

The commons today

Commons registration and the 1965 Act

It is impossible to understand the contemporary property rights subsisting over Cwmdeuddwr Common without an appreciation of the historical context within which they have been generated and adapted to meet the local needs of the agricultural and wider local community. This is a theme that runs through all four of the case studies presented in this work, and is clearly presented here.

The starting point for a discussion of contemporary property rights and governance must be, as in the other case studies, the Commons Registration Act 1965 and its impact upon the nature and structure of land use-rights over the common. In this respect, at least, Cwmdeuddwr is for historical reasons quite unique. The manner in which common property rights were registered for Cwmdeuddwr Common (RCL36) reflects the fact that the surviving common is an entirely modern creation.

Pasturage

There are registered rights to pasture 10,844 sheep on RCL 36 (or parts of it). A total of 10,304 of these are registered as rights appurtenant to dominant land identified in the register (in most cases with identification of the relevant acreages of the dominant land to be benefitted). There are only two entries of grazing rights in gross, giving grazing for 540 sheep. These are expressed as exercisable over two small parcels of land on the western fringes of the common along the watershed of the Elan catchment and are rented by the Welsh Water Elan Trust to tenants on the adjoining Elan Estate.

Most of the grazing rights are registered as exercisable over part of the common, not the whole common land (CL) unit. The areas of land over which the rights are expressed as being exercisable reflect the former division between the two manors – 'over part of this unit, namely waste of the manor of Grange of Cwmteuddwr' or over the 'waste of the Manor of Cwmteuddwr' – representing in each case the manor of which the farm holding the rights originally formed part. In law, pasturage rights are, in principle, exercisable over the whole CL unit against which they are registered. A commoner can, however, abandon his right to graze over the whole of the land which he is otherwise entitled to use, and RCL 36 provides a good example of this phenomenon (see Gadsden, 1988, §3.112). There are only two registrations of grazing rights over the whole of Cwmdeuddwr Common (i.e. over land comprising the former wastes of both manors). The right to turbary and estovers in both of these entries is, however, only exercisable over land that is waste of the manor of Cwmdeuddwr.

The commons register discloses no temporal restrictions on when ewes, lambs or rams may be put to the common or removed (e.g. for overwintering). And unlike the registrations in some other CL units, it does not record additional rights to graze lambs (compare the register for CL 58 (Eskdale), where the entries are more specific, recording, in many cases, rights to graze 'breeding ewes or other sheep aged 1 year and over 1 year', 'sheep and followers', 'sheep and lambs'; see Chapter 6 pp99–100). There are also no registered rights to graze cattle or horses. As we have seen earlier, historically cattle and horses were grazed on Cwmdeuddwr Common; but customary practice has not, in this case study, been recorded in the commons registration process. This may prove of considerable importance in the context of modern priorities for the ecological improvement of the common; the Tir Gofal agri-environment scheme, for example, envisages mixed grazing with cattle and sheep as a strategy for managing bracken and molinia encroachment and controlling gorse. None of the commoners currently have registered rights to put cattle to the common.

Estovers

There are 43 entries of rights of estovers in the rights section of the register for RCL 36. All are expressed in general terms to be either for 'estovers (including the rights to cut bracken)' or for 'estovers (including the rights to cut fern)'. Although the cutting of ferns and bracken is the right of estovers of most value in this case, the right is not expressed as exclusively limited to bracken or fern ('including the right ... '). The legal form taken by the registrations would suggest a general (i.e. unlimited) right of estovers – potentially including greater and lesser house bote, plough bote and hedge or hay bote – with the cutting of fern or bracken the only right specified by name. This is unlikely to be representative of the rights claimed, however, which may well have been intended to be limited to cutting bracken or ferns for animal bedding. The register for RCL 36 therefore provides a good example of another point made by Gadsden – that in many cases rights of estovers were registered under the 1965 Act without refining the term further and that 'it is necessary to look behind the register to discover the scope of the right' (see Gadsden, 1988, §3.66). In practice, these rights are rarely exercised today, and whether evidence could be adduced on which to base a wider claim to estovers – other than a right to ferns or bracken – must be doubtful.

Turbary

All the registered pasture rights on RCL 36 also record a generic right to turbary, without specifying the site from which peat may be taken. Turbary rights have not been used to extract peat in modern times, and their exercise would, in any event, breach the terms of the SSSI notification for the Elenydd SSSI and the terms of the current ESA management agreement for Cwmdeuddwr Common. The environmental governance mechanisms discussed below effectively override the property rights recorded in the commons registers. As with the registered rights to estovers, it would, in any event, be necessary to look behind the register in order to discover the precise nature and ambit of the turbary rights registered under the 1965 Act.

Adaptations of property rights

In the modern context, the resource allocation reflected in common property rights over RCL 36 has been subject to substantial modification. Not only has customary agricultural practice changed considerably over the past century, property rights have also been substantially remodelled under agri-environment management agreements for the conservation of the natural features of the common. The impact of management agreements and environmental management techniques is discussed further below. This section concentrates on modern adaptations in agrarian practice that are reflected in property rights, drawing on qualitative research data in the case study.[38]

The exercise of turbary rights certainly took place within living memory. None of the commoners exercise rights of turbary and estovers today, although there is some limited evidence of the use of bracken for animal bedding and as a covering for potatoes and turnips. The only common right of substantial agronomic value is pasturage, which is exclusively used to graze sheep on the common. In practice, the commons registers have little impact upon agricultural management, and very few of the current graziers have consulted it or possess a copy. The majority of graziers identify the number of rights that they possess through alternative sources, including principally rent negotiations with their landlords or the terms of the Environmentally Sensitive Area (ESA) agreement for the common (as to which, see further below).

There is no evidence of the transfer of common rights between commoners, or between commoners and other farmers. The rights in gross recorded in the commons register, which in principle would be transferable without appurtenant land, are, in practice, leased to existing tenants of the adjoining Elan Estate who also hold other common rights over RCL 36. They have therefore been retained within the local farming community as a local resource to be allocated as part of an integrated strategy for the management of the common land and the adjoining Elan Estate. Common property rights are also strongly identified, in this case study, with a sense of locality and community. The importance to local stakeholders of retaining the connection between common rights and local community interests is strongly reflected in their attitude to the potential severance of common rights from the land they have historically benefitted. The anti-severance policy reflected in the Commons Act 2006, which attaches common rights to the dominant tenement and prohibits severance, was strongly supported by commoners with rights on RCL 36.

Modern management is heavily conditioned by the terms of the ESA management agreement for Cwmdeuddwr Common that was concluded in 2001. This replaced an ESA agreement negotiated in 1990/1991. The agreement reduced livestock on the common, but its provisions were individually tailored by allocating to each farmer a number of 'grazing days' per annum to be selected at their choice. By contrast with ESA agreements elsewhere (e.g. in Eskdale; see Chapter 6, p105), individual farmers were given limited freedom to manage the necessary stock reductions. Some agreed to remove all stock from the common in winter and limit their grazing to the summer months, while others use their grazing days selectively throughout the year. The commons register has, in practice, very little impact upon land management issues. It is, for example, impossible to calculate how many registered (but unused) grazing rights each commoner possesses as grazing will change seasonally.

The inclusion of the former (deregistered) CL 66 within the case study enabled an assessment to be made of the impact upon land management of the special status of common property rights (in this case, over RCL 36) when compared to land management outwith the common. Many of the graziers on RCL 36 also farm land on the adjoining Elan Estate, that is within the former CL 66. Farmers in our research sample noted the Elan Trust's strong focus on water quality issues, a factor that is also reflected in their tenancy agreements, which contain detailed provisions targeted at water protection (e.g. by restricting the use of inorganic fertilizers and pesticides). They also noted the lower priority given by the landlords to the profitability of agricultural production. Aside from this special situation, however, little difference in land management practices can be attributed to the special status of the common land within RCL 36. The farming operations of those common graziers who own or rent land within CL 66, and who also farm on RCL 36, are closely integrated. There are some differences attributable to the legal status of RCL 36 as common land, however. There is no formal restriction on the burning of molinia for heather regeneration on former CL 66, whereas this is impermissible on RCL 36 (unless consented by the owner of the soil) because of its status as common land. And farmers on the former CL 66 can graze both cattle and sheep, whereas only grazing rights for sheep are recorded in the common rights register for RCL 36 and permissible on the common. This could prove important in the negotiation of a future agri-environment scheme for the common on expiry of the current ESA agreement in 2011.

Commons governance

Until 1990 a single association, the Elan Valley Graziers' Association, oversaw management of both the Elan Trust Land (former CL 66) and Cwmdeuddwr Common (RCL 36). Today the Elan Valley Graziers' Association represents farm tenants on the Elan Estate, including those who farm the former CL 66. Tir Gofal agreements have been negotiated for individual farms within this part of the case study (discussed below). On Cwmdeuddwr Common itself the need to negotiate a single, collective, ESA management agreement led to the formation of a new and separate body in 1990: the Cwmdeuddwr Commoners' and Graziers' Association. The relatively recent division in the collective management structures reflects the fact that the creation of RCL 36 as a discrete and freestanding common is itself a relatively modern development, born largely out of Birmingham Corporation's (and latterly Welsh Water's) requirements for the water catchment and its efficient organization. It also demonstrates the potential for agri-environmental schemes to shape and influence not only agricultural practice, but also the creation and structure of local governance institutions.

The Cwmdeuddwr Commoners' and Graziers' Association actively manages the common, but not in a strongly formalized manner. It has a formal written constitution stipulating its officers, the quorum for meetings and voting procedures, but this does not lay down detailed rules for the governance of its member's common rights. The association's management committee intervenes if there are breaches of the ESA agreement in relation to grazing or bracken control. Prior to the conclusion of the first ESA agreement in 1991, two specific problems appear to have affected the common:

sheep scab was prevalent, and some graziers were keeping sheep on the common for long periods because they did not want them to lamb too early. These problems were resolved through informal internal negotiation that resulted in the setting of dates for rams to be put to the common and collectively agreed gathering dates.[39] The Association also attempts to regulate traffic on the metalled road crossing the common, and has put up traffic signs on the byway which runs over the common.

Environmental governance

Modern governance is dominated by two management paradigms: first, environmental regulation to protect and enhance the wildlife habitats the common encompasses; and, second, rules introduced under the Common Agricultural Policy (CAP) to promote sustainable agriculture in the wider sense of balancing the protection of agricultural resources with environmental protection.

Statutory environmental designations (see Figure 8.1)

There are three environmental designations of relevance to the modern governance of this case study, as listed below.

Special Protection Area (SPA) The Elenydd-Mallaen SPA, classified in 1996, covers over 30,000ha and is one of the most important sites in Wales for the protection of European breeding raptors. The predominance of sheep rearing in the case study has contributed to the conservation of the carrion-feeding red kite. Current feeding habitats and carrion availability are sufficient to support the breeding population of kites in the long term, and the principal land management objectives are the maintenance of suitable woodland management and grazing levels to maintain the bird habitats. The farmers' perception, on the other hand, is that the substantial reduction in sheep grazing levels in recent years has reduced available carrion, and that this is detrimental to the bird population.

Special Areas of Conservation (SACs) The Elenydd SAC (8609ha) was designated in 2004 in order to protect large and ecologically significant areas of blanket bog. Overgrazing, grass burning and winter livestock feeding are the principal threats to the site's habitats and species (JNCC, 2006a), while recreational activities (such as motorbike scrambling) and deposits of atmospheric pollutants also render the habitats vulnerable. Damage by grazing is being addressed through agri-environmental agreements, as discussed below. Both the Elenydd SAC and the nearby Coetiroedd Cwm Elan/Elan Valley Woodlands SAC are in unfavourable conservation status (Countryside Council for Wales, 2008).

Sites of Special Scientific Interest (SSSIs) The Elenydd SSSI, originally notified in 1954, is one of the largest SSSIs in Wales, at 22,770ha in extent, and includes the Claerwen National Nature Reserve. It has multiple features of special interest and many of European-level significance, such as broadleaved semi-natural woodland, breeding red kites, merlin and peregrine, a variety of epiphytic lichens, and blanket bogs covering 20 per cent of the Elenydd moorland plateau. The SSSI habitat is currently in unfavourable conservation condition, due largely to the encroachment of purple moor-grass (*Molinia caerula*) caused by the management effects of sheep grazing (Countryside Council for Wales, 2008, para 5.2). Bog vegetation is very sensitive to sheep grazing and so are the nests and young of ground-nesting birds, which can be damaged by sheep trampling. Limited grazing is, however, necessary to prevent the colonization of bracken and shrubs.

The ecological management sought by the Countryside Council for Wales (CCW) is aimed at establishing a balanced grazing regime across the Elenydd with mixed grazing by cows and sheep. Cattle grazing will control the spread of molinia as well as bracken and causes less damage to heather than sheep, whose selective grazing patterns damage dry heath. Ponies can also provide low-intensity year-round grazing, and this solution has been adopted in the Claerwen National Natural Reserve. Claerwen is within former CL 66, and grazing limitations imposed by the commons registers do not, therefore, apply. Mixed grazing would be more difficult to implement on RCL 36 (Cwmdeuddwr Common), where all registered pasture rights are exclusively for grazing sheep.

The legal mechanisms for controlling land management in SSSIs have very little impact upon the agricultural management of the common and of land within former CL 66. No management agreements have been entered into under the legislation on SSSIs,[40] and none of the current graziers have served a notice of their intention to carry out operations likely to damage the special conservation interest (OLDSIs), thereby triggering a statutory consultation with CCW under section 28 of the Wildlife and Countryside Act 1981. Most farmers were aware of the existence of the SSSI. Few had a detailed knowledge of the restrictions in the list of OLDSIs served on them with the site notification, and most did not consider that they limited their customary management practices. Some thought the restrictions 'pretty minimal'.[41] The only OLDSI they strongly disagreed with was the prohibition on burning vegetation, which they consider to be a more effective way of controlling molinia than cattle grazing.

Negotiations between individual farmers and CCW over notified OLDSIs are invariably informal. This is perhaps surprising as the list of OLDSIs for the Elenydd is very extensive, prohibiting 28 operations, including changes in grazing intensity and the extraction of peat or turf. It therefore reallocates to CCW decisions on the exercise of rights of turbary, as well as increases in grazing numbers that are within the limits set in the commons registers. It also provides a good example of the lack of integration between the common property entitlements and nature conservation law. The 1981 Act makes provision for the service of a single list of OLDSIs for each SSSI, and it is not possible to have differentiated lists of OLDSIs for common land and non-common land within an SSSI. In cases where an SSSI covers a geographically large area – such as the Elenydd SSSI – this inevitably increases the potential for there to be a mismatch between the prescriptions in the list of OLDSIs and the land use-rights of common graziers. Many OLDSIs in the Elenydd SSSI are, consequently, operations which commoners have no legal capacity to perform given the status of the land as common land (e.g. supplementary feeding of livestock and the burning of vegetation on the common).

There are also two smaller SSSIs within the case study. The Coed y Cefn SSSI is the only oak woodland site in Powys supporting a population of hairy wood ants and invertebrates associated with woods and nests. The site has been assessed by CCW as in favourable and improving condition, and a woodland management plan and periodic sheep grazing are targeted for its maintenance. The Cerrig Gwalch SSSI, on the other hand, has three special features: broadleaved semi-natural woodland (supporting a variety of breeding birds), lily-of-the-valley and mountain melick. This SSSI is also in favourable conservation condition, but CCW management objectives seek to avoid continuous grazing and identify atmospheric pollution as a further threat.

The Environmentally Sensitive Area (ESA) scheme

The Cambrian Mountains ESA was designated in 1987 and revised in 1993/1994. The area was designated in order to maintain and enhance areas of semi-natural rough grazing as well as broadleaved woodlands, under the threat of agricultural intensification. Until the 1994 revision of the Cambrian ESA, however, the risk of intensification was still high in non-ESA areas since the ESA management agreements were applied only to eligible land and not to the whole of each farm (Wilson, 1997, p73).

Cwmdeuddwr Common is one of only four commons in Wales to conclude an ESA management agreement with the Welsh Assembly Government (Countryside Council for Wales, 2007, para 3.5). The ESA agreement is the principal mechanism for regulating the environmental impacts of land management in the case study, and is of far greater practical significance than the SSSI mechanisms discussed above. The limited number of graziers on the Cambrian Mountains ESA is an important variable for understanding the reaching of an ESA agreement (Wilson and Wilson, 1997). Qualitative research confirmed the degree of familiarity existing between the common graziers, noting that despite the remoteness of some farms, they all knew each other personally and cooperated in their daily management of the common. A related variable explaining the success of ESA in Cwmdeuddwr Common is the communal sense of 'belonging' expressed by the farmers and a shared economic situation. Sheep grazing on Cwmdeuddwr Common is only marginally profitable, and agri-environmental schemes such as ESA are vitally important to the continued viability of hill farming. The administration of the ESA agreement, which has standard terms and applies equally to all participating graziers, is administratively simpler and less time consuming for the public agencies than preparing and monitoring individual SSSI management agreements with each farmer. And, by binding non-active graziers, the collective ESA agreement negotiated in 2001 prevents them from interfering with the agreed management of the common.

The Cwmdeuddwr Common ESA agreement is a ten-year Tier 1 and Tier 1A agreement. Tier 1 offers payments of £20 per annum per hectare over the first 20ha; £10 per annum per hectare on land over 20ha but less than 51ha; £5 per annum per hectare on land which exceeds 50ha but less than 101ha; and £3 per annum per hectare on land which exceeds 100ha. For Tier 1A, payments increase to £25 per annum per hectare for unenclosed semi-natural rough grazing without heather and £35 for that with heather. The land management prescriptions are wide-ranging and include maintaining existing hedges, walls, fences, lakes and ponds. There are also prohibitions on the removal of broadleaved trees and ploughing, to cultivating, installing new drainage systems or applying fertilizers.

The ESA grazing prescriptions are particularly important to the environmental management sought for the common. Under Tier 1 it is an obligatory requirement that the level of grazing livestock cannot be increased without prior written approval. Tier 1A seeks to prevent overgrazing by imposing an average stocking rate of 0.375 livestock units (LU) per hectare on unenclosed semi-natural rough grazing, and 0.22 LU per hectare on unenclosed semi-natural rough grazing where heather is present. The supplementary feeding of livestock is only to be undertaken in areas agreed in advance with the Welsh

Assembly Government (WAG). The ESA prescriptions, like those in the SSSIs (see above), conflict both with environmental law and common property rights, and further illustrate the lack of integration between property rights, environmental law and economic instruments. Supplementary feeding is an OLDSI in the Elenydd SSSI and will constitute a criminal offence if carried out without the permission of CCW – this will be the case whether or not it is carried out with WAG consent under the terms of the ESA agreement. And it is, in any event, an activity that a common grazier cannot lawfully undertake as an attribute of their common property right. The Tier 1 ESA obligations permit stocking increases with WAG consent; but the agreement does not expressly recognize that the registered grazing rights of individual graziers cannot legally be exceeded. Other Tier 1 obligations – for example, the prohibitions on ploughing and cultivation – fail to take account of the fact that these operations are already prohibited as OLDSIs in the Elenydd SSSI and are, in any event, beyond the rights of common exercisable by farmers.

In addition to the standard ESA prescriptions, on Cwmdeuddwr Common each grazier was allocated a number of grazing days to be used whenever preferred. Although some farmers decided not to put livestock on the common between 15 October and 15 April annually, there is no formal 'closed period', and the farmers have considerable freedom to manage their grazing practices. It was initially proposed to cut livestock grazing by a flat rate of 25 per cent; but this was considered unfair to those who did not graze up to their full commons entitlement. The approach to grazing control on Cwmdeuddwr Common differs markedly from that in the Ingleton case study (see Chapter 7), where the common grazing has been closed for fixed periods annually in order to prevent overgrazing.

The ESA agreement has been an important financial instrument that has greatly benefitted the farming economy. Has it, however, delivered environmental benefits beyond those already secured through the SAC, SPA and SSSI notifications in the case study? The ESA agreement has not, on its own, prevented overgrazing, and it has been supplemented by management agreements with individual farmers under the Countryside Act 1968 and, more recently, Tir Gofal agreements with WAG. Tir Gofal agreements have been negotiated with most of the farmers on former CL 66 and on the other non-common land farmed by graziers on RCL 36. The ESA agreement is, however, the only instrument for regulating grazing levels on Cwmdeuddwr Common itself.

The views of common graziers and estate managers as to the environmental impact of the ESA varied. Many did not think the ESA had made a great difference to livestock management or the environmental quality of the common. The introduction of the single farm payment has arguably had a greater impact than the ESA agreement in reducing livestock levels.[42] Some farmers had a positive view that the ESA had contributed to the regeneration of the heather on parts of the common. Although the agreement did not require the off-wintering of all stock from the common, many farmers have opted to do so. Views as to the environmental benefits of off-wintering varied. Some thought less winter grazing was bad for the common's vegetation because the smaller number of sheep concentrated on the 'sweeter' grass, leaving large areas of common ungrazed. The majority thought, however, that reduced winter grazing had a variety of positive effects: it ameliorated the conditions of the sheep, producing a higher percentage of lambs, and with regard to the environmental quality of the common it improved the status of the vegetation and encouraged heather regeneration.[43]

Impact of the Single Payment Scheme
Reform of the European Community's Common Agricultural Policy (CAP) and the implementation of the new Single Payment Scheme (SPS) for farm support have had a major impact upon land management in the case study. The 'cross-compliance' conditions that must be observed by farmers as a condition of payment under the SPS appear, in particular, to have had an important impact in reducing grazing pressure on Cwmdeuddwr Common. Of particular relevance are the cross-compliance conditions on overgrazing and unsuitable supplementary feeding methods (see the Common Agricultural Policy Single Payment and Support Schemes (Cross-Compliance) (Wales) 2004, regulation 4, schedule, para 6). These require farmers to refrain from overgrazing, defined as 'grazing with so many livestock that the growth, quality or diversity of natural or semi-natural vegetation is adversely affected'. The WAG has power to give farmers written directions concerning the management of land that is overgrazed. The SPS appears to have had a substantial impact upon livestock levels on Cwmdeuddwr Common and the adjacent former CL 66.[44] When the price of sheep meat is very low, there is no financial incentive to keep sheep as almost the whole of each producer's income is derived from the SPS and from agri-environmental payments under Tir Gofal agreements and/or the ESA agreement for the common. Indeed, there is evidence that the SPS has had a greater role in reducing grazing pressures than either the ESA or Tir Gofal schemes. Some farmers have maintained livestock numbers that are the minimum permissible under their Tir Gofal agreements. Even in the summer months, many farmers maintain minimum winter stock levels because if they do not own or rent land elsewhere, it is not economically efficient to away-winter the additional stock.[45] These dynamics will change, of course, if the market for sheep meat improves.

Environment governance: The future

Looking forward, two issues will dominate the future management of Cwmdeuddwr Common. The first is the prospect of the entry of the common into the Glas Tir agri-environment scheme (the successor to Tir Gofal), and the changes in land management that this will require. And, second, would the management of the common benefit from the establishment of a commons council under Part 2 of the Commons Act 2006? The majority of commoners viewed entry into Tir Gofal, or its successor Glas Tir, as essential both for the economic sustainability of their enterprises and for the future sustainable management of the common. And, with some caveats, they view the possible establishment of a commons council positively. The outcomes of a focus group to consider the advantages and disadvantages of the establishment of a statutory commons council were discussed in Chapter 5 (pp78–79).

The WAG has reviewed axis 2 (landscape and environment) of the *Rural Development Plan for Wales 2007–2013* in order to align it with reform of the Common Agricultural Policy and emerging policies for combating climate change. Section 5.2.42 of the plan proposed the pilot use of co-operative land management schemes for common land, recognizing the unique demands of common land management. It also supported the development of a top tier scheme, going beyond the current scope of Tir Gofal, to promote management solutions at a landscape or river catchment scale to address environmental problems. One of the measures that a top tier scheme might include is 'co-operative action to achieve improvements on common land, including support for initiatives undertaken by commoners' associations to mobilise farmers to act together' (Welsh Assembly Government, 2007, para 5.2.52). This suggests that revisions incorporated in the new Glas Tir scheme might build on the peculiar institutional basis of common land in order to address environmental problems. Those Welsh commons that lack a commoners' association could be marginalized by this proposal, and the option to establish common councils under the 2006 Act could be particularly important in providing the organizational infrastructure for delivering the emerging targets for land management established in the revised plan.

Most farmers in the case study currently have Tir Gofal agreements on their inbye land and, when the Cwmdeuddwr Common ESA expires in 2011, it is hoped that the whole common can be entered into a single collective agreement. Glas Tir includes an All-Wales Common Land Element, which facilitates applications by commons or graziers associations that have registered as a customer with WAG. Participation will be limited from the beginning of 2014 to commons with established grazing associations (although applications in the period prior to 31 December 2013 will be accepted from a lead grazier on behalf of groups of commoners). Associations that have registered with WAG and expressed interest in Glas Tir will receive application packs in 2011, and the first available contract start date will be 1 January 2012. Contracts will be for five years. The scheme will offer two entry-level management options for common land under the All Wales Element (Welsh Assembly Government, 2010, Section C, p13). Option 1 will offer payments in return for the management of sward height throughout the year. This is the likely option that will be applicable to Cwmdeuddwr Common. CCW has suggested that the management option for the common would be a combination of restoration of semi-improved grassland to unimproved grassland with heathland vegetation on acid grassland.[46] Option 2 will require the imposition of a closed grazing period for three months between 1 November and 31 March annually – this is unlikely to be attractive as it would require a substantial change in the grazing management currently applied under the Cwmdeuddwr ESA agreement.

An important variable determining farmers' willingness to join the scheme will be the extent of the changes in land management that it would require. Further reductions in livestock rates were anticipated by the majority of commoners in the research sample. These are likely to be required by the WAG, which views reductions in winter grazing as fundamental to heather regeneration.[47] Controlled burning to control molinia vegetation will not be permitted, as this is contrary to the list of OLDSIs for the Elenydd SSSI. Mixed grazing with cattle will, however, be permitted as a strategy for molinia control. The introduction of cattle grazing – either with or without controlled burning as a molinia control measure – would only be possible in two situations:

1 if new rights of common are created under the Commons Act 2006; or
2 if any surplus grazing accruing to the owner of the soil is used to license additional grazing to graziers wishing to stock cattle on the common.

The creation of new rights will depend upon a sustainability appraisal being carried out by CCW under the 2006 Act, and will be impossible if the cumulative impact of the exercise of existing rights, and such new rights as are sought, will be unsustainable (2006 Act, section 6(6); see also Chapter 4, pp61–62). The second option depends upon the existence of surplus grazing over and above the extent of registered rights on the commons register for RCL 36. CCW recognizes not only the limitations imposed by the commons register and the lack of fencing against cattle straying, but also potential issues for reduced water quality if cattle grazing is reintroduced to the common – especially important given the status of the former CL 66 and parts of RCL 36 as part of the Elan reservoir catchment.

Bracken control may also be required under a prospective Glas Tir agreement. None of the common graziers exercise rights of estovers, and bracken encroachment is currently minimized by controlled spraying under the terms of the ESA agreement.

Finally, the successful conclusion of a Glas Tir agreement will depend upon the commoners' ability to reach a consensus on a joint application. Unanimity is not required; but the WAG requires that applications for the All-Wales Common Land Element be made by a grazing association with participation from at least 80 per cent of active common graziers (Welsh Assembly Government, 2010, Section C, p12).

Conclusions

In conclusion, what can the history of commons governance, and its contemporary challenges, in this case study tell us about changing conceptions of 'sustainable' commons management and the manner in which cultural, legal and societal perceptions have changed – often subtly – over time?

The dominant feature of this case study is, of course, the dramatic impact of the wholesale reorganization of property ownership and common property rights by the Birmingham Corporation Water Act 1892. The 1892 Act instituted one of the largest civil engineering infrastructure projects undertaken in Victorian Britain, remodelling not only the landscape itself, but also redrawing the intricate pattern of landownership and resource allocation represented in common property rights over much of the land involved. Another unique feature of the 1892 Act was the grant of statutory rights of access and recreation to the local population – a factor that removed some of the 'contest' from the multiple (and sometimes conflicting) land uses to which commons have historically been put, and which we have seen in the other case studies in this work. The purchase of many common rights and sheepwalks by Birmingham Corporation under the1892 Act meant that most of the open hill land ceased to be common at all – as recognized in the deregistration of CL 66 following the introduction of commons registration in 1965. And although Cwmdeuddwr Common itself remained 'common', that status is now overlaid with additional statutory rights granted to the public under the 1892 legislation.

Another curious feature of this Welsh case study is the idiosyncratic nature of the property rights that it manifests. Peculiar to the Welsh context is the phenomenon of 'sheep walks' and the ambiguities that they raise when considered in the context of definitions of 'common' land. The disconnectedness between the legal status of most sheepwalks as simply manorial waste (and, hence, 'common' land, although farmed by one occupier) and their customary profile as tantamount to the exclusive property of the farm to which they are attached, is symptomatic of the tensions to which legal conceptions of common property can give rise. This is a curious feature of the property rights regime that has yet to be satisfactorily resolved.

Although the landscape of the Elan Valley is an iconic one, in general terms 'recreational' activities do not impinge heavily upon the common. As a result, the tensions between recreational and other competing land uses (typically, but not exclusively, agriculture) that we see in the other case studies is largely absent. Some recreational uses are problematic – for example, 'off-roading' by cyclists and, particularly, motorists; but most recreational land uses are uncontroversial. The principal driver of cultural change in the area, and of the way in which its 'common' land is perceived, is water supply. The need to preserve a clean and sustainable water supply for human consumption defines the landowner's approach to sustainable land management across the whole case study area, and underpins all other aspects of the environmental governance of the contemporary commons. This can be seen, for example, in the relatively minor role played by farm diversification in the rural economy. Diversification of the rural economy is not integral to the landowner's perception of a 'sustainably' managed common, in which matters of water quality preservation are paramount. It follows that the emphasis on a holistic approach to the sustainability of rural communities seen in, for example, the Eskdale case study, where it is driven by the National Trust's stance as the primary landowner in that context, is simply absent in the Elan Valley case study.

Notes

1 Powys County Archives [hereafter PCA], R/D/LEW/3/106, searches, 27 July 1892.

2 PCA, R/D/LEW/3/96, boundaries of manor of Grange of Cwmdeuddwr, 1797; PCA, R/D/LEW/2/694 Draft Maps for Vesting Assent', undated [mid 20th century]. The boundaries of the manor of Grange are described in Banks (1880, p32).

3 See www.cpat.org.uk/projects/longer/histland/elan/evintr.htm, accessed 16 May 2010; Banks (1880).

4 Elan Estate Office [hereafter EEO], Plan of Manorial Boundaries and Manorial Rights acquired by the Corporation of Birmingham [circa 1900].

5 PCA, R/D/LEW/3/107 'Notes by R. S. Lewis prepared for evidence in *Lewis v. Pugh* relating to Trefelgwyn sheepwalk', undated [post-1967].

6 Powys County Council Common Land Register [hereafter Powys CLR], RCL 66, entry no 1; objections nos 947, 967; file of papers re RCL 66; Commons commissioner decision reference no 276/D/321-323.

7 Powys CLR, RCL 36 Cwmdeuddwr Common, Land Section: Sheet 1, and accompanying registration maps: sheet nos 36, 38, 40, 41.

8 Powys CLR, RCL 36 Cwmdeuddwr Common, Land Section: Sheet 1. See also registration maps: sheet nos 36, 38, 40, 41.

9 National Library of Wales [hereafter NLW], BRA 259/74.

10 PCA, R/D/LEW/3/96 presentments book 1722–1817, [no day/month given] 1807; R/D/LEW/2/171.

11 PCA, R/D/LEW/1/41; R/D/LEW/5/147.

12 PCA, R/D/WWA/1A/A8: Elan Estate sheep stock accounts, 1917, 1960–1961.

13 PCA, R/D/LEW/02/228. Lluest-aber-caethon (at SN 875 687) is recorded as 'Clettwr Mawr' on the Tithe Plan of 1838: PRO, IR 30/55/34.

14 Ordnance Survey 1:10,560 map, Radnorshire Sheet XIV SW. Clwyd-Powys Archaeological Trust report that the chimney stack in the house at Lluest-aber-caethon (now derelict) includes a stone with the inscription: 'D.E. 1814 CLETTWR', preserving its older name. See CPAT, *The Elan Valley: Landed Estates and Agricultural Improvements of the 18th and*

19th Centuries, www.cpat.org.uk/projects/longer/histland/elan/evesta.htm (accessed 16 May 2010).

15 EEO, Estate plans and terrier, covering dates circa 1892–1913 (with additions to 1932).

16 Summing-up of the Lord Chief Justice, *Ecclesiastical Commissioners v. Griffiths and Others*, Cardiganshire Assizes, 1875 (Westminster, Nichols and Sons, 1875) [printed transcript]. We are grateful to Gwyn Jones (Scottish Agricultural College) for drawing our attention to this case. See also Gadsden, 1988, §3.108–3.112.

17 NLW, Mayberry (3) 7201: brief for petitioners, 1902, p1.

18 NLW, Mayberry (3) 7201: brief for petitioners, 1902, p7.

19 Banks 1880, p9; PCA, R/D/LEW/3/96.

20 Information from Mr J. Pugh, Parc Farm and Mr G. Evans, Pant-y-dwr, 2008.

21 55 & 56 Vict., Ch.clxxiii, clause 54.

22 For example, see the Second and Third Readings (HC Deb, 8 March 1892, vol 2, cc266–307; HC Deb, 26 May 1892, vol 4, cc1857–1883; HC Deb, 31 May 1892, vol 5, cc338–348).

23 Powys CLR, RCL 66, entry 1.

24 Records survive in NLW (e.g. presentment, 1757: Dolaucothi MSS and Papers, schedule II, p16, MS vol 12 (57)) and PCA (e.g. list of farms, 1600–1700: R/D/LEW/5/135; list of lords and stewards, 1722–1889: R/D/LEW/5/133–134; presentment book, 1722–1817: R/D/Lew/3/96–97; courts rolls, extracts related to boundaries, 1809–1839: R/D/LEW/5/136; precepts to summon court (3) 1837–1844: R/D/LEW/5/138–140; court roll, 1873: R/D/LEW/5/141; court roll, 1878: R/D/LEW/5/142).

25 E.g. court rolls, 1688 (NLW, Powis Manorial records group II, p179, various manors); extracts from court rolls, 1780–1878 (PCA, R/D/Lew/5/145); court rolls, 1873, 1878 (PCA, R/D/LEW/5/143–144); estreat rolls, various years, 1530–1688, (PRO, SC 2/227/50; 227/67; 227/71; LR 11/55/795; 56/809; 57/812–813; 57/820–822); presentments, 1780–1786 (PRO, CRES 5/192).

26 PCA, R/D/LEW/5/141–144, court rolls 1873 and 1878.

27 Birmingham Water Act 1892, clauses 48–51. The Elan Estate is unaware of such by-laws ever being introduced; we are grateful to Michael Rolt for this information.

28 PCA, R/D/LEW/3/96, presentments book 1722–1817; R/D/LEW/5/141, court roll 1873; R/D/LEW/5/142, court roll 1878.

29 NLW, MS 12878 D: legal papers re: encroachments, undated [circa 1837–1838].

30 PCA, R/D/LEW/3/96, presentments book 1722–1817, 14 October 1791, 17 May 1725, 3 May 1729, 28 April 1741, 26 October 1742, 20 October 1804.

31 PCA, R/D/LEW/3/96, presentments book 1722–1817, 9 October 1797, 3 May 1811.

32 PCA, R/D/LEW/5/142 court roll, 18 July 1878. A building and an adjacent small enclosure at Lluest Cwm Bach are marked on the tithe plan of 1841.

33 55 & 56 Vict., Ch.clxxiii, clause 53.

34 PCA, R/D/WWA/1A/A7/47/1. Parc tenancy agreement, 1902, clauses 6, 10, 31.

35 55 & 56 Vict., c. clxxiii, section 48.

36 Information from Cwmdeuddwr Commoners, 2009. The washfold is at SN 933 697.

37 PCA, R/D/WWA/1A/A7/47/1. Parc tenancy agreement, 1902, clauses 18–21, 23, 24, 26–28.

38 For full data analysis and further detail, see http:commons.ncl.ac.uk/case studies/elanvalley/qualitativedata.

39 Semi-structured interview, 2009.

40 For example, under Section 15, Countryside Act 1968 and the *Guidelines for Payments under Management Agreements and Associated Matters* (Defra/WAG, 2001).

41 Semi-structured interviews, 2009.

42 Semi-structured interview, 2008.

43 Semi-structured interviews, 2008.
44 Semi-structured interview, 2008.
45 Semi-structured interview, 2008.
46 Semi-structured interview, 2008.
47 Semi-structured interview, 2008.

9

Brancaster and Thornham, Norfolk

The focus of this case study lies on the coast fringing Brancaster Bay, an area of high conservation value, designated as Heritage Coast and falling within the North Norfolk Area of Outstanding Natural Beauty (AONB).[1] In marked contrast to the upland case studies, the surviving common land represents only a fraction of the land over which common rights formerly existed. Enclosure of commonable arable land in the 18th century resulted in the extinguishment of common rights over the bulk of the land, with the result that only the saltmarshes and smaller vestigial areas of inland common remain. The surviving commons (see Figure 9.2) thus represent only fragments of a system of communal resource management which operated before circa 1750. At Brancaster, a total of 1746ha of coastal marshes and dunes are registered as common in three common land units (CL 65, CL 124 and CL 161), the bulk of which comprises Scolt Head Island National Nature Reserve; a further 300ha of saltmarsh common survives at Thornham (CL 41 and CL 56). Smaller patches of common land survived inland, including Barrow Common (CL 159), near Brancaster Staithe, which is included in the case study, and Thornham Ling Common (CL 55), the attempted registration of which failed.[2]

Brancaster and Thornham lie in the 'sheep-corn' country of north-west Norfolk, on light sandy soils overlying boulder clay (Postgate, 1973; Williamson, 2006). In broad outline, the parishes from Holme-next-the-Sea to Burnham Deepdale exhibited similar patterns of historic land use. Each consisted of a transect across the countryside, from the coastal saltmarshes in the north to an undulating plateau at approximately 50m above sea level in the south. The villages, aligned east–west, lay at the junction between the coastal marshes and the higher land. Before enclosure in the 18th century, the coastal parishes contained three distinct land-use zones: first, the coastal marshes, only capable of agricultural use if reclaimed by embanking and drainage, but valuable for a wide range of resources; second, the rising ground immediately south of the villages, which formed the core of the open arable fields; and finally the rolling plateau on the southern edge of the parishes, formerly heathland, much of which had been divided into blocks of land ('brecks') which were cultivated on a long ley rotation by the early-modern period.

Enclosure in the 18th century transformed the open fields and the heathland 'brecks', leaving the coastal marshes largely untouched. The environmental character of commons that survive is markedly diverse. The coastal marshes include both salt water and freshwater marsh and embrace a spectrum of vegetation types, from comparatively

Figure 9.1 *Brancaster Marsh from the air*

Source: Ben George Photography

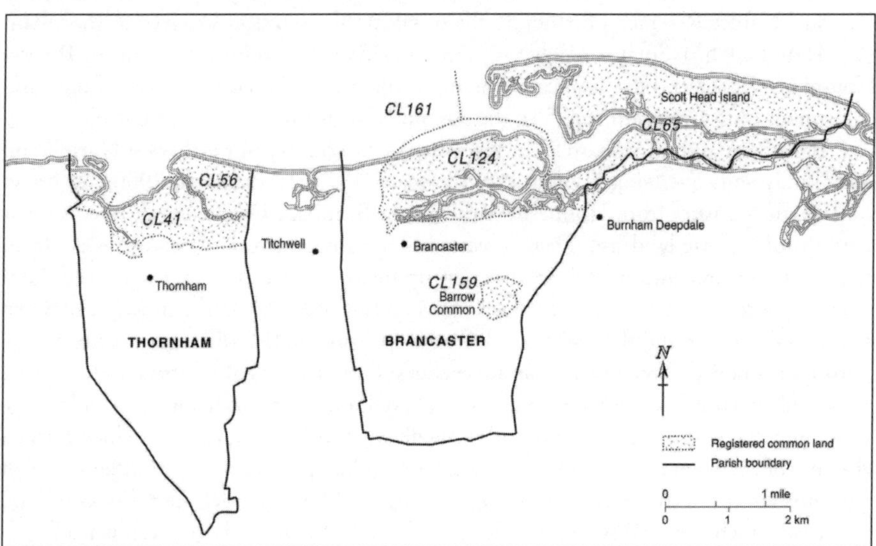

Figure 9.2 *Brancaster and Thornham: Parish boundaries and common land (CL) units*

Source: Norfolk County Council, Common Land Register

dry pasture to fragmented mud flats, where the marshes merge into the foreshore. They also include sand dunes fronting the sea, known in the vernacular as 'meals' (from the Old Norse *melr*: 'sand hill'). The heathland character of the inland commons is recorded in the name 'ling' (Old Norse for 'heather') borne by several areas of former common land on the inland plateau. 'The Lyng', 214 acres of waste on the southern edge of Brancaster parish, was described in the 17th century as 'a greate pece of heath and furzy ground' and 'all whinnie grounds' (i.e. gorse-covered land).[3] Identically named commons are recorded at Thornham and at Holkham (Faden, 1797; Allison, 1957, p17).

One of the themes running through this case study is the distinctive character of coastal common land and rights, which stands in marked contrast to the upland commons which were the focus of preceding chapters. The exercise of grazing rights, which dominates the other three study areas, and is a major driver of common land policy nationally, is of much less importance here, where issues such as wildfowling and samphire collecting are more pertinent. The perceived relationship between community and property rights is also often at variance with the upland pattern, with a greater emphasis on personal rights held and shared between members of families.

A second, related, theme is the reinvention and adaptation of commons and common rights over time, pointing to a more unstable legal context than was seen elsewhere. There is a measure of uncertainty about the relationship between historical commons and the common land and common rights registered under the Commons Registration Act 1965. The county of Norfolk appears to have experienced a dramatic increase in the number of commons as a result of registration, in part because parish councils 'often felt obliged to register land rather than run the risk of losing it for the parish'. Perhaps as few as 46 out of almost 500 commons registered in the county have a history as true commons (Birtles, 1998, pp89, 91–2). Of the registered commons in Brancaster and Thornham, only Barrow Common (CL 159) and Brancaster Marsh (CL 124) possess an undoubted unbroken heritage as common land. The others include stinted pastures created under an enclosure act (at Thornham), land which was historically the lord of the manor's several ground (such as Little Ramsey and other parts of CL 65), or land with historically obscure legal standing, such as Scolt Head Island (Hoskins and Stamp, 1963, pp135–136). Similar discontinuities may exist between historic practices and registered common rights. The register contains a large number and range of common rights entries for the coastal commons (including rights to gather a wide range of products which are difficult to classify under the normal legal categories – such as rights to take samphire, seaweed, shellfish, sea lavender, fish, bait, wildfowl, sand, shingle and reeds) which probably point to a mass registration of rights which may have had little historical precedent as legally recognized common rights. It has been suggested that the long lists of finalized rights attached to the coastal commons 'is due more to lack of objection or negotiated settlement than to any universally recognised rights of common' (Birtles, 1998, pp88–89). Whereas deep-seated tradition runs as a theme through the upland case study areas, transformations in the legal framework of common land in these coastal communities occurred twice, at enclosure in the 18th century and at registration in the late 20th. These discontinuities provide the opportunity to explore the reinvention of customary rights and changing cultural conceptions about the characteristics and 'ownership' of common land since the 18th century. Each of the commons in

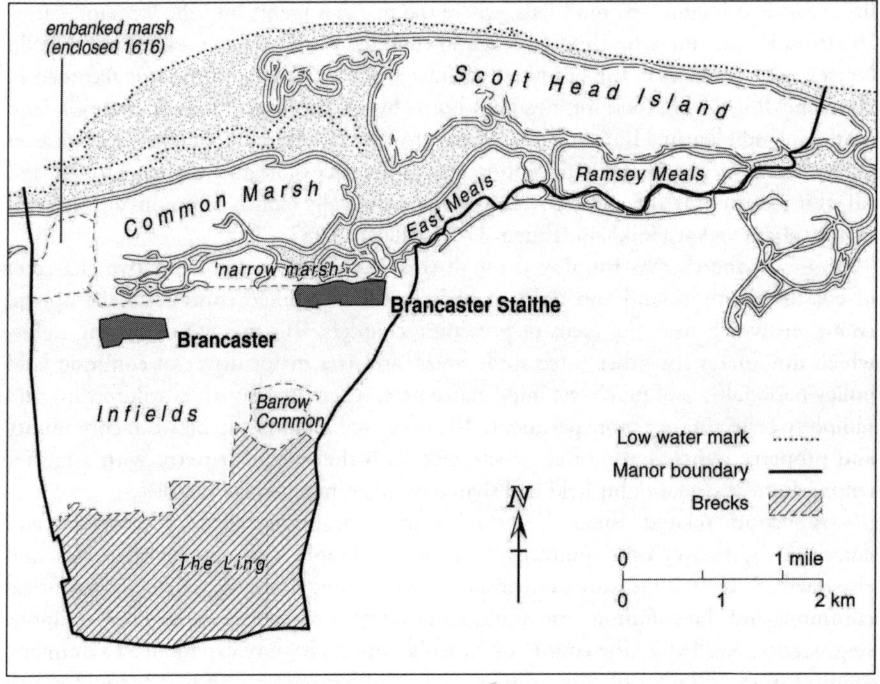

Figure 9.3 *Brancaster: Reconstruction of land use and common land in the 17th century, based on surveys of 1630 and 1663*

Source: Reconstructed from GA, D 2700, MJ19/3 and 5.

Brancaster and Thornham possess a distinct history, so the following account discusses each separately.

Common rights and governance to 1965

Property rights

Brancaster

The coastal commons at Brancaster are unusual in that their boundaries extend to the low tide mark, thus including the foreshore. This is a legacy of the quasi-regal rights over the foreshore held by the lords of Brancaster, which derived from Edward the Confessor's charter to Ramsey Abbey in 1053, granting the monks royal liberties, including 'wreck of the sea' (the right to ships and goods cast ashore in storms), at Brancaster and Ringstead (Hart and Lyons, 1884–1893, I, pp219, 241). Within the manor, the division of the Brancaster saltmarshes into separate CL units reflects their different histories (see Figure 9.3). Despite now being registered as common land, much of the saltmarsh appears to have been considered to be the lord's several freehold in the 17th century.

Only Brancaster Marsh Common (CL 124) has a history of common use back to the 17th century.[4] In 1630 it comprised two distinct marshes belonging to the lords of Brancaster, first the 'common marsh' (370 acres), which is to be identified with the dunes and marshland north of Mow Creek, including the area occupied by the Royal West Norfolk golf course. Under an agreement of 1616, whereby the lord of the manor gained exclusive use of newly embanked and reclaimed marsh to the west of this area, the lord's sheep were excluded from the common marsh.[5] The marshes immediately behind the villages of Brancaster and Brancaster Staithe were known as the 'narrow marsh' (estimated at 183 acres), which was in the lord's private ownership, though it was said in 1670 that the tenants had 'feed for their great cattell' there.[6] Under the Brancaster enclosure act of 1755 the lord of the manor relinquished his grazing rights over these sections of marsh, but presumably retained his rights in the soil. Indeed, the lords subsequently proposed draining large areas of the common marsh. Proposals drawn up by the lady of the manor circa 1783 reveal an intention to reserve a mere 50 acres for cottagers' use, limiting them to the same stint as had been applied to Barrow Common under the 1756 award.[7] Nothing appears to have come of the proposal; indeed, there are suggestions of a strengthened sense of 'ownership' among the commoners as a result of the release of grazing rights. In the tithe apportionment of 1841, the words 'Marsh Common' were entered under 'landowner' and the occupier was stated to be 'The Parish': the then lord of the manor appears not to have objected to this designation, as he confirmed the tithe award.[8] Nevertheless, when the Royal West Norfolk Golf Club developed a golf course on the links towards the end of the 19th century, the lord of the manor's ownership of the soil was implied, if not stated explicitly. The golf club paid both the lord and the parish council for the privilege of golfing on the common and when a formal agreement was entered into in 1902, it was with both the parish council (as representative of the commoners) and Simms Reeve, as lord of the manor. Later agreements were, however, between the golf club and the parish council alone.[9] Ownership of the common was claimed in the 1920s by Rose Sutherland, who had purchased the saltmarshes, beach and foreshore in 1923, becoming lady of the manor of Brancaster. In the resulting lawsuit, the disputed ownership of the links was settled when the golf club, which had claimed that the freehold of the links was not part of the manorial estate, purchased the freehold and manorial rights over the links from her.[10] In 1964, a local syndicate purchased the manorial estate at auction in order to pass it to the National Trust. At registration, ownership of CL 124 was registered as being divided between the Royal West Norfolk Golf Club and the National Trust.

The second major area of coastal common land at Brancaster covers Scolt Head Island and the marshes south of Norton Creek (CL 65). During the 17th century there is no indication that any of this area was deemed to be common. In 1630, its constituent elements were described as follows. 'Ramsey Meels' (now Little Ramsey), a 100 acre marsh, was lord's freehold: its name presumably refers to Ramsey Abbey, the pre-Dissolution owner of the manor, suggesting a history of seigniorial ownership since the medieval period. 'East Meels' was also the lord's freehold marsh and its private status can be traced back to circa 1240, when Robert of Brancaster, the largest freeholder in Brancaster, held 'a marsh called Estmeles' as a pasture for 600 sheep (Hart and Lyons, 1884–1893, I, p413). In the tithe apportionment of 1841, both Ramsey Meals and East Meals were recorded as belonging to the lords of Brancaster Manor and were said to be occupied by themselves.[11] Scolt Head Island, which forms the bulk of CL 65, is nowhere recorded in the 17th-century sources: indeed, Ramsey Meals and East Meals were said in

1630 to abut upon the sea, suggesting that Scolt Head did not exist at that time. It seems likely that much of the island is the result of more recent accretion of coastal deposits. If that were the case, it may explain the disputes over ownership in the 20th century. On the death of Simms Reeve, lord of Brancaster, in 1922 it was agreed that the north part was owned by Lord Orford and the southern part by the executors of Reeve's Brancaster Hall Estate. Scolt Head Island and other nearby lands were bought by Lord Leicester, who sold the major part of the island to the National Trust in 1923 in order to create a nature reserve (Steers, 1960, pp1–2). At registration, ownership of CL 65 was divided between the Norfolk Naturalists Trust, Lord Leicester (who had retained some areas of Scolt Head Island) and the National Trust.

In its current form, Barrow Common (CL 159) was created by the Brancaster Enclosure Act of 1755. In 1630, much of the 'Sheepe Pasture' or 'the Brecks' in the southern part of the parish was cultivated; yet some substantial areas of 'heath and furzy ground' survived. Two of these, 'Barrowe' (containing 47.5 acres) and a common pasture called 'the common hills' (38.75 acres),[12] were combined to create Barrow Common. The 1755 Enclosure Act redefined rights in the southern section of the parish, granting Barrow Common to the use of the poor in exchange for converting the rest of the 'brecks' into 'the sole property of the Lord of the Manor'.[13] The act stated that the lord owned the 'piece of unenclosed land ... called Barrow-hills' which was to become common land; but it did not state explicitly in whom ownership was to be vested after the creation of Barrow Common. By 1841 the lord's ownership appears to have been forgotten, as the tithe apportionment stated that Barrow Common was both owned and occupied by the 'Common Rights Owners'.[14] Nevertheless, during the 20th century ownership of the soil of Barrow Common has been with the owners of the Brancaster Hall Estate, with which it was sold in 1922 and 1991, and registered under the Commons Registration Act in 1968.[15]

Thornham

In contrast to those at Brancaster, the coastal commons at Thornham (CL 41 and CL 56) were subject to enclosure. The Thornham Enclosure Act (1794) and Award (1797) divided the marshes in two, awarding the lord of the manor, George Hogg, the 'Commonable Marshes or Low Common' west of Staithe Road, while decreeing that the marshes lying to the east 'shall be and remain Common of Pasture, to be used and enjoyed as a Stinted Common by the several Proprietors thereof'.[16] The award evidently extinguished the lord of the manor's interest in the grazing to the east; what is not clear is whether the award intended to extinguish his ownership of the soil and replace that with ownership by the stintholders in undivided shares. The wording used in later Thornham manorial court books when transfers of stints were recorded suggests that it was assumed that the marsh was, indeed, still common land.[17] But uncertainty persisted, even after registration. In 1975 the commons commissioner noted that 'the 1797 Award contains no clear indication as to how the ownership of [CL 41] was to become vested, probably because nobody at that time thought that the ownership was of any practical consequence.' He judged that the common was a stinted pasture, and that ownership should be vested in the Public Trustee (under the terms of the Law of Property Act 1925, which prevented the holding of land in undivided shares).[18]

Grazing rights

If complexity and a degree of uncertainty characterize the evolution of property rights, the patterns of use-rights in Brancaster and Thornham exhibit similar characteristics. The role of common land in the local agrarian economy changed at enclosure, while the range and variety of resources yielded by the coastal commons, in particular, has meant that grazing (the dominant and persisting economic value of common land in the uplands) has played a much smaller part in the spectrum of use-rights in this case study.

Before enclosure, however, pasture rights dominated. Grazing rights in the early-modern period have to be viewed in the context of a distinctive feature of Norfolk sheep-corn husbandry, the 'foldcourse' system. A foldcourse was a section of a village's lands over which a sheep flock (often the lord of the manor's demesne flock) had exclusive grazing rights. Folding sheep on the arable land played an important part in the sheep-corn system, the sheep fertilizing the land with their dung and breaking the soil down with their hooves – the combined process known as the 'tathe'. Each foldcourse needed to include both open field arable land, which provided grazing in autumn and winter, and heathland or marsh, to provide summer grazing. In some parishes only parts of the fields and waste were assigned to particular flocks; in others (such as the nearby manor of Holkham), the entire parish was divided into foldcourses (Allison, 1957).

Foldcourses are recorded in both Brancaster and Thornham. By the mid 17th century the lord of Brancaster had two, referred to in 1663 as 'The Marsh Pasture or weather Grownd' and 'The Ewe Pasture or Linge Grownd'. Surveys of that year and 1670 show that the ewe foldcourse (for 700 ewes) covered the western part of the 'brecks' and the wether foldcourse (for 600 wethers) included the eastern part of the 'brecks', including Barrow Hills, and the saltmarshes (the lord's several marshes in Ramsey and East Meals, and the 'narrow marsh').[19] The traditional grazing arrangements at Thornham were described in 1730. There, a flock of 900 sheep was kept on the Ling Common and the 'brecks' and could also graze the 'half year lands', between Michaelmas (29 September) and Lady Day (25 March), when not sown with corn.[20]

The tenants had grazing rights of 'shack' or 'shackage' for their cattle on the stubble of the open fields after the crop was harvested. The normal season for 'shack' ran from Michaelmas to Lady Day, during which time enclosures were to remain open to allow livestock freedom to graze.[21] On the marshes and on the inland heaths, tenants' pasture rights were closely defined. At Brancaster they were restricted to the common marsh (from which the lord's sheep were excluded) and to grazing for 'great goods' (horses and cattle) on the 'narrow marsh' behind the village.[22] In the 'uplands' they could graze their milk cattle in Barrow and Crowsnest (a small area of common pasture adjoining to Barrow) across the autumn and winter from Michaelmas to 1 May, and in the Ling from 1 November.[23] How the size of an individual's grazing right was determined is not made explicit in the manor court records, though linkage to the size of the holding can be assumed. In 1598 an individual was said to have overcharged the common shack at Brancaster by keeping 60 cattle, when 'by reason of his holding' he should not have kept so many; while a presentment in 1606, in which a man was accused of overcharging the common pasture with 'more beasts than by right he ought to according to the rate and quantity of land in his tenure' may hint at stinting.[24]

Enclosure resulted in a major reconfiguration of grazing arrangements in both Brancaster and Thornham during the 18th century. In 1730 the lords of the manor and the landowners of Thornham came to an agreement whereby enclosure of arable land was accompanied by the removal of all sheep from the common land. At the same time the shack period for great cattle was reduced to the weeks between corn harvest and 20 November annually.[25] But completely new grazing rights regimes accompanied the formal enclosure awards of 1755 at Brancaster and 1797 at Thornham. At Brancaster the act preserved Barrow Common for the poorer commoners, permitting each eligible household rights for 'Two commonable Cows or Heifers, or for a Mare and Foal, or for Two Horses'.[26] Whereas the Brancaster enclosure made no arrangements for the marsh commons, that at Thornham instituted a stinting system on the marshes, as noted above. There were to be 49 grazing rights on the commonable marsh in respect of the common-right houses in Thornham, the owners of each house being permitted to graze 'two Cows or heifers or one Cow or one heifer and one Gelding colt Mare filly or female ass with or without a foal'.[27] The owners of the grazing rights were to have power, as a body, to lessen or increase the value of stints and to alter the kinds of animals permitted to be grazed, introducing a degree of flexibility not always found in stinting awards. As often occurred once grazing rights were expressed in numerical terms, a market in stints developed, leading to a monopoly of rights coming into the hands of the lords of the manor.[28] By the time of registration under the Commons Registration Act 1965, the lord had acquired almost all of the 49 stints.[29]

Other common rights

The wide range of ecosystems represented on the different areas of common provided a variety of other resources which could be exploited, some under common of estovers, others apparently by local custom, which it is difficult to categorize under the normal classification of common use-rights. Manor court orders and presentments referring to the taking of gorse ('whin' or 'furze'), bracken, rushes and reeds make it clear that these species were exploited and that access to them was controlled by by-law by the 16th century. The Brancaster Enclosure Act of 1755 formalized fuel rights on Barrow Common for the poorer inhabitants (those occupying houses with an annual value of less than £5), confirming their right to cut 'furze' for fuel for their dwelling houses in perpetuity.[30]

Frequent references occur in 16th- and 17th-century sources to the gathering of other resources from the marshes, dunes and foreshore – for example, fishing with stake nets and by spearing, collecting shellfish, shooting and snaring wildfowl and collecting marram grass. References to digging the roots of 'sea hulver' (sea holly, *Eryngium maritimum*), suggest that local men might respond to a new market for a local resource: presentments are recorded at Brancaster across the 17th century from 1625 to 1689, probably reflecting the fashion for candied 'eryngo' as a cure-all and aphrodisiac (Thirsk, 2007, pp199, 352, note 8).[31] The legal basis for the gathering of these resources is by no means clear: some probably represent customary practice rather than formal common right; but they appear to have been viewed as communal resources nonetheless. Deep-seated custom thus probably underlies the assemblage of rights on both Brancaster and Thornham marshes, referred to collectively as 'samphire rights', which were registered by numerous individuals under the Commons Registration Act 1965. The spectrum of rights included gathering vegetation, taking wildlife, and digging sand and shingle. Specific rights claimed included rights to take samphire, seaweed, sea lavender, estovers, fish, bait and shellfish, wildfowl and game, and sand and shingle. Both marsh samphire (a local delicacy) and sea lavender ('sold in bunches to tourists, as a popular radiator adornment after a coastal holiday') (Mabey 1996, pp97–99, 111–112) had a monetary value as a cash crop, stretching the concept of 'necessary' use-rights. Despite the fact that collecting samphire and sea lavender appears to have been a deeply rooted tradition in north Norfolk (de Soissons, 1993, p58), no references to either species has been found in the earlier sources recording the local management of common rights.

Governance

Active manorial governance was in evidence at Brancaster during the 16th and 17th centuries. Courts leet, generally held annually in the autumn, include presentments against breaches of agrarian by-laws and the imposition of new orders, and a separate court, the *curia admiralitatis* or 'Port Court', protected the lord's rights and the exercise of 'good neighbourhood' on the foreshore.[32] The frequency of orders and presentments concerning common land in the manor court records declines from the mid 17th century and later court books (covering the years 1860 to 1935) are largely silent on common land management, save for the occasional appointment of a pinder or common reeve.[33] No agrarian orders or by-laws have been found in early-modern court records from Thornham;[34] but the court there made orders on a range of offences in 1785 and 1786, including grazing, estovers, the taking of clay and gravel, and use of oyster lays, perhaps indicating a growing emphasis on establishing property rights on the eve of parliamentary enclosure.[35] The key agents in enforcing the orders of the manor courts were the 'pinders' (*imparcatores*) appointed by the courts. Their role was spelled out by the court leet at Brancaster in 1565 as 'taking all cattle grazing at large in the closed season (*tempore seperali*) causing damage in the corn and cornfields of the lord's tenants and impounding those cattle in the lord's pound (*parco*)'.[36] The emphasis of the policing they undertook was thus predominantly on the protection of open fields and shack lands, rather than the management of the saltmarsh commons.[37]

Regulation of common rights

The early-modern manor court records for Brancaster are rich in orders and presentments concerning the regulation of common rights. The familiar litany of offences associated with grazing rights is recorded: overcharging the common, allowing diseased animals to graze and infringing by-laws (the substance of which is not always stated) that regulated the types of animals or the times at which grazing was permitted. A presentment of 1603 which stated that the offender had acted 'against the custom formerly used by the lord's tenants and inhabitants of the vill of Brancaster' suggests a strong tradition of local regulation.[38]

The manor court's numerous references to the exercise of common of estovers illustrate some of the thinking underpinning the management of these rights in the early modern period. As elsewhere in lowland England, 'whins' or 'furze' (i.e. gorse, *Ulex europeanus*) was valuable as a fuel resource, particularly among the rural poor (Neeson, 1993, pp159–160, 174–176; Shaw-Taylor, 2002, pp75–76). A series of court orders between 1556 and 1598 is probably to be interpreted as an attempt to preserve gorse on the common as a resource for the poor, the implied assumption being that those with holdings of land would have access to gorse on their own property. As was the case elsewhere, the Brancaster court forbade the taking of gorse by cart, but allowed the poor to collect it as long as they carried it in bundles on their heads. In each case the ban on taking the fuel by cart was time limited – for three years in 1556, 1567 and1569, and for four years in 1598, perhaps suggesting that these were periodic attempts to allow the gorse to regenerate.[39] Pressure on the resource is implied by the order of 1567, which limited the amount to be taken to what one man could take in one day, and the thrust of the court's regulation of the resource seems to have been specifically to ensure a fuel supply for the poor. The order of 1569 drew a distinction between inhabitants who had horses and carts (and were forbidden from taking gorse for three years) and the poor, who could take it in bundles. This order should be seen in the context of other entries concerning the exploitation of gorse. The previous spring, the court had forbidden inhabitants from collecting whins on the lord's or the tenants' several lands under a penalty of 3d per bundle, and the following spring ten men were presented and amerced because their wives had taken whins growing on the lord's several lands, contrary to the court's by-law.[40] The landed had access to whins on their own land; the landless, excluded from these private resources, were therefore given priority on the common. When fuel rights on Barrow Common were formalized by the Enclosure Act of 1755, there are even hints that the species was being deliberately planted: the expenses of enclosure included the cost of sowing 'whin seeds'.[41]

The late 18th-century verdicts of Thornham court illustrate continuing pressure on gorse. Market demand for the fuel is in evidence in an order from 1785, which imposed heavy fines (£2 for every cart load; £3 for every wagon load) on anyone caught selling whins from Thornham Lings 'to any out town person'. But the driving force behind the order may not have been simply preservation of fuel for the local community. The same court also recorded an agreement between the tenants and the lord, allowing the lord to stake out an area of 10 acres of the Ling common from which no whins were to be cut by anyone in the parish, the aim being to create an exclusion zone to provide cover for game.[42]

Pressure on other species of vegetation is also in evidence. Between 1598 and 1603 the Brancaster court imposed seasonal (and, in one instance, quantitative) restrictions on the taking of rushes, reeds and bracken.[43] In 1627 the same principle that applied to whins – namely, that they could be taken 'by burdens' carried on the back, but not by cart – was applied to the cutting of bracken and rushes.[44] All suggest that demand for these resources was sufficiently high to require sophisticated regulatory regimes by the early 17th century.

The need to foster 'good neighbourhood' between those exploiting communal resources is also apparent in the work of the 'port court' or *curia admiralitatis* in managing the use of the foreshore in Brancaster. Fishing rights, some of which were held as tenancies of the manor,[45] were closely controlled. Outsiders (like the man from Burnham Deepdale presented for spearing flat fish ('prickinge for buttkyns') in 1567) were amerced.[46] The court oversaw the placing of stake nets across the creeks, forbidding anyone from lifting nets set in place by someone else, from digging up another's stakes, or from placing his nets where they annoyed others, and fining people for taking fish from other people's nets.[47] Similar entries, both against outsiders and against breaches of 'good neighbourhood', occur in relation to fowling and the taking of shellfish. Two entries from the same sitting of the court in 1570 illustrate different aspects of the court's concerns. A desire to punish un-neighbourly conduct is implied by the presentment of one individual, who was also amerced for removing fish by night from another man's net, and for taking a curlew from a snare set by another; a concern for environmental damage which threatened the sustainability of the resource is seen in the case of two men who had collected shells with iron rakes, so that the 'shelf' or shellfish bed was 'utterly ruined and devastated'.[48]

The complexity of the factors which lay behind the court's attempts to manage the exploitation of the foreshore is illustrated in relation to the digging of sea holly roots from the dunes at Brancaster during the 17th century. The wording of the presentments suggests, first, that offenders were infringing upon the lord of the manor's rights by digging the roots without licence. In the earliest, from 1625, two men were presented for digging the root in the Meals 'without licence of the lord of this manor, and they carried them away to the prejudice of the lord and in bad example to others'.[49] The core of the offence lay in 'breaking the lord's soil', a general prohibition on manorial waste, except in particular circumstances, such as when exercising turbary rights. One of the offenders continued to dig and in 1629 the court noted that environmental damage had resulted from his activities: 'the Meeles are greatly decayed'.[50] Since most of the dunes at Brancaster were deemed to be the lord's freehold in the 17th century, digging sea holly root infringed the lord's privileges. The earlier presentments may therefore have been attempts to prevent the taking of sea holly from developing into a customary right, by repeatedly amercing an offender (perhaps one among many) to establish that the gathering of the newly valuable roots represented an unwarranted infringement of the lord's rights. However, some of the presentments from the 1650s onwards were against men from neighbouring villages, in one case (in 1651) their exploitation of the plant being not only to the lord's damage, but also to the 'prejudice of his tenantes'.[51] It seems very possible that digging the roots had by then become a customary practice, which only in some circumstances entered the court record. Perhaps the actions of neighbouring villagers conflicted with the interests of Brancaster men, for whom sea holly roots provided a useful source of income. Certainly, taking sea holly roots is thought to have continued in Norfolk until the 19th century, strongly suggesting that it came to be accepted as a customary right on the seaboard commons despite manor court presentments such as those at Brancaster.[52]

Post-manorial governance

At Brancaster the parish council seems to have assumed some responsibility for the management of the commons by the early 20th century. It entered into agreements with the Royal West Norfolk Golf Club over the use of the dunes, as noted above, and negotiated with the War Department between 1949 and 1952 to remove the legacy of barbed wire left by the World War II radar station on Barrow Common.[53]

At Thornham there was a sharp break in the institutional framework as a result of the enclosure award in 1797, which established a new management institution on the newly stinted common marshes by requiring annual meetings of common rights owners, and regulation by elected reeves. The new institution was relatively resilient, and continued to operate into the 20th century despite the diminishing number of stint owners. Three 'Commons Reeves', elected annually by a meeting of common right owners held in the porch of Thornham church, were charged with improving and regulating the common, ensuring that no cattle strayed from the common, impounding trespassing stock, and maintaining a rule book.[54] Income was raised by an annual fee paid by the common-right house owners for each animal grazed on the marsh. The surviving minute book, covering the years 1924 to 1951, reveals the concerns occupying the minds of stint owners and reeves in the first half of the 20th century. As stints came to be concentrated in the hands of the lords of the manor, so the annual rights holders' meeting came to be dominated by the lords, their representative chairing the meetings and signing the minutes. Reeves continued to be elected into the 1940s, though the number fell from three to two, and on one occasion only the two reeves attended and they were obliged to reappoint themselves. There was a high degree of stability with only three individuals performing this role, one of them, the lord of the manor's bailiff Jacob Walker, serving as reeve almost continually throughout this period.[55]

The minute book shows the stint owners actively managing Thornham Marsh. During the early 1920s they took two villagers to court over alleged trespasses with geese, in contravention of the 1797 Enclosure Award, which forbade the grazing of geese or goats. When, in 1929, a discrepancy was found between a grazier's entitlement and the number of animals he was grazing, he was required to pay for the surplus stock 'at the usual rate of £1 per head', suggesting that the stint owners were willing to take a flexible approach. In 1930, the opening of the common to livestock was put back from 1 May to 13 May, since 'this Extra fortnight would make all the difference in the growth of the feed on the Common'. In 1951 it was agreed that all cattle should be treated for warble fly before being turned onto the common and tagged, and the number recorded. The stint owners' meeting oversaw the repair of gates, fences, roads and culverts and the maintenance of the 'fen eyes' which drained the common, as well as dealing with a range of wider environmental maintenance matters affecting open spaces, such as the removal of rubbish, manure heaps, tents and unwanted electricity poles. They negotiated with central government over military use of the Low Common during and after World War II.[56] The presence of a local management institution created by the Enclosure Award of 1797 appears to have enabled active and effective management of Thornham Common across the first half of the 20th century.

The contrasting histories exhibited by the commons within the case study are striking. The formalization of rights in Thornham and Barrow commons under parliamentary enclosure awards and, in the case of Thornham, the creation of an active and effective management body contrasts strongly with the strength of custom in the uses of the marshes at Brancaster and the role that it played in the evolution of property rights.

The commons today

Commons registration and the 1965 Act

As might be expected, given the distinctive historical development of land management in Brancaster and Thornham, the commons registers produced by the registration process under the Commons Registration Act 1965 contrast strongly with those of the upland case studies – both as to the types of rights registered and the manner of registration.

The form in which registrations were entered in the commons registers is relatively standardized and therefore suggestive of the coordination of claims organized by the parish councils of Thornham and Brancaster. Many common rights are registered to the sole owners of properties – some in the immediate locality, and some in distant locations (e.g. Derby and London). In many cases different members of the same family registered common rights separately, and therefore hold discrete rights in their own name. In other cases, however, common rights were registered in the names of five or more members of the same family. The register for Brancaster Common (CL 65) discloses numerous examples of this phenomenon: one entry[57] records a right to herbage, estovers, samphire, soil, fish, shellfish, bait and wildfowl registered in the names of five different members of one family at a single address; another[58] records a common right vested in seven family members, and one[59] vests a common right in no fewer than nine members of one local family. In these cases the registrations, having become final without amendment, give each rights holder a proportionate share of the common rights. As far as the individual ownership of rights is concerned, therefore, the outcome of the registration process seems somewhat arbitrary. This highlights a defect in the registration process under the 1965 Act, which provided no mechanism for the correction of this sort of anomaly where the error had been subsequently discovered.

The type of common rights registered under the 1965 Act displays, in each case, a significant departure from the organization of land management in the manorial past. There are very few pasture rights, and the majority of registered rights (such as wildfowling and 'samphire rights') are un-quantified and unique to this locality. They are also difficult to categorize within the accepted parameters of common rights recognized in English law.

Pasture rights

In striking contrast with the upland case studies, where common pasture rights dominate the commons registers, in the Norfolk case study, they today constitute a marginal category. The register for Brancaster Common (CL 65) records five entries of grazing rights; three of these record rights to graze small numbers of cattle (five in each case) and geese, another a right to graze two cows or two horses, and one a right to graze one horse and one foal. Similarly, there are only five entries of grazing rights on the Thornham Common register (CL 41), two of which also extend to Thornham Low Common (CL 56). There are, however, a large number of pasture rights registered on the Brancaster Saltings and Foreshore (CL 124). There is some grazing on Thornham Common; but the grazing rights on the other commons in the case study – for example, those registered on Barrow Common (CL 159) – are not exercised today.

Samphire rights

The registers in this case study are unique in recording 'samphire rights', not found elsewhere in England or Wales. The extent of the samphire rights claimed is not, however, uniform across the registers for the commons at Brancaster and Thornham, and there are also variations within each register. On Brancaster Common (CL 65) the 'standard' registration of samphire rights comprises 'herbage, estovers, samphire, soil, fish, shellfish, bait and wildfowl'. The samphire rights registered on Thornham (CL 41) also include seaweed, sea lavender, game, sand and shingle, but do not include herbage. There are very large numbers of samphire rights on both registers: 117 samphire rights on that for CL 41 and approximately 300 on the register for CL 65. There are also large numbers of samphire rights registered on Brancaster Marshes (CL 124) and on the intertidal area north of the marsh (the 'Saltings and Foreshore', CL 161). There is less uniformity in the way in which the rights have been recorded in these two cases. On CL 124, for instance, the majority of entries record rights to samphire, seaweed ('tangle'), shellfish, sea lavender, fish, bait, estovers, wildfowl and game. Some entries also reserve rights to soil, sand and/or shingle, some to take reeds, and a few to 'herbage' (which is otherwise undefined).

There are some variations in the land over which the samphire registrations apply within each register. At Brancaster, although full samphire rights apply across the whole common in the majority of cases, rights claimed over the National Trust land on CL 65 are limited in some cases to herbage, estovers and samphire – the remaining common rights claimed in these cases having been declared unproved by a commons commissioner's ruling in 1980.[60] This concerned objections to the provisional registration of rights against different parts of the common. The decision of the commons commissioner recognized a differentiation of rights registered over:

- the area of land owned by the Nature Conservancy Council in the north of the CL unit, including Scolt Head Island;
- the 'Holkham Land' in the east of the unit belonging to the Holkham Estate; and
- the National Trust land to the south of Scolt Head island owned by the Trust.

The subdivision of CL 65 into three units is also reflected in the fact that there are a small number of entries recording full samphire rights over the Holkham land and not the remainder of the CL unit.

The proprietary character of the registered samphire rights is also unusual. On Brancaster Common (CL 65) they are registered as rights in gross. On Thornham Common the rights were initially claimed as rights in gross. These were challenged and commons commissioners' hearings were held in 1974 and 1975. The commons commissioner's decision, given in 1975, [61] confirmed an agreement reached between counsel for the landowners and the commoners which varied the samphire rights in order to convert them into rights appurtenant to the homes/addresses of the various claimants. The rights, when confirmed, were therefore registered as rights appurtenant to specific addresses.

It is clear from the evidence presented to the commons commissioners in both the Brancaster and Thornham cases that the claim to common rights was put forward 'on the basis of a customary right for local inhabitants'.[62] A customary right of common for a fluctuating body of persons is not recognized by English law, however, and the only legal basis on which rights in gross of the kind claimed could be proved would be either under the common law of prescription, or the doctrine of lost modern grant. In both cases, the common law rules proceed on the basis of a presumed grant by the landowner at some point in the past. In order to establish a prescriptive right, the claimant to a right in gross must show that he has acquired the right by exercising it[63] for the requisite period (in practice, 20 years, as presumptive evidence of user since time immemorial) (Megarry and Wade, 2000, para 18–132). The commons commissioner in the Brancaster case found sufficient use for these purposes in only two cases. Additionally, the user by the claimant must have been 'as of right' (*nec clam, nec vi, nec precario*) – it will not suffice if the exercise has been tolerated by the landowner, as this will imply permission. The use of the foreshore for bait digging, fishing and recreation is not usually an exercise 'as of right' – its use by the public for such purposes is tolerated by the Crown and is not a matter of 'right'. In the Brancaster case the commons commissioner therefore concluded, on the evidence:[64]

> *If it is sought to establish the rights as rights by prescription then on my view of the evidence … and having regard to the situation and character of the Unit Land and the normal activities of persons living on or near the sea coast, creeks and marshland, it seems to me that the enjoyment of these activities is more readily attributed to tolerance or tacit permission by the landowner, than to use as of right. On this ground … I hold that the claim to rights if based on prescription fails.*

Accordingly, the objections to the rights claimed over the foreshore land (i.e. the land below the median high water mark), over land to the east of Burnham Harbour and over a strip of land north of Deepdale marsh were all upheld and confirmation of the registrations was refused.

Estovers and ancillary rights

Sarah Birtles notes, in her analysis of the statutory commons in Norfolk, that estovers present particular problems (Birtles, 1988, p88). There are 24 commons in Norfolk, including those in this case study, that are subject to rights of estover (such as a right to take underwood or bracken). The right, like turbary, is traditionally attached to property and qualified by the principle of necessity – its extent is determined by the needs of the dominant tenement at the time of the grant. These characteristics are often absent in Norfolk and the commons in this case study provide a good example of the problems to which this gives rise.

There are 52 entries of estovers on the register for CL 124 (the saltings and foreshore), 298 entries on the register for CL 65 (Brancaster Common), 20 for CL 159 (Barrow Common), 51 for CL 56 Thornham Low Common, and 39 confirmed registrations of estovers on CL 41 (Thornham Common). Except on Barrow Common, where they are described as rights 'to take fuel' or 'to cut furze', 'estovers' are not further defined in the registration entries; but this category of right traditionally applies to give the holder the right to take the produce from the land of another – usually timber, firewood, bracken or rushes. The right to estovers – especially for fuel or wood – is usually attached to a building and is an appurtenant right (Gadsden, 1988, §3.67). And in most cases the right is limited to what is necessary for the support and repair of the building to which the right is attached. It is extremely unusual to come across rights of estovers that are not attached to specific tenements or buildings – partly because the nature of the right itself renders this a necessary qualification, and partly because the courts have been reluctant to recognize the right to sever estovers from land.

It should also be noted that the commons commissioner in the Thornham Common case expressed clear reservations as to whether the samphire rights under consideration there could, as a matter of law, subsist as rights in gross (as opposed to rights appurtenant to land – for example, to a cottage or house owned by the claimant): [65]

> *These registrations are ... as they now stand, of rights in gross (not attached to any land). Those who took samphire etc. from the Unit Land did so or may have done so because they thought that this was the right of any member of the public or of any inhabitant. There was no evidence to establish any such right on this basis, even if (which I doubt) it is recognised by law. Nevertheless, a person who in fact takes a profit from the land of another in circumstances in which such taking can properly be regarded as referable to the land he owns or occupies may by prescription acquire the right to such profit, notwithstanding that the things he did were done by him supposedly because he was an inhabitant or member of the public.*[66]

Yet, all of the rights of estovers on CL 65, and the other constituent rights in the standard 'samphire rights' entries, are registered as rights in gross (i.e. as personal rights) separate from property. Birtles (1998, p88) concludes that 'the registers chronicle the breakdown of the original understanding about rights which has been going on slowly since the Middle Ages and which has accelerated since the decline of manorial discipline'. The registers for Brancaster and Thornham illustrate this anomaly very clearly. Quite apart from the problem of the nature of the rights themselves (discussed below), the fact that many of the rights (e.g. to take samphire or sea lavender) are registered as rights held in gross would appear to represent an abrogation of the traditional principles by which common rights were managed. This also reflects the fact that if no objection was made to the provisional registrations claimed under the 1965 Act these became final and effectively created new common rights in some cases, or reinvented existing common rights with the additional *characteristics* (e.g. as freely transferable property rights) claimed when the first registrations were made.

Adaptations of property rights

The uncertainty about the relationship between the historic commons and the rights registered under the Commons Registration Act 1965, many of which do not appear to have any basis in historical precedent, highlights a facet of the 1965 Act not seen in the other case studies: its use to turn social practices of unproven legal provenance into common property rights, and to reinvent rights of surer customary origin in ways that changed their essential attributes. This is a story about the (re)invention of property rights as much as it is about their adaptation. The use of the registration process to reinvent property rights in this manner had two consequences meriting closer examination: the rights it created are unique and difficult to categorize within the accepted parameters of common property rights, and they find their expression in a different sense of locality and community than common rights found elsewhere.

The unique nature of the rights in the Norfolk registers is reflected in the difficulty one encounters when trying to categorize them within the accepted legal categories of right in English law. Most common rights are *profits à prendre* – the right to take the produce of land belonging to another (see Chapter 4, p52). Rights to collect samphire, sea lavender, soil, bait and shingle might properly be viewed as profits; but their legal classification remains elusive. Gadsden (1988, §3.76) comments of samphire rights that 'this type of right does not fall into any of the normal classes of rights but, as water related products are concerned, it may be possible to view them as an exceptional variant of the right to take fish'(i.e. the common right of piscary). Categorizing rights to take fish or shellfish in this way may – just – be feasible; but samphire, sea lavender and shingle are simply products of the soil and therefore difficult to view as derivative of a right of piscary. The right to take wildlife found on another's property (animals *ferae naturae*) is also problematic: it can subsist as a *profit à prendre* and as such is registrable as a common right, but must be distinguished from a sporting right, which is neither. A right to take game (such as wild ducks) by shooting, which is exercised principally for pleasure and not to provide food, is not a profit and therefore not properly a right of common (*Re Lustleigh Cleave* [1978]). Although the registers for Brancaster Common, Brancaster marshes and the foreshore (CL 65, CL 161 and CL 124), and also Thornham (CL 41), contain numerous rights to wildfowl, these are, in practice, used mainly for sporting purposes. Whether they should have been given the legal status of common rights is questionable. The decisions of various commons commissioners elsewhere on this subject are difficult to reconcile and unsatisfactory (they are reviewed by Gadsden, 1988, §3.87, 3.88).

The link between the common resource represented by common land and notions of 'community' and 'locality' is usually captured by the fact that common rights are appurtenant to land adjacent (or near) to the common, and limited in extent to the needs of the dominant land. Modern statutory law on commons also starts from the assumption of an indissoluble link between local management and the character of rights as appurtenant to land. This is exemplified by section 9 of the Commons Act 2006, which prohibits the severance of appurtenant rights from the dominant tenement. The strong association between notions of locality, sustainable management and the nature of rights as appurtenant to locally held land is very clearly seen in the Eskdale and Elan Valley case studies (see pp102–103, 150). This feature of common rights on many agricultural commons, such as Eskdale, was also expressed through rules such as levancy and couchancy and the manner in which livestock grazing was formerly controlled by the manorial courts.

The Norfolk registers offer an entirely different perspective on issues of community and locality. The rights registered at Brancaster were mostly expressed as rights in gross, and *not* attached to specific dominant tenements (such as land, houses or cottages). This has had the effect of maintaining rights within local families in a period of property price inflation, when they may (if attached to specific houses or land) have passed out of the control of the local community, given the number of local properties purchased as holiday or second homes by people living far from the Norfolk coast. This phenomenon raises interesting (and difficult) issues, however, given the nature of the rights that have been registered.

It requires us to rethink the assumed link between local management and the nature of common rights as appurtenant to land, thereby departing from a territorial understanding of 'locality' and stressing the importance of social ties. On the other hand, the manner of registration has, to some extent, contributed to a weakening of the link between community, locality and rights. Some rights were registered in multiple names (examples given above include rights registered to up to nine members of a family), and many rights have subsequently been divided and sold, passing into the hands of owners with no local connection. This has proved to be controversial and problematic. Guidance was issued by Norfolk County Council in April 2009 that they will recognize a maximum of four persons as the owners of registered common rights (Norfolk County Council, 2009, p4). If a right is registered to more than four persons, therefore, it cannot be transferred unless the current rights holders clarify which four of them constitute the legal owners of the right. In cases of joint ownership or multiple registrations, in principle the joint owners of a single registered right cannot take more produce from the common than an individual holder of a similar right. In the case of rights that are unquantified by reference to the number, volume or quantity of produce that may be taken from the common – such as the right to take wildfowl or samphire – it is difficult to see how this rule could be enforced where the right has been partitioned and sold, and there must be a theoretical potential for the sustainable management of the common to be affected if this practice became widespread.

According to local commoners, the division and sale of rights endangers the social sustainability of local commons management, and the Scolt Head Common Right Holders' Association opposes this practice as applied to unquantified wildfowling rights. [67] The policy of Norfolk County Council is also controversial. The division and sale of wildfowling rights is mainly attributable to people without local connections whose primary consideration is their monetary value. It is profitable to bring people to Brancaster to shoot for sporting purposes, and little income is generated from the birds themselves (whose carcasses are sometimes left on the common). The apportionment of rights means that the number of rights holders has multiplied. And although purchasers acquire a proportion of an unquantified wildfowling right, this inevitably increases the pressure on the common resource. The commoners in the research sample were aware that the rights of common are, by custom and their nature as *profits à prendre*, limited to the satisfaction of the holder's essential needs – and that wildfowling as a purely sporting activity is not within the ambit of the common rights.

These concerns will to some extent be addressed by Part 1 of the Commons Act 2006. The 2006 Act provides for the apportionment of common rights that are appurtenant to land where the dominant land is severed on sale or transfer – but there is no provision for the apportionment of rights in gross (2006 Act, section 8). It permits the transfer of rights in gross; but a transfer will only be legally effective upon registration of 'the transferee' as the owner of 'the right' in the commons register (2006 Act, section 12). An application to register a transfer can be made by 'the registered owner of the right of common in gross' or 'the transferee' of that right (SI 2008/1961, schedule 4, para 6). There is no provision for the registration of ownership of an apportioned part of a right in gross. Moreover, when updating the registers during the transitional period following the bringing into force of Part 1 of the 2006 Act, the only prior transactions that can be entered on the register are transfers of 'the right' – not transfers of an apportioned part of it (2006 Act, schedule 3, para 3 (d)).

It follows that where a change in the ownership of an apportioned part of a right has taken place, it will be necessary for all co-owners of the right to act together to register alterations in the registered identity of the rights holders – they will collectively constitute 'the owner' for these purposes. Transferring an apportioned part of an unquantified right (e.g. to take wildfowl) will therefore be impossible in a form having legal effect, without the cooperation of all owners of the unquantified right to which it relates. Whether an unquantified right (such as that to take wildfowl or samphire) can be apportioned at common law in the first place remains an open question. The guidance note on Part 1 of the Commons Act 2006 issued by the Department for Environment, Food and Rural Affairs (Defra) to commons registration authorities is clear on this point:

> *... a right of common can be apportioned only if it is quantified, and attached to land. Common law provides that a right cannot be apportioned if it is unquantified ... because apportionment of such rights would be likely to increase the burden on the common. In particular, the following rights cannot be apportioned, and any application for that purpose must be refused: an unquantified right of turbary, an unquantified right of estovers ... or an unquantified right of piscary.* (Defra, 2010b, para 8.3.21)

This guidance will be applicable to many of the registered common rights in the Norfolk case study. Where an unquantified right (e.g. to take wildfowl, sea lavender or samphire) has not been apportioned prior to the coming into force of Part 1 of the 2006 Act, it seems clear that its apportionment thereafter will be impermissible.

Commons governance

Three voluntary associations play a large part in the management of the commons at Brancaster. Local control of wildfowling is maintained through the local gun club, and shooting is only permitted over the common saltmarshes by its members. The legal basis of this institution has never been tested, but it provides evidence, nevertheless, of 'good neighbourliness' being used to control external influences on the commons management. The Scolt Head and District Common Rightholders' Association also plays a leading role in managing the exercise of common rights. The large number of rights holders (over 300), coupled with the fact that the commons register is outdated, makes it difficult to either identify all the commoners or to monitor their activities. These difficulties are reflected in the slowness of the local processes for making communal decisions on commons management. This is viewed in a positive manner by the association, however, and is good for precautionary reasons.

The third body with an active role is the Brancaster Commons Committee, founded in 2000. It is an executive committee bringing together various stakeholders, and to some extent embodies many features (in a non-statutory form) of a statutory commons council as envisaged by Part 2 of the Commons Act 2006. The stakeholders who participate are the National Trust's area manager; five members of the common rights holders' association (one of whom acts as chairman); the parish council, district council and county councils; the Brancaster fairways advisory committee; the Royal West Norfolk Golf Club (as invited); Natural England (as invited); and the National Trust property manager (as an observer only). Its proceedings are governed by formal constitution: the *Brancaster Commons Committee Rules for the Conduct of Business*.[68]

The committee is a very effective forum for resolving environmental governance issues and raising management questions with Natural England. The discussion often revolves around the harbour and mooring, issues that are claimed to be interfering with the exercise of common rights to shellfish and other rights, as the common rights holders find it difficult to claim their own mooring rights. The biggest challenge today is the management of recreational aspects of the commons use (sailing, power boating and the impact of access under the Countryside and Rights of Way Act 2000). Access to the common land owned by the National Trust is governed by the National Trust Act 1907, and therefore falls outside the 'right to roam' under the 2000 Act (2000 Act, section 15). Recreational fishing is also a management problem.

Barrow Common (CL 159) provides an interesting example of a lowland common that formerly provided rough livestock grazing, but which has fallen largely into disuse. The regeneration of the common as a community resource for open-air recreation is being overseen by the Barrow Common Management Committee, a body established in 2004 with a membership comprising a representative of the landowners (the Hartop Trust), two Brancaster parish councillors and four members of the Barrow Common Right Holders' Association. The committee adopted a management plan for the regeneration of the common in 2005. This divides the common into eight management zones and prioritizes work in each zone to eradicate invasive saplings, prevent further gorse and bracken encroachment, and improve footpaths. The management plan is based on the premise that 'it is extremely unlikely that the area will be required for grazing by any of the common right holders and ... the primary aim of management is to retain the common as a pleasant place for air and recreation for the whole village, providing well maintained footpaths and encouraging a diverse wildlife population' (Barrow Common Management Committee, 2005, p7). The emphasis is on achieving a balance between recreational use and the promotion of biodiversity, and the wholesale clearance of trees and vegetation is not to be promoted, especially where it provides valuable nesting sites and cover for birds and mammals. This initiative, like the Brancaster Commons Committee, is a good example of a voluntary management model for non-agricultural commons that displays many of the features sought by the Commons Act 2006 for statutory management through commons councils.

Environmental governance

The application of environmental governance mechanisms in the Norfolk case study is less visible than in the upland case studies. This is explicable, in part, by the fact that none of the Common Agricultural Policy instruments are deployed to promote sustainable management – there are no management agreements within the Rural Development Plan for England and the land-use controls introduced elsewhere through the single payment scheme have no application. Because the common is not agricultural in orientation, as is reflected by the registered rights and the fact that (with the exception of Thorham Common) no sheep or cattle are grazed by the commoners today, there are no single farm payment entitlements registered on most of the land within the case study. The principal governance mechanisms therefore flow from the statutory environmental designations within the case study, of which there are a number. As we shall see, although the case study hosts a large number of environmental designations, the practical impact of statutory conservation measures upon daily management is negligible.

Statutory environmental designations

North Norfolk Coast Special Area of Conservation (SAC)[69]

The site covers a large area – 3207.37ha – and is characterized by coastal and sand dunes, tidal rivers, mud and sand flats, lagoons, machair, marshes and shingle. The North

Norfolk SAC is one of only two sites representing embryonic shifting dunes in the east of England and shifting dunes along the shoreline with white dunes. Fixed dunes with herbaceous vegetation are a priority feature.

North Norfolk Coast Special Protection Area (SPA)[70]
The North Norfolk Coast SPA extends far beyond the parameters of the case study. It contains extensive shingle deposits at Blakeney Point and (within the case study itself) major sand dunes at Scolt Head and extensive reedbeds at Brancaster. Because of the diversity of intertidal and marine habitats on the saltmarshes, the site has an enormous biodiversity importance. Large numbers of protected bird species breed on the saltmarshes, including various species of terns, waders, bittern and wetland raptors. Migratory waders that overwinter on the site include large numbers of Icelandic pink-footed geese.

North Norfolk Coast Ramsar Wetlands[71]
The North Norfolk Coast Ramsar Wetlands is a low-lying barrier coastal site extending for 40km from Holme to Weybourne. It encompasses a variety of freshwater and marine habitats, which support wildfowl in winter and several nationally rare breeding bird species. It supports at least three *British Red Data Book* and nine nationally scarce vascular plants, one *British Red Data Book* lichen and 38 *British Red Data Book* invertebrates. It supports almost 100,000 waterfowl in winter each year.

North Norfolk Coast Site of Special Scientific Interest (SSSI)
The SSSI in its current form was notified in 1986 and is a composite site made up of two National Nature Reserves at Scolt Head and Holkham, and a number of former SSSIs at Holme Dunes, Thornham Marshes, Titchwell Marshes, Brancaster Manor, Stiffkey Saltmarshes, Morston Saltmarshes, Blakeney Point, and Cley and Salthouse Marshes, with substantial additions. It includes all the common land in the case study except Barrow Common. Because of its extent, the site is divided for monitoring purposes into 73 units, the majority of which are in favourable conservation condition (96.62 per cent).

Despite the enormous differences in terms of geography, flora and fauna, the operations likely to damage the special conservation interest (OLDSIs) served with the SSSI notification mirror those in the upland case studies. In practice, their relevance to environmental management is minimal as none of the commoners were notified when the SSSI was re-notified in 1986. This is not considered to be problematic by Natural England. Natural England employs the concept of sufficiency of the common in informal discussions with the commoners so that they are aware that they can exercise their rights in so far as the environmental value of the common remains sufficient (semi-structured interview, July 2009).

The only potential problem from a conservation standpoint would be the exercise of grazing rights, which would contravene the SSSI management statement.[72] But a pragmatic view is that the reintroduction of grazing livestock on the common grazing marshes (other than Thornham Common) will never happen – and attempting to prevent the exercise of grazing rights by notifying OLDSIs to those commoners with registered grazing rights is not therefore worthwhile. The difficulties of managing cattle and sheep on the common, given the nature of the land, are such that graziers are very unlikely to reintroduce stock onto the common. At Thornham Common the position is different, as farming is still a key activity. Environmental management is delivered through a single Wildlife Enhancement Scheme (WES) agreement with the Thornham cattlegate holders, which regulates both grazing rights and reed cutting.

Scolt Head Island National Nature Reserve[73]

Scolt Head Island National Nature Reserve is the prime example of an offshore barrier island in the UK and is part of the North Norfolk Coast SSSI. Several species of terns raise broods in the shingle and sand dunes, which are two of the four habitats identified in the reserve, the other two habitats being intertidal mud and sand flats. Its international importance is due to overwintering populations of geese. The reserve is managed by Natural England. Although it is classified as a non-intervention reserve, rights of common are exercised and control of predator species is required.

Commons registration and future environmental governance

A study of Thornham Common by the Rural Planning Service in 1985 concluded that the final registers for CL 41 and CL 56 (Low Common) were 'unreliable', 'incomplete, legally questionable and out of date'. The same criticism may be made of the registers for the much larger area of common land comprising Brancaster marshes CL 65, CL 124 and CL 161. The CL 65 register records almost 300 individual entries in the rights section, but identifying the current holders of the rights recorded would be extremely difficult from the information given – many entries are no longer current and are marked by notes such as 'Moved 16 years ago, 22/8/91'[74] and 'Gone away'.[75] The difficulty in identifying current rights holders is also compounded by the fact that the rights are registered as rights in gross. It is not therefore possible to trace ownership of rights by means of tracing the transfer of ownership of the property to which they would otherwise attach – as is the case elsewhere (e.g. in the other three case studies, where the majority of rights are registered as rights appurtenant to land).

Although, as noted above, Natural England has not sought to notify the North Norfolk SSSI to individual commoners, it is clear that the problems of identifying commoners from the registers would, in any event, frustrate any attempt to do so and make it too burdensome to be of practical utility. The strategic approach used by Natural England in the upland case studies is irrelevant here due to the non-agricultural use of the common and the success of the pragmatic approach embraced by stakeholders. Ideally, reed cutting should be legally controlled in Brancaster, and to further this aim entering the common into a WES agreement could be a management priority for the future. However, the National Trust, as landowner, already monitors reed cutting and this is not therefore necessary. Local disinterest in the development of an environmental management scheme also means that the prospects for establishing statutory commons councils are of marginal importance compared to the other case studies. Voluntary bodies such as the Brancaster Commons Committee and the Barrow Common Management Committee already deal with most matters in an efficient and pragmatic way.

Conclusions

The Norfolk grazing marshes present a unique perspective on the history of sustainable land management and common rights. It is the only case study in this work in which the predominant land use is non agricultural. The commons here present a picture of a constantly shifting reinvention of property rights. And they offer an example of common land which has survived parliamentary enclosure. They also offer a different perspective on the contested nature of land use on the commons – for example, of the tension between commercial exploitation of the common resource as opposed to the primacy of the concept of 'necessary' use (as reflected, for example, in estovers as a category of common right). The coastal context also generates a different range of contested issues – for example, between mooring rights, foreshore ownership (which is itself in places uncertain) and land-use rights. Given the unique and shifting nature of the land forms over which many of the common rights are exercised, accretion and erosion are also important and sometimes problematic. The environmental management problems that they present are also quite different. Under-grazing by livestock is, for example, a problem on Barrow Common and presents issues quite different from the problems of overgrazing seen on most upland commons (including those in the other three case studies presented in Chapters 6 to 8). The coastal environment also presents a range of issues that are unique and are valued for different reasons than the upland habitats in the other case studies (e.g. as breeding and migratory habitats for wildfowl, in the context of the 1972 Ramsar Convention on International Wetlands).

This case study represents an 'invention of tradition' in relation to common land (Hobsbawm, 1983, pp1–14). Both during the enclosure movement and then during the process for the registration of common land under the Commons Registration Act 1965, the boundaries of common land and common rights have been reinvented in North Norfolk – so much so that the modern commons and common rights, far from reflecting ancient custom, are largely the product of modern phenomena. Barrow Common and Thornham Common were created by parliamentary enclosure, and many of the common rights subsisting over the common land on the nearby Brancaster marshes were created during the registration process triggered by the Commons Registration Act 1965. This reinvention of tradition both created and legitimated communal practices, and it had important social and legal consequences. The registration of rights as rights in gross permitted the development of a different conceptualization of the link between community and locality, and facilitated the maintenance of common rights within local families in subsequent periods of house price inflation. This provides a contrast to the conceptualization of property rights in many upland commons, exemplified by Eskdale and the Elan Valley (see Chapters 6 and 8) where the appurtenant character of common rights has always been understood as a prerequisite for the sustainable management of the common resource. The North Norfolk case study shows us that a de-territorialized understanding of property rights can nevertheless enhance the concept of locality. In this it aligns itself with the Ingleton case study (see Chapter 7) where the stinting system of livestock management also gave rise to a conceptualization of common rights as personal property. At the same time, the registration of common rights as personal rights with multiple owners has subsequently presented its own challenges to the maintenance of social ties of 'locality' and community, in as much as it has permitted the sale of wildfowling rights to purchasers external to the local community and with no interest in the sustainable management of the common.

The reinvention of common land was facilitated by the Commons Registration Act 1965, and, in particular, by the fact that it failed to provide for an audit of customary practices prior to provisional registration. The confirmation of rights that went unchallenged had interesting legal consequences, seen here in the creation of rights that are difficult to classify within the accepted parameters of common rights in English law, and permitting exploitation that goes beyond that normally recognized (e.g. by linking rights claimed as profits to concepts of necessary use). It is important to recognize, however, that although this might position the North Norfolk case study outside an orthodox understanding of common land, it is the case study that demonstrates the strongest sense of community in which the emphasis is on the 'commonality' of common land.

Notes

1 See http://www.defra.gov.uk/wildlife-countryside/issues/common/pdf/norfolk.pdf, http://www.norfolkcoastaonb.org.uk/mediaps/pdfuploads/pd000125.pdf, pp5–6.
2 Decision of the Commons Commissioner, Thornham Ling Common (CL 55) 1972, ref 25/D/7, http://www.acraew.org.uk/uploads/Norfolk.
3 Gloucestershire Archives (hereafter GA), D 2700, MJ19/3 and 5: Brancaster surveys 1630 and 1663, parcel no 93.
4 The following summaries are drawn from the 1630 survey of the manor: GA, D 2700, MJ19/3.
5 NRO, PD 379/86.
6 GA, D 2700, MJ19/6.
7 GA, D2700/QS3/5: Proposal to drain Brancaster salt marsh, [undated] (accompanying documents dated 1771–1788). The proposal is possibly contemporaneous with, and relates to, a map of the Duchess's Brancaster Estate which was drawn up in 1783 (D2700/QS7/2).
8 NRO, PC 86/3, parcel no 151; confirmation of tithe award, 1841 (courtesy of Brancaster Parish Council, 2010).
9 NRO, PC 86/5 (agreement, 1902); /9 (agreement, 1937); /10 (agreement, 1948).
10 PRO, CRES 58/346: Mr Simms Reeve – Crown Estates Foreshore Rights File, 1891–1962; letter, Mills and Reeve, Solicitors, to Secretary Board of Trade, 28 April 1927.
11 NRO, PC 86/3, parcel no 331.
12 GA, D 2700, MJ19/3 (Brancaster survey, 1630) and MJ19/5 (Brancaster field book, 1663).
13 NRO, PD 379/36.
14 NRO, PC 86/3, parcel no 267.
15 NRO, PD 379/89; http://www.northcoastal.co.uk/barrowcommon.htm; Register of Common Land, Norfolk County Council, Register Unit CL 159, ownership section, entry no 1.
16 NRO, PC 9/1–2, Thornham enclosure award and map, 1797.
17 As in references to 'Copyhold or Customary right of Common of Pasture for two Head of Stock in over and upon the Common and Salt-Marshes'; 'a Common Right over the Commons of Thornham': NRO, H. Bett 14/6/79/4, Thornham court book, 1894–1925, pp3, 29 (17 November 1894; 4 August 1897).
18 Decision of the Commons Commissioner, Thornham Common (Norfolk CL 41), 18 December 1975, ref 25/D/79-95, p5, http:// www.acraew.org.uk/uploads/Norfolk.
19 GA, D 2700, MJ19/5 and 6.

20 NRO, H. Bett 14/6/79, Deeds: G (2), Thornham agreement, 10 August 1730.

21 In 1598 three individuals were presented for keeping land in Brancaster field enclosed 'in le shack tyme', where the lord's sheep ought to have had 'shack': NRO, HARE 6345 (16 January 1598).

22 GA, D 2700, MJ19/3 (Brancaster survey, 1630), f. 95; MJ19/6 (estate particulars 1670).

23 GA, D 2700, MJ19/2, court book, 1626–1630 (court leet, 18 October 1627); NRO, HARE 6338 (13 November 1567).

24 NRO, HARE 6345 (16 January 1598); GA, D 2700, MJ19/2, court book 1603–1608 (court leet, 20 October 1606).

25 NRO, H. Bett 14/6/79, Deeds: G (2), Thornham agreement, 10 August 1730.

26 NRO, PC 86/1: Brancaster Inclosure Act 1755, pp3–4.

27 NRO, PC 9/1–2, Thornham enclosure award and map, 1797.

28 For example, in the Thornham manor court book 1894–1925, entries dated 22 May 1918 record the lady of the manor's recent purchase of seven stints in five separate lots; NRO, H. Bett 14/6/79 (4).

29 Decision of the Commons Commissioner, Thornham Common (Norfolk CL 41), 18 December 1975, ref 25/D/79-95, p5, http://www.acraew.org.uk/uploads/Norfolk.

30 NRO, PC 86/1: Brancaster Inclosure Act 1755, pp3–4, 6.

31 GA, D2700/MJ/19/1–2.

32 An incomplete run of court rolls survives for Brancaster Manor from 1540 to 1687: PRO, LR3/48/2–3 (1540–1544); NRO, HARE 6334-6344 (covering 1548–1586); HARE 6345–6348 (1598–1614), HARE 6349 (1622–1623); HARE 6350 (1634–1635); HARE 6354 (1668–1670); HARE 6355 (1685–1687); GA, D 2700, MJ19/1 (1625–1628); MJ19/2 (1603–1608, 1621–1624, 1626–1630, 1630–1633, 1637–1639, 1641–1659, 1660–1682, 1683–1690).

33 NRO, MC 1813/29, Brancaster court book, 1860–1895; MC 1813/30, Brancaster court book, 1895–1935.

34 Court records consulted were those for Thornham Priory Manor 1613–1633 (NRO, DCN 60/36/17), 1626–1629 (NRO, BRA 981/1) and 1654–1719 (NRO, CHC 135539).

35 NRO, H. Bett 14/6/79/2, Thornham court book, 1777–1841 (2 December 1785), pp77–78; H. Bett 14/6/79/12, Thornham verdicts, list of common rights, 1 December 1786.

36 NRO, HARE 6339.

37 Further references to the work of pinders are found in NRO, MC 1813/29 Brancaster court book, 1818/29, 30 October 1894, p478; H. Bett 14/6/79/2, Thornham court book, 1777–1841, 6 November 1777, 2 December 1785, p80.

38 GA, D 2700, MJ19/2, court book 1603-8 (11 October 1603).

39 NRO, HARE 6334 (September 1556); 6338 (13 November 1567, 27 October 1569); 6345 (11 October 1598).

40 NRO, HARE 6338 (8 April 1569; 1 April 1570).

41 GA, D2700/QS6/3 (account of the charges and disbursement of inclosing Barrow Common, 1756).

42 NRO, H. Bett 14/6/79/2, Thornham court book, 1777–1841, 2 December 1785.

43 NRO, HARE 6345, 11 October 1598; 1 October 1599; GA, D 2700, MJ19/2, court book 1603–1608 (11 October 1603)

44 GA, D 2700, MJ19/2, court book 1626–1630 (18 October 1627).

45 Compare admittances to 'fish stalls', each containing 12 nets: GA, D2700/MJ19/2, court books 1626–1630, 18 December 1626; 1637–1639, 11 October 1637.

46 NRO, HARE 6338 (14 November 1567). 'Butt' is recorded as a dialect term for 'flounder' in Norfolk (Wright, *English Dialect Dictionary*); 'buttkyn' may therefore refer to a small flatfish, such as a dab.

47 NRO, HARE 6337 (1 May 1556); 6338 (14 November 1567); 6342 (15 November 1574); 6345 (1 October 1599).
48 NRO, HARE 6338 (5 December 1570).
49 GA, D2700/MJ/19/1, 5 October 1625.
50 GA, D2700/MJ19/2, court roll 1626–1630, 16 April 1629.
51 GA, D2700/MJ19/2, court book 1640–1659, f. 38v.
52 Norfolk Wildlife Trust (2009) *Natural Connections – Sea Holly*, http://www.norfolkwildlifetrust.org.uk/naturalconnections/species_profiles/sea_holly.
53 Correspondence with War Department, 1941–1952, copies in possession of Brancaster Parish Council, 2010.
54 The rule book, if it survives, has not been located.
55 NRO, H. Bett, 14/6/79/28, *Thornham Common Minute Book, 1924–1951*.
56 NRO, H. Bett, 14/6/79/28, *Thornham Common Minute Book, 1924–1951*.
57 Register of Common Land, Norfolk County Council, Register Unit CL 65 (Brancaster), rights register, entry 78.
58 Register of Common Land, Norfolk County Council, Register Unit CL 65 (Brancaster), rights register, entry 145.
59 Register of Common Land, Norfolk County Council, Register Unit CL 65 (Brancaster), rights register, entry 159.
60 *In the Matter of Creeks Foreshore and Salt Marshes, Burnham Overy, Burnahm Norton and Brancaster Norfolk* (1980) 25/D/105-11.
61 Reported as *Re Thornham Common, Thornham North Norfolk District* (1975) 25/D/79-95 (Commissioner Baden Fuller).
62 (1980) 25/D/105-111 at 121 (Commissioner L. J. Morris Smith); (1975) 25/D/79-95 at 72 (Commissioner Baden Fuller).
63 Or showing that his ancestor or forefathers had acquired it by use for the relevant period).
64 (1980) 25/D/105-111 at 122–123 (Commissioner L. J. Morris Smith).
65 *Re Thornham Common, Thornham North Norfolk District* (1975) 25/D/79-95 (Commissioner Baden Fuller) at 72.
66 See *de la Warr v. Miles (1881) 17 ChD 535*. This case was also cited in the Brancaster litigation (above).
67 See http://commons.ncl.ac.uk/?q=system/files/BrancasterQualitativeAnalysis.pdf (semi-structured interviews, July 2009).
68 NRO, PC86/12.
69 The factual information contained in this section is extrapolated from *Natura 2000 Standard Data* form, http://www.jncc.gov.uk/ProtectedSites/SACselection/n2kforms/UK0019838.pdf.
70 The factual information contained in this section is extrapolated from an SPA description published in 2001 by the Joint Nature Conservation Committee, http://www.jncc.gov.uk/default.aspx?page=2008.
71 The factual information contained in this section is a summary of the *Information Sheet on Ramsar Wetland (RIS)* completed in 1976 by Joint Nature Conservation Committee, http://www.jncc.gov.uk/pdf/RIS/UK11048.pdf.
72 *North Norfolk Coast SSSI Views about Management*, http://www.sssi.naturalengland.org.uk/Special/sssi/sssi_details.cfm?sssi_id=1001342.
73 Additional information on Scolt Head Island National Nature Reserve is available at http://www.naturalengland.org.uk/ourwork/conservation/designatedareas/nnr/1006129.aspx.
74 Register of Common Land, Norfolk County Council, Register Unit CL 65 (Brancaster), rights register, entry 153
75 Register of Common Land, Norfolk County Council, Register Unit CL 65 (Brancaster), rights register, entry 127

Part III

Conclusions

10

Sustainable Commons: Reflections on History, Law and Governance

The research presented in this book is premised on the understanding that cultural assumptions concerning the value of common land are not stable but have changed across the centuries, with profound consequences for the law, for land management and for the exercise of common rights. The distinctive legal status of 'common' land poses a puzzle for a society in which concepts of private property are dominant, giving rise to a series of tensions that have emerged at different times: between public and private rights and interests; between concepts of common rights as appurtenant to property and as personal rights; between limitations on their use based on necessity and commercial exploitation. The sustainable governance of common land therefore presents us with a complex set of problems reflecting many conflicting interests – public and private, national and local, recreational and economic, ecological and agricultural, to name but a few. Common land is, in this sense, a truly 'contested' resource. The 'stakeholders' of today – whether land users, policy-makers or the public – are the inheritors of this complex cultural legacy, and must negotiate diverse and sometimes conflicting objectives in their pursuit of a potentially unifying goal: a secure future for the commons.

In drawing this study together, this chapter will argue for a wider public debate on the sustainability of our commons – an important facet of the British landscape – and how it might be promoted. It will also look beyond the narrow focus of the English and Welsh commons, and consider the potential impact of the research presented in the earlier chapters on the wider debate about the institutional governance of common pool resources.

Common land governance: Some key themes

Several key themes emerge from the case studies presented in Chapters 6 to 9. The first is the persistence of custom and its importance in the governance of the commons. Related to this is the role of 'good neighbourhood' as a key ingredient in good common pool resource management. Custom is often expressed differently at different times, and its relationship with governance institutions is sometimes complex and shifting. Another theme linking the case studies is the complex interrelationship between the changing nature of customary land-use practices, on the one hand, and the legal and/or institutional form in which they are captured, reflected and (in some cases) shaped by governance institutions and norms, on the other.

The complexity of these interrelationships can be very clearly seen if we consider the relationship between customary land-use practice and the property rights captured by the Commons Registration Act 1965, and reflected in the contemporary commons registers. The 1965 Act has been described as the true 'tragedy' of the commons, in an English context, and its impact upon the sustainable management of the commons was almost wholly negative (Rodgers, 2010, p436). The relationship of the commons registration process to customary land management practices that were prevalent, prior to 1965, in many different parts of England and Wales was, however, highly complex, as was its impact.

On many commons registered under the 1965 Act, the registration procedure had the effect of suppressing local custom, either wholly or in part. The case studies presented in this work offer many examples of this phenomenon. Once the registration process had closed it was provided that rights not registered would 'not be exercisable' (1965 Act, section 1(2)). There can be no doubt that many rights that had existed in customary practice prior to 1965, but which were not registered, were thereby extinguished. In practice, some of these may have been abandoned prior to 1965, as the use of rights changed in step with changing agricultural technology and practice. For a right of common to be abandoned at common law requires very clear evidence of an intention to relinquish its future use, however, and long periods of non-usage will not in themselves suffice to extinguish a right (*Tehidy Minerals Ltd v. Norman* [1970]). The abandonment of rights to turbary in our three upland case studies illustrates the somewhat arbitrary impact of the 1965 Act in this context. Although the digging of peat was widespread in past centuries, the right had been unused by most commoners for some considerable time. The registration of a large number of entries for turbary on the registers for both Eskdale and Cwmdeuddwr commons therefore clothed with unquestionable legal validity a right that has for all practical purposes been abandoned by commoners (see pp100, 149). In the Ingleborough case study, in contrast, few rights of turbary were registered: whether or not the rights had been abandoned as a matter of common law, the failure of commoners to register them resulted in their extinguishment.

In many cases where customary rights *were* registered under the 1965 Act, local custom was only partially captured in the registers. This gives rise to a situation where knowledge of local custom remains essential today, both to identify the rights accurately, and to establish any qualifications and restrictions to which they may be subject – the importance of customary heafs and sheepwalks in effectively restricting the rights of an individual to a defined section of the common is a case in point. Consequently, it is often necessary to go 'behind' the registers to establish the precise nature of the registered rights and their full extent. Rights to estovers provide a classic example of this problem, which all four of the case studies in this work illustrate. 'Estovers' is potentially a wide category of right, but it is rarely defined with any precision in those commons registers where the right was claimed. In the Norfolk case study, for example, there are large numbers of generic entries of 'estovers' in the commons registers. No detail is given in the registers; but the rights were, historically, focused mainly on collecting rushes, reeds and bracken. On Cwmdeuddwr Common, similarly, the registration of estovers was expressed in general terms (e.g. 'estovers (including the rights to cut bracken)'), reflecting local practice, which in the upland context was, in effect, limited to taking bracken for animal bedding. Establishing the exact nature of the registered rights in such cases therefore requires an examination of historical practice going beyond what is stated in the commons register.

If the 1965 Act sometimes had a destructive impact upon rights, it also had creative potential too. It could be (and was, on occasion) used to turn unwritten traditional land uses into legally enforceable rights, or to radically change their nature. And in so doing it could also be used to turn land that was not, in legal terms, 'common' into common land through the simple expedient of its registration as such under the Commons Registration Act 1965. The Norfolk case study provides an excellent example of both creative facets of the registration process, and supports the observations of some commentators:

> *Most observers would accept that not only have many unused rights been registered and consequently given a fresh lease of life, but many claims to rights which would not have borne close legal examination have slipped into registration through lack of objection. The overall result of the 1965 Act may well have been to create more rights than it extinguished.* (Gadsden, 1988, §5.110)

The evidence from Brancaster and Thornham (see Chapter 9) supports the conclusions reached in the wider context of common land registration across Norfolk as a whole (see Birtles, 1998). There is little documentary evidence that rights to estovers and samphire in the Norfolk case study were held as personal rights (rights in gross) in earlier centuries – indeed, estovers are, elsewhere, invariably recognized as a category of right that is always appurtenant to specific dwellings and limited to what was necessary for the enjoyment of that property by its occupants. Their registration as rights in gross at Brancaster therefore represents a break with tradition and the conversion of the rights into a new species of property right. It is also noteworthy that in those cases where the rights were challenged, the commons commissioners doubted whether (as a matter of law) they could subsist in gross, found little evidence of customary use, and refused to confirm many of the registrations – and in the case of Thornham Common, specifically directed that those rights that were proven should instead be registered as appurtenant to the dominant land they were intended to benefit. Those rights that went unchallenged were, nevertheless, registered as rights in gross – and were therefore not limited by conditions of necessity, while being freely transferable without land. Furthermore, the historical evidence shows that some of the land registered under the 1965 Act in the Norfolk case study was not 'true' common land before registration: much of the land registered at Brancaster had been the lord of the manor's several property in the 17th century, while the registered common at Thornham had, in fact, been subject to parliamentary enclosure. Customary perceptions of the land in question were presumably stronger than strict legal definitions.

The requirement to quantify common grazing rights upon registration (1965 Act, section 13) also had an important (and destructive) impact upon the ability of customary practices to supply the sustainable management of the common. The requirement to register fixed grazing numbers effectively abolished levancy and couchancy (and represented a significant break with customary practice) (*Bettison v. Langton* [2001]), and on stinted commons it destroyed the inherent ability of stinting to act as a reflexive mechanism to adjust grazing pressures in response to ecological changes in the common grazing.

In cases where excessive registrations of pasture rights were made, the property rights reflected in the commons register will also now fail to perform the former distributive functions of levancy and couchancy, and of stinting, in equitably allocating land-use rights between competing appropriators. If each commoner has more than sufficient registered rights for all foreseeable purposes, and cumulatively with others more than the grazing can sustain, then the property rights reflected in the register will cease to have any meaningful allocative function in terms of regulating access to the land resource. The allocative function formerly performed through property rights will therefore be exercised by alternative means – in a contemporary context, typically, through publicly funded environmental management schemes. This is clearly illustrated by the upland case studies (Chapters 6 to 8). Where environmental management agreements have been concluded, the allocation of common pool resources is accomplished by the terms of the agreement, which also adjust the commoners' property rights in return for publicly funded management payments. Paradoxically, therefore, commons registration has contributed to a position where it can be claimed that instruments promoting the environmental sustainability of the commons have superseded, and subsumed the functions of, those with a focus solely on common resource protection and allocation (i.e. on economic and social sustainability). This supports the argument that ecological sustainability is now the dominant paradigm for the sustainable future management of the commons (see Bosselman, 2008; Ross, 2009; Rodgers, 2010)

The relationship between law as a social construct and custom

The close examination of the relationship between law, governance institutions and customary usage undertaken in the earlier chapters also draws attention to the problematic nature of the relationship between law (especially when viewed as a social construct) and custom. Social organization and customary practice – key facets of commons management – are inherently reflexive and iterative. They are not only subject to constant change, but are also inherently flexible. When assimilating customary practice into legal principles, the law clothes it with normative force: for example, as case law, as in the assimilation of the rule of levancy and couchancy into the common law; or by statute, a contemporary example of which would be the adoption of management rules based on customary practice by a commons council under the Commons Act 2006. Once assimilated into a legally enforceable rule, custom will not necessarily cease to be reflexive – but it will be capable of modification and adaptation only in accordance with the rules appropriate to the particular normative legal order of which it now forms part. In the case of a management rule adopted by a commons council under the 2006 Act, for example, changes are subject to approval by the national authorities if they are to be legally enforceable (2006 Act, section 34(2)). In the case of a common law rule reflected in case law, it would be subject to the doctrine of precedent (*stare decisis*). This would not necessarily render the rule incapable of revision to meet changing social conditions: it would, however, render such change conditional upon a later case presenting an issue for a decision by the courts that necessitated a revision to the rule in question, and the ability of the court to adjust the rule (e.g. by distinguishing the earlier case on the facts from that now requiring its decision).

The ability of custom and agrarian practice to develop and change over time – for example, in response to changing social and economic circumstances and land-use pressures, and advances in agricultural management techniques and technology – is what has made them such valuable tools for the governance of the commons. But it follows from the discussion above that changes will not necessarily be reflected in the normative order within which the law has captured a particular customary practice, or within the common property rights recognized by the legal order. Clothing social practice with normative (legal) force will capture key aspects of a custom at a specific point in time and be informed by the wider cultural context (e.g. the primacy of the quest for environmental sustainability, in the case of the 2006 Act). Where land-use practice has continued to develop and adapt, this may lead to a mismatch between local custom as practised by appropriators and the legal rules that apply, in theory, to adjust property rights in the commons. The absorption of the rule of levancy and couchancy into the common law provides a good example of this phenomenon. The earliest articulation of the rule is in a mid 15th-century report from the court of common pleas (*lour bestes la couchants and levants*: Yearbook 37 Henry VI 34). The rule was well established, and commented upon in reported case law by the late 16th century (see *Smith v. Bensall* [1597]; *Cole v. Foxman* [1618]) and was certainly well established in manors such as Eskdale (see Chapter 6) by the 16th century. Changes in agricultural management practices in successive centuries, including the away-wintering of livestock and the taking of additional animals 'on tack' in the summer, meant, however, that in practice the numbers admitted to the common ceased to be regulated by reference to the capacity of the farms to which common rights attached to fodder livestock over the winter. Even by 1600, the rule was out of step with agricultural practice and could not be strictly enforced (see Winchester, 2000, pp81–82). Other customary practices, such as limiting an individual's grazing right to a 'heaf' or sheepwalk, were perhaps of greater practical significance on upland commons by the 18th century, as in the Elan Valley (see Chapter 8). Nevertheless, levancy and couchancy remained the legal principle by which grazing was – at least notionally – regulated on many open upland commons right down to the passage of the 1965 Act.

An analysis that sets the relationship between social custom, governance institutions and legal principles in historical context inevitably highlights the need for legal governance rules to reflect the flexible and iterative nature of customary practice. It also emphasizes the inherent difficulties that they have in doing so. The relationship between case law and custom (discussed above) illustrates this, and emphasizes the importance of adopting a dynamic model of property rights that is capable of reflecting the constantly changing agricultural, social and environmental requirements of common resource management. This is even more clearly seen in the relationship between statutory law and commons management. One of the principal weaknesses of the Commons Registration Act 1965 lay in the manner in which, through the registration of rights, it created a fixed and static model of property rights in the commons. This approach was flawed because it attempted to define the *substance* of property rights in common land, rather than confining itself to the legal *form in which* those rights are expressed. As a consequence, the registers captured property rights in a fixed and inflexible form that is unresponsive and incapable of further change as customary land management practice evolves. As discussed in Chapter 3, manor court by-laws had typically combined quantitative, seasonal and spatial restrictions in order to manage potential conflicts over the exercise of rights, adjusting the limitations as circumstances changed. Registrations under the 1965 Act could not incorporate that flexibility.

The 1965 registration model also has difficulty in capturing and reflecting the local diversity of the commons. Even as an attempt to impose a standardized approach to the form in which rights were recorded by commons registration, moreover, the 1965 Act was unsuccessful – because no standardization was required for the form in which entries were made on the individual registers, the commons registers kept by different local authorities use different types of entry and reflect different levels of detail. The problems to which this can give rise are also amply demonstrated by the four case studies in this work.

The Commons Act 2006 offers the prospect of a new approach to capturing both the inherent flexibility, and the diversity, of customary land-use practice. It also offers opportunities for the representation of customary practice within a more dynamic model of property rights, one by which property rights can be adapted to meet the changing demands of sustainable commons governance. The approach adopted in the 2006 Act differs because it fixes the *legal form* within which governance rules can be expressed by a commons council (as management rules made under section 31 of the 2006 Act); but it does not seek to define the substance or content of the management rules adopted by different commons councils. These can be collectively agreed, implemented and given legally binding force through the agricultural management rules adopted by each commons council (2006 Act, sections 31(3) and 34(2)). Should a commons council be established in an area, local agricultural practice would have an important role in shaping property rights adapted as a result of the introduction of management rules under the 2006 Act. Customary management practices, such as seasonal restrictions or sheep heafs and sheepwalks, could, for example, be accommodated within the management rules adopted by a commons council, even though they may not be reflected in the property rights captured in the formal commons registers originally established under the 1965 Act. And, of course, a commons council would be able to adapt and change these rules if necessary, thereby ensuring that the legal expression of management rules and property rights kept in step with changing local practice.

Some lessons for common pool resource (CPR) scholarship

What lessons can we draw from this study of the environmental governance of the English and Welsh commons in historical perspective? And what is the potential impact of the research presented in the earlier chapters on the wider debate about the institutional governance of CPRs?

Beyond an institutional approach to commons governance

The relevance of institutional and neo-institutional theory for the successful governance of CPRs was highlighted in Chapter 1. The significance of the principles established by recent neo-institutional scholarship can be reassessed in the light of the historical and empirical research presented in the case studies in Chapters 6 to 9. A significant theme that emerges from the case studies is the importance of the cultural heritage reflected in differing systems of common property rights for successful CPR management. These include both differences in the formal conceptions of use-rights (stinting in North Yorkshire; levancy and couchancy in Wales and Cumbria) and local management practices with deep roots in custom, such as heafing in Eskdale and the sheepwalks of mid-Wales. The legacies of these can be seen in the importance attached to tradition and the impact that this has upon both the cultural perceptions of appropriators towards property rights (either as personal or appurtenant rights) and the organization of 'sustainable' collective management. The impact of different property rights traditions on cultural attitudes to CPR management has largely been ignored by neo-institutionalists, who tend to characterize the CPR actor merely as an appropriator and assume the primacy of narrow economic concerns among resource users. This ignores the importance of cultural factors to collective choices and decision-making and of collective perceptions as to the nature of common property rights – which may differ from place to place, and from time to time.

Although the neo-institutionalist literature recognizes the relevance of wider cultural elements to CPR governance, such as appropriators' shared knowledge of the environment, reciprocity and trust in robust CPRs, their importance is seen as reflected primarily in their instrumental value. From a neo-institutionalist standpoint, the resource users' cultural heritage is simply a background factor – a resource bank from which social capital can be drawn to facilitate the implementation of effective resource management. Social capital is, moreover, often viewed as a single homogeneous element. This type of analysis therefore excludes the multiplicity of cultural elements, the divergent claims and the differing constructions of the resource system within each 'community' of stakeholders. These are all, it is suggested, fundamentally important to successful CPR management.

Another shortcoming of the neo-institutionalist approach, illustrated by the case studies, is its assumption that the constitution of each CPR institution and of its community of users is self-contained. The neo-institutionalist analysis emphasizes a reflexivity which is interior and local, and only produced by the closed system of each CPR. This fails to take into consideration how external factors and other variables may contribute to the establishment of CPR management institutions and the process of CPR management. The case studies demonstrate the relevance of external economic and environmental instruments in shaping CPR institutions – both as stimuli for appropriators to establish CPR institutions, and in shaping the allocation of common resources implicit in sustainable management. External cultural factors, both printed treatises on manorial administration and oral folk culture, played a part in the evolution of manor court by-laws across the centuries, and, in the modern context, these external stimuli were frequently state mediated. The influence of external factors on recent local governance is illustrated in the proliferation of commoners' associations in the second half of the 20th century, many of which were established primarily in response to the need to organize the registration of rights under the 1965 Act, or to negotiate a collective agri-environment agreement for the common in 1990 (see Chapters 6 and 8). Neo-institutionalist scholars, by focusing attention primarily on the self-enclosed relationship between CPR institutions and their members at the local level, have tended to ignore the multiplicity of influences, land uses and governance rules that play a role in establishing complex CPR institutions.

Although recent scholarship has recognized that exogenous factors affect the institutional design and management of CPRs, they do not explore in depth how 'locality' is created in conjunction with different external contexts (Ostrom et al, 2002, p47; see Box 1.1, p12, above). Ostrom's design principles focus on the internal and local scale of CPR institutions, only two of which (Ostrom et al, 2002, principles 7 and 8 expressly address the legal recognition of CPR institutions by the public authorities and the recognition of 'nested' institutions. Although Ostrom's seventh design principle refers to the wider political environment, its role is envisaged as limited merely to acting as a facilitator of local autonomy in successful CPRs. Governmental bodies are conceived of as external entities whose only role consists in recognizing the rights of appropriators to form their own institutions. This assumption is reiterated by other neo-institutionalist scholars, who agree that resource appropriators' self-determination of access and harvesting rules, if not undermined by external authorities, is conducive to the formation and success of self-governing associations (Wade, 1994; Meinzen et al, 2002). Here, neo-institutionalists construct a dichotomy between the external political authorities and the local and supposedly apolitical CPR. If the external cultural and political realm is assigned a marginal and external role in this way, the impact of economic factors is also often dismissed in the neo-institutionalist analysis of CPRs. This ignores the relevance of the external economic climate within which CPRs are embedded, and its role in shaping collective action and the formation or dissolution of CPR institutions. As the case studies in this work have shown, this is not the case in England and Wales, where the public authorities, through positioning themselves as facilitators, and emphasizing the active role of the local CPR community in forming statutory commons councils, have an important role in shaping the practice and principles of future environmental governance as applied to common land.

This study of common land in England and Wales has demonstrated not only that economic instruments are sometimes a key factor in the formation of CPR institutions, but also that the public authorities, by positioning themselves as facilitators and emphasizing the self-regulatory role of CPR users, can (and often do) play an active part in the institutional design and management of individual CPRs. Indeed, the potential role of public bodies, such as the Department for Environment, Food and Rural Affairs (Defra) and the Countryside Council for Wales and Natural England, will be considerably expanded by the Commons Act 2006. They already have an important role in securing the environmental governance of common land – through the designation of land for legal protection – as Sites of Special Scientific Interest (SSSIs), Special Areas of Conservation (SACs), etc., and the conclusion with CPR users of management agreements to promote nature conservation. Their role in the establishment and subsequent functioning of statutory commons councils will be considerable. As we have already seen, the constitution of each commons council must be approved by the secretary of state or Welsh Assembly Government prior to its establishment, and the exercise of its powers to introduce binding land management rules will also require their approval.

The increasing prominence of public bodies in determining management practices on common land brings us back to the cultural paradigms which underpin conceptions of common land. Taking the long view, it is important to remember that these are not static or, in any absolute sense, objective. They reflect the priorities of a particular point in time and raise questions about the assumptions underlying policy-making. What should be sustained and for whom? Who should be the arbiters of ecological value and of taste in determining what constitutes 'good' or desirable landscape character? Tensions continue between the objectives of 'use' (the commoners' perspective) and 'delight' (the conservation and recreational perspective). For example, agri-environmental schemes that are designed to achieve particular ecological results that reflect the priorities set by public agencies can impact upon commons management in ways which might be perceived as detrimental in the eyes of graziers. Reductions in sheep numbers break down the integrity of heafs or sheepwalks; stock from outside move in to fill the gaps; and shepherding becomes increasingly labour intensive and costly (Natural England, 2008a, pp32–33).

The endurance of custom and tradition has been a central theme of this book, yet the survival of traditional ways of life centred on common land, especially in hill farming districts, is at risk (Commission for Rural Communities, 2009, pp48–51). The value of hill farming culture is increasingly being recognized, as in Cumbria, where it is seen as a key element in the 'outstanding universal value' of the Lake District in framing its prospective World Heritage inscription proposal. On many commons today there is a tension between local self-governance and external authority, expressed in differing perceptions and priorities: the traditional commoning culture, underpinning local management by experienced but untrained practitioners, on the one hand, and decision-making by external professionals, pursuing the objectives of ecological conservation, on the other.

Commons governance: A legal pluralist analysis

Successful models for CPR governance can be most effectively identified and analysed if we accept the limitations of the neo-institutionalist approach, and instead study the interplay between the cultural, historical, political and economic contexts of each common and their relevance to CPR institutional design. This can be accomplished by employing the analytical framework of legal pluralism. A legal pluralist analysis can extend the study of commons governance beyond formal legal structures, emphasizing the importance of customs, cultural practices and other informal or 'soft law' mechanisms in sustainable commons governance. When using a legal pluralist methodology (e.g. to study colonial legal governance), anthropologists have often, however, overlooked the interpenetrations between formal and informal legal orders, and have tended to portray them as existing in separate hermetic domains. It is, nevertheless, clear that multiple systems of legal and normative rules can exist in society and interpenetrate (Moore, 1978; Merry, 1988). The notion of the 'semi-autonomous social field' has been employed, for example, to identify the connections between the internal workings of an observable normative domain and its points of intersection and articulations with larger settings (see Moore, 1978).

The difficult relationship between 'formal' legal structures and customary practice emerges very clearly from this study of commons governance. A particular problem when viewing the relationship between formal law and informal normative orders (such as customary practice) in a legal pluralist context is the hierarchy of legitimacy and enforceability conferred by the legal system on different formal and informal normative orders. The assumption of the primacy of formal legal rules is sometimes referred to as the 'ideology of legal centralism' (Griffiths, 1986, p3). There is, however a growing recognition among legal scholars (as well as anthropologists) of the importance of recognizing both the pluralities of the sources of law and the pluralities of legal interpretation (Cotterrell, 2006; Mellisaris, 2006). In the context of commons governance, a legal pluralist analysis highlights the socially constructed nature of law and its practical consequences. In particular, it enables us to retain the neo-institutional focus on CPR governance rules, while recognizing that management rules are the product of more than simply local decisions. Viewed in historical context, the management rules adopted by the manor courts in the early modern period, by contemporary commoners associations, and in the future potentially by statutory commons councils, can best be understood as the institutional products of a variety of normative orders – including customary and soft law, legislation and economic governance mechanisms (such as management agreements) introduced through agricultural and environmental law.

The intersections between formal and informal law, between custom and legislation, and between historical and contemporary practice, are to be found in all aspects of contemporary commons governance, and are essential to an understanding of its future sustainable governance and how this might be achieved. The point of departure for the analysis of contemporary commons governance in Chapter 5 was the Commons Act 2006, and the development of a policy for sustainable commons management based on the formation of statutory commons councils. It is important to recognize, however, that customary and soft law have played an important part in shaping the collective organization of grazing management and other common resource use across the centuries, and that they have defined the role of the different types of voluntary commons associations found today in many parts of England and Wales. Similarly, although the modern policy focus on the environmental sustainability of the commons has been pursued through legislation (such as the Wildlife and Countryside Act 1981) and the use of land management agreements and other economic instruments, their implementation and impact is wholly dependent on interactions with informal normative orders. The impact of management agreements to promote environmental management is, for example, conditioned by the property rights subsisting in the commons: and these have been developed out of, and reflect, customary land-use practices in each locality but may not capture them in full (as in the invisibility of heafs and sheepwalks in the formal commons registers established under the Commons Registration Act 1965).

Finally, even where a future commons council is established under the 2006 Act and adopts management rules based on local custom, the interpenetrations between customary local practice and 'formal' law must still be recognized – for the 2006 Act requires commons councils to have regard to the 'public interest' when carrying out their functions. The 'public interest' is expressly defined to include nature conservation and public access, and reflects the importance of environmental legislation (formal law), itself an expression of the dominant cultural paradigm at the start of the 21st century, in shaping the institutional structure and functions of otherwise self-regulating commons councils (2006 Act, section 31(7)).

A sustainable future for the commons?

The research presented in this book has highlighted the importance of custom and its persistence as a driver underpinning more formal conceptions of property rights and governance systems across the centuries. Its survival has provided a degree of continuity, varying in strength from place to place, bridging the void between the collapse of effective regulation by manor courts in the 18th century and the present day. Although some commons benefited from new forms of governance, either formal bodies created by statute or informal commoners' associations, many suffered from an institutional vacuum which custom alone could not fill. By the late 20th century, a lack of effective management resulted in many upland commons experiencing serious overgrazing, while many lowland commons were, in practice, abandoned and left to revert to scrubby wilderness.

The use of commons councils based on the model in the Commons Act 2006 has the potential to lead to the development of a new institutional approach to sustainable commons management. Its success will require local approaches that are sensitive to the distinctive property rights, customary practices and governance rules that have, in each case, shaped commons management over the centuries – and produced the landscapes and biodiversity for which we value our commons so highly. Taking the wider view and considering models for successful commons governance at a national scale, it is also important to recognize the wide diversity of types of value attached to commons in England and Wales: some are primarily recreational, many primarily agricultural, and others have a variety of mixed land uses. This has not always been recognized by policy-makers. The Commons Act 1876 assumed, for example, that all commons were akin to metropolitan commons where access was the key issue. The model for commons management set out in Part 2 of the Commons Act 2006 focuses heavily on 'agricultural' commons and issues of environmental improvement, and says little about the problems of recreational commons. As we have seen, on commons where agricultural land use is minimal, such as those in our Norfolk case study, the management powers granted to commons councils by the 2006 Act have little relevance. There is, clearly, a need for a more sensitive taxonomy of common land in England and Wales, and a clearer recognition of the differential impacts of the land uses and cultural influences that will shape its sustainable future.

There is also a need for a clearer taxonomy of common land in different parts of the world. Many of the questions addressed in this work through case studies of commons management in England and Wales are highly relevant to the environmental governance of CPRs around the world. What are the special characteristics of property rights in the commons, how have they developed historically, how do they interrelate with modern legal and economic instruments for land management and environmental protection, and how might the sustainable future of the commons be secured? Comparative study of the international commons should be targeted to investigating and answering these important questions. Before this can be achieved, however, archival and contemporary research data will be required to securely ground comparative CPR research in its historical and modern policy contexts.

References

Adams, J. (1988) *Mines of the Lake District Fells*, Clapham: Dalesman

Aglionby, J. C. W. (2009) 'Commons Councils a new era for the management of common land?', *RICS Rural Research Conference March 2009*, www.rics.org/site/download_feed.aspx?fileID=3481&fileExtension=PDF

Agrawal, A. (2003) 'Sustainable governance of common-pool resources: Context, methods, and politics', *Annual Review of Anthropology*, vol 32, pp243–262

Agrawal, A. and Ostrom, E. (2001) 'Collective action, property rights, and decentralization in resource use in India and Nepal', *Politics and Society*, vol 29, no 4, pp485–514

Aitchison, J. W. (1990) 'The commons and wastes of England and Wales 1958–1989', *Area*, vol 22, no 3, pp272–277

Aitchison, J. and Gadsden, G. S. D. (1992) 'Common land' in W. Howarth and C. P. Rodgers (eds) *Agriculture Conservation and Land Use: Law and Policy Issues for Rural Areas*, Cardiff: University of Wales Press, pp165–185

Aldred, D. H. (1990) *Cleeve Hill: The History of the Common and its People*, Stroud: Alan Sutton

Allen, R. (1997) 'The battle for the common: politics and populism in mid-Victorian Kentish London', *Social History*, vol 22, no 1, pp61–77

Allison, K. J. (1957) 'The sheep-corn husbandry of Norfolk in the sixteenth and seventeenth centuries', *Agricultural History Review*, vol 5, pp12–30

Altenburg, K. (2003) *Experiencing Landscapes: A Study of Space and Identity in Three Marginal Areas of Medieval Britain and Scandinavia*, Stockholm: Almqvist and Wiksell International

Anon (1720) *The Law of Commons and Commoners or a Treatise shewing the Original and Nature of Common*, 2nd edition, London

Arora, V. (2006) 'The forest of symbols embodied in the Tholung Sacred Landscape of North Sikkim, India', *Conservation and Society*, vol 4, no 1, pp55–83

Ault, W. O. (1960) 'Village assemblies in medieval England', *Album Helen Maud Cam,* vol 1, p13–35, Louvain: Studies Presented to the International Commission for the History of Representative and Parliamentary Institutions XXIII

Ault, W. O. (1965) *Open Field Husbandry and the Village Community: A Study of Agrarian By-Laws in Medieval England*, Philadelphia: Transactions of American Philosophical Society, Series 55, Part 7

Banks, R. W. (1880) 'The Grange of Cwmtoyddwr', *Archaeologia Cambrensis*, 4th ser. XI, pp30–50

Balderston, R. R. (undated) *Ingleton: Bygone and Present*, Skipton: Simpkin & Marshall

Barrow Common Management Committee (2004), 'Management Plan for Barrow Common' (unpublished)

Batterick, E. (1987) *Guardian of the Lakes: A History of the National Trust in the Lake District from 1946*, Kendal: Westmorland Gazette

Becker, C. D. and Ostrom, E (1995) 'Human ecology and resource sustainability: The importance of institutional diversity', *Annual Review of Ecology and Systematics*, vol 26, pp113–133

Birtles, S. (1998) 'The impact of commons registration: A Norfolk study', *Landscape History*, vol 20, pp83–97

Birtles, S. (1999) 'Common land, poor relief and enclosure: The use of manorial resources in fulfilling parish obligations 1601–1834', *Past and Present*, vol 165, pp74–106

Blackstone, W. (1792) *Commentaries on the Laws of England*, vol 2, http://avalon.law.yale.edu/subject_menus/blackstone.asp

Bonfield, L. (1996) 'What did English villagers mean by 'customary law'?', in Z. Razi and R. Smith (eds) *Medieval Society and the Manor Court*, Oxford: Oxford University Press, pp103–116

Bosselmann, K. (2008) *The Principle of Sustainability – Transforming Law and Governance*, Aldershot: Ashgate

Bowden, M., Brown, G. and Smith, N. (2009) *An Archaeology of Town Commons in England: 'A very fair field indeed'*, Swindon: English Heritage

Bromley, D. W. (1991) *Environment and Economy: Property Rights and Public Policy*, Oxford and New York: Basil Blackwell

Brown, G. (2009) *Herdwicks: Herdwick Sheep and the English Lake District*, Kirkby Stephen: Hayloft

Butler, J. (2007) *Interactions between Ecological Condition and the Management of Grazing Rights on Eskdale Common in the Lake District National Park*, MSc thesis, Newcastle University, September 2007

Carr, J. (1896) 'Personal recollections of Ingleton for over sixty years', *Lancaster Guardian*, 28 March 1896 (vol LIX, no 3013), 'Supplement', p1

Clark, J. (1794) *General View of the Agriculture of the County of Brecknock, with Observations on the Means of Its Improvement*, London: Board of Agriculture

Clayden, P. (2003) *Our Common Land: The Law and History of Common Land and Village Greens*, Henley-on-Thames: Open Spaces Society

Clwyd-Powys Archaeological Trust (undated) *The Making of the Elan Valley Landscape*, www.cpat.org.uk/projects/longer/histland/elan/evintr.htm

Coleridge, S. T. (1956) *Collected Letters of Samuel Taylor Coleridge Volume II 1801–1806*, Earl Leslie Griggs (ed), Oxford: Oxford University Press

Colgrave, B. (ed) (1985) *Felix's Life of Saint Guthlac*, Cambridge: Cambridge University Press

Commission for Rural Communities (2009) *Inquiry into the Future of England's Upland Communities: The Views of the Communities*, Report prepared by Step Ahead Research Ltd, www.ruralcommunities.gov.uk/files/CRC%20Uplands%20Communities%20-%20Final%20Report%2017%2007%2009.pdf, accessed 27 April 2010

Cosgrove, D. and Daniels, S. (eds) (1988) *The Iconography of Landscape: Essays on the Symbolic Representation, Design and Use of Past Environments*, Cambridge: Cambridge University Press

Cotterrell, R. (2006) *Law, Culture and Society: Legal Ideas in the Mirror of Social Theory*, Aldershot: Ashgate

Countryside Commission (1986) *Common Land: Report of the Common Land Forum* (Cheltenham, Countryside Commission)

Countryside Council for Wales (2007) *Report of the Pori Natur a Threftadaeth (PONT) Conference to discuss the implications of the new provisions within Part 2 (Management) of the Commons Act 2006 to facilitate the sustainable grazing management of Wales' commons*

Countryside Council for Wales (2008) *Core Management Plan (Including Conservation Objectives) Incorporating: Elenydd-Mallaen SPA, Elenydd SAC, Elan Valley Woodlands SAC, Cwm Doethie – Mynydd-Mallaen SAC* (17 April 2008), www.ccw.gov.uk/about-ccw/search-results.aspx?txtSearchTerms=Mallaen SPA

Cousins, J. (2009) *Friends of the Lake District: The Early Years*, Lancaster: Centre for North West Regional Studies

Cowell, B. (2002) 'The Commons Preservation Society and the campaign for Berkhamsted Common, 1866–70', *Rural History*, vol 13, no 2, pp145–161

Cunningham, W. (1910) 'Common Rights at Cottenham and Stretham in Cambridgeshire', *Camden Miscellany XII* (Camden Society, 3rd series, volume XVIII), pp169–296

Davies, E. (1980) 'Hafod, Hafoty and Lluest: Their distribution, features and purpose', *Ceredigion*, vol 9, no 1, pp1–41

Davies, W. (1815) *General View of the Agriculture and Domestic Economy of South Wales Volume I*, London

De Moor, M., Shaw-Taylor, L. and Warde, P. (eds) (2002) *The Management of Common Land in North West Europe, c. 1500–1850*, Turnhout: Brepols

de Soissons, Maurice (1993) *Brancaster Staithe: The Story of a Norfolk Fishing Village*, Brancaster: Woodthorpe Publishing

Defra (Department for Environment, Food and Rural Affairs) (2003) *Consultation on Agricultural Use and Management of Common Land*, London: Defra

Defra (2005) *Single Payment Scheme: Information for Farmers and Growers*, London: Defra

Defra (2006a) *Draft West Barsetshire Commons Association Establishment Order 2006*, www.defra.gov.uk/rural/documents/protected/common-land/cc-draftsi-westbarset.pdf

Defra (2009a) *Cumbria Commons Shadow Council: A Proposal for Consultation* www.defra.gov.uk/rural/documents/protected/common-land/ccouncil-flyer.pdf

Defra (2009b) *Shadow Commons Council Project: The Regulations as Prepared under Section X of the Establishment Order for the Cumbria Commoners Council* (draft), www.defra.gov.uk

Defra (2010a) *Part 2 of the Commons Act 2006: Commons Councils. Technical Guidance on Setting Up a Commons Council* (February 2010), www.defra.gov.uk/rural/documents/protected/common-land/cc-techguide.pdf

Defra (2010b) *Part 1 of the Commons Act 2006: Guidance to Commons Registration Authorities and the Planning Inspectorate for the Pilot Implementation* (March 2010), www.defra.gov.uk/rural/documents/protected/common-land/pilot-craguide.pdf

Defra (2010c) *Explanatory Memorandum to the Commons Associations (Standard Constitution) (England) Regulations 2010*, www.opsi.gov.uk/si/si2010/em/uksiem_20101204_en.pdf

Demsetz, H. (1967) 'Towards a theory of property rights', *American Economic Review*, vol 57, no 2, pp347–359

DETR (Department of the Environment, Transport and the Regions) (2001) *Guidelines on Management Agreement Payments and Other Related Matters*, HMSO, London

Dilley, R. S. (1973) *Common Land in Cumbria, 1500–1850*, MPhil thesis, University of Cambridge, Cambridge

Dilley, R. S. (1991) *Agricultural Change and Common Land in Cumberland 1700–1850*, PhD thesis, McMaster University

Done, A. and Muir, R. (2001) 'The landscape history of grouse shooting in the Yorkshire Dales', *Rural History*, vol 12, no 2, pp195–210

Evans, T. P., York, A. M. and Ostrom, E. (2008) 'Institutional dynamics, spatial organisation, and landscape change', in J. L. Westcoat Jr and D. M. Johnston (eds) *Political Economies of Landscape Change: Places of Power*, New York: Springer, pp111–129

Everitt, A. (2000) 'Common land', in J. Thirsk (ed) *The English Rural Landscape*, Oxford: Oxford University Press, pp210–235

Faden, W. (1797) *Map of Norfolk*, www.fadensmapofnorfolk.co.uk/, accessed 12 May 2010

Fleming, A. (1998) *Swaledale: Valley of the Wild River*, Edinburgh: Edinburgh University Press

Fraser, C. M. and Emsley, K. (eds) (1977) *Court Rolls of the Manor of Wakefield Vol I (1639–40)*, Leeds: Yorkshire Archaeological Society

French, H. R. (2003) 'Urban common rights, enclosure and the market: Clitheroe Town Moors, 1764–1802', *Agricultural History Review*, vol 51, no 1, pp40–68

Gadsden, G. D. (1988) *The Law of Commons*, London: Sweet and Maxwell

Gardner, A. (1942) *Britain's Mountain Heritage and its Preservation as National Parks*, London: Batsford

Getzler, J. (1997) 'Judges and hunters: Law and economic conflict in the English countryside, 1800–60', in C. Brooks and M. Lobban (eds) *Communities and Courts in Britain 1150–1900*, London: Hambledon, pp199–228

Gibbs, C. J. N. and Bromley, D. W. (1989) 'Institutional arrangements for management of rural resources: Common-property regimes' in Berkes, F. (ed) *Common Property Resources: Ecology and Community-Based Sustainable Development,* London: Belhaven Press

Gifford, G. (1582) *A Brief Discourse of Certaine Points of the Religion which Is among the Common Sort of Christians …*, London

Gray, K. (1994) 'Equitable property', *Current Legal Problems*, vol 47, pp157–214

Griffith, J. (1986) 'What is legal pluralism?', *Journal of Legal Pluralism*, vol 24, pp1–55

Gulliver, D. (2007) *Cononley Manorial Courts: A Selection of Transcriptions of Manor Court Records Relating to Cononley and Neighbouring Parts of South Craven*, Cononley: Kiln Hill

Hallam, H. E. (1963) 'The fen bylaws of Spalding and Pinchbeck', *Lincolnshire Architectural and Archaeological Society*, vol 10, pp40–56

Hankinson, A. (1988) *A Century on the Crags: The Story of Rock Climbing in the Lake District*, London: Dent

Hardin, G. (1968) 'The tragedy of the commons', *Science*, vol 162, pp1243–1248

Harris, J. W. (1996) *Property and Justice*, Oxford: Clarendon Press

Harrison, C. (1997) 'Manor courts and the governance of Tudor England', in C. Brooks and M. Lobban (eds) *Communities and Courts in Britain 1150–1900,* London: Hambledon, pp43–59

Hart, W. H. and Lyons, P. A. (eds) (1884–1893) *Cartularium Monasterii de Ramseia,* Rolls Series 79 (3 vols)

Hill, C. (ed) (1973) *Winstanley: 'The Law of Freedom' and other Writings*, Cambridge: Cambridge University Press

Hindle, S. (2003) '"Not by bread only"? Common right, parish relief and endowed charity in a forest economy, c. 1600–1800', in S. King and A. Tomkins (eds) *The Poor in England 1700–1850: An Economy of Makeshifts*, Manchester: Manchester University Press, pp39–75

Hobsbawm, E. (1983) 'Introduction: Inventing traditions' in E. Hobsbawm, and T. Ranger (eds) *The Invention of Tradition*, Cambridge: Cambridge University Press

Honore, A. (1961) 'Ownership' in A. Guest (ed) *Oxford Essays in Jurisprudence*, Oxford: Oxford University Press

Hoskins, W. G. and Stamp, L. D. (1963) *The Common Lands of England and Wales*, London: Collins

Howells, E. (2005) *Good Men and True: The Lives and Tales of the Shepherds of Mid Wales*, Aberystwyth: privately printed

Humphries, J. (1990) 'Enclosures, common rights, and women: The proletarianization of families in the late eighteenth and early nineteenth centuries', *Journal of Economic History*, vol 50, no 1, pp17–42

Hunt, I. (ed) (1991) *Norman Nicholson's Lakeland: A Prose Anthology*, London: Robert Hale.

Hunter, R. (1897) 'The movement for the inclosure and preservation of open lands', *Journal of the Royal Statistical Society*, vol 60, no 2, pp360–431

Hurle, P. (2007) *The Forest and Chase of Malvern*, Chichester: Phillimore

Johnson, D. (2008) *Ingleborough Landscape and History*, Lancaster: Carnegie

Johnson, M. (2007) *Ideas of Landscape*, Oxford: Blackwell

Johnston, J., Webb, S. and Hunt, D. (2006) *English Nature's Sustainable Grazing Initiative in Cumbria – A Review of the Success of Grazing Agreements for Upland SSSIs,* Peterborough, English Nature

Joint Nature Conservation Committee (2006a) *Natura 2000 Site Data Assessments, Elenydd SAC,* www.jncc.gov.uk/protectedsites/sacselection/n2kforms/UK0012928.pdf

Joint Nature Conservation Committee (2006b) *Natura 2000 Site Data Assessments, High Fells SAC*, www.jncc.gov.uk/ProtectedSites/SACselection/n2kforms/UK0012960.pdf

Joint Nature Conservation Committee (2006c) *Natura 2000 Site Data Assessment Ingleborough Complex SAC*, www.jncc.gov.uk/protectedsites/sacselection/n2kforms/UK0012782.pdf

Keohane, R. O. and Ostrom, E. (eds) (1995) *Local Commons and Global Interdependence: Heterogeneity and Cooperation in Two Domains*, London: SAGE Publications Ltd

Leist, A. and Holland, A. (2000) *Conceptualising Sustainability*, Cambridge Research for the Environment, Environmental Valuation in Europe Policy Research Brief No 5

Leland, J. (1964) *The Itinerary of John Leland*, L. Toulmin Smith (ed), London: Centaur Press (5 volumes)

Liddell, W. H. (1966) 'The private forests of south–west Cumberland', *Transactions of the Cumberland & Westmorland Antiquarian & Archaeological Society*, vol 66, pp106–130

Mabey, R. (1996) *Flora Britannica*, London: Sinclair-Stevenson

McCay, B. J. and Acheson, J. M. (eds) (1987) *The Question of the Commons: The Culture and Ecology of Communal Resources*, Tucson: University of Arizona Press

Megarry, R. and Wade, H. W. R. (2000) *The Law of Real Property* (6th edition), London: Sweet & Maxwell

Meinzen, D. K., Raju, V. and Gulati, A. (2002) 'What affects organization and collective action for managing resources? Evidence from canal irrigation systems in India', *World Development*, vol 30, pp649–666

Mellissaris, E. (2009) *Ubiquitous Law: Legal Theory and the Space for Legal Pluralism,* Aldershot: Ashgate

Merry, S. E. (1988) 'Legal pluralism', *Law & Society Review*, vol 22, pp869–896

Moore, S. (1973) 'Law and social change: The semi autonomous filed as an appropriate field of study', *Law and Society Review*, vol 7, no 4, pp719–746

Moore, S. F. (1978) *Law as Process: An Anthropological Approach*, London: Routledge

Murdoch, J. (1984) *The Discovery of the Lake District*, London: Victoria & Albert Museum

Natural England (2005a) 'A statement of English Nature's views about the management of Scafell Pikes Site of Special Scientific Interest (SSSI)', *Countryside and Rights of Way Act 2000*, Schedule 11(6) (16/09/05), www.sssi.naturalengland.org.uk/Special/sssi/sitedocuments.cfm?type=vam&sssi_id=1001922

Natural England (2005b) 'A statement of English Nature's views about the management of Wasdale Screes Site of Special Scientific Interest (SSSI)', *Countryside and Rights of Way Act 2000*, Schedule 11(6) (27/04/05), www.sssi.naturalengland.org.uk/Special/sssi/sssi_details.cfm?sssi_id=1002125

Natural England (2008a) *Trends in Pastoral Commoning in England: A Study for Natural England*, The Pastoral Commoning Partnership with H&H Bowes, Carlisle

Natural England (2008b) *The State of the Natural Environment 2008*, Natural England Research Report NE85, Peterborough

Natural England (2009) *Scafell Pikes SSSI Condition Assessment*, www.sssi.naturalengland.org.uk/Special/sssi/reportAction.cfm?report=sdrt18&category=S&reference=1001922

Natural England (2010a) *Whernside SSSI Condition Assessment*, www.sssi.naturalengland.org.uk/Special/sssi/reportAction.cfm?report=sdrt18&category=S&reference=1004533

Natural England (2010b) *Ingleborough SSSI Condition Assessment*, www.sssi.naturalengland.org.uk/Special/sssi/reportAction.cfm?report=sdrt18&category=S&reference=1001537

Natural England (2010c) *Wasdale Screes SSSI Condition Assessment*, www.sssi.naturalengland.org.uk/Special/sssi/scsi_details.cfm?Sssi_id=1002125/

Nature Conservancy Conservation (1991) *Press Statement PPG 4/91*

Neeson, J. M. (1993) *Commoners: Common Right, Enclosure and Social Change in England, 1700–1820*, Cambridge: Cambridge University Press

Newsome, D. (1980) *On the Edge of Paradise: A. C. Benson, The Diarist*, London: John Murray

Norden, J. (1618) *The Surveiors Dialogue*, London

Norfolk County Council (2009) *Common Concerns*, Commons Registration Authority for Norfolk, Norfolk County Council

North, D. (1990) *Institutions, Institutional Change and Economic Performance*, Cambridge: Cambridge University Press

Office of the Deputy Prime Minister (2005) *Planning Policy Statement 9 – Biodiversity and Geological Conservation*, UK

Olwig, K. R. (2003) 'Commons and landscape', in *Landscape, Law and Justice: Proceedings from a Workshop on Old and New Commons, Centre for Advanced Study, Oslo, 11–13 March 2003*, pp15–22

Ostrom, E. (1990) *Governing the Commons: The Evolution of Institutions for Collective Action*, Cambridge: Cambridge University Press

Ostrom, E. (1999) 'Coping with tragedies of the commons', *Annual Review of Political Science*, vol 2, pp493–535

Ostrom, E. (2005) *Understanding Institutional Diversity*, Princeton, NJ: Princeton University Press

Ostrom, E., Dietz, T., Dolsak, N., Stern, P. C., Stonich, S. and Weber, E. U. (eds) (2002) *The Drama of the Commons*, Washington: National Academy Press

Pearce, D. (1993) *Blueprint 3 – Measuring Sustainable Development*, London: Earthscan

Penner, J. (1996) 'The "bundle of rights" picture of property', *UCLA Law Review*, vol 43, no 3, pp711–820

Pieraccini, M. (2010) *A Legal Pluralist Analysis of Upland Commons in England, Wales and Northern Italy*, PhD thesis, Newcastle University, Newcastle, UK

Pollard, S. (1997) *Marginal Europe: The Contribution of Marginal Lands since the Middle Ages*, Oxford: Oxford University Press

Poos, L. R. and Bonfield, L. (1998) *Select Cases in Manorial Courts 1250–1550: Property and Family Law*, London: Selden Society, vol CXIV

Postgate, M. R. (1973) 'Field systems of East Anglia', in A. R. H. Baker and R. A. Butlin (eds) *Studies of Field Systems in the British Isles*, Cambridge: Cambridge University Press, pp281–324

Raff, M. (1998) 'Environmental obligations and the western liberal property concept', *Melbourne University Law Review*, vol 22, pp657–692

Ravensdale, J. R. (1974) *Liable to Floods: Village Landscape on the Edge of the Fens, AD 450–1850*, Cambridge: Cambridge University Press

Reay, B. (1996) *Microhistories: Demography, Society and Culture in Rural England, 1800–1930*, Cambridge: Cambridge University Press

Ritvo, H. (2009) *The Dawn of Green: Manchester, Thirlmere and Modern Environmentalism*, London: University of Chicago Press

Roach, P. C. (ed) (1959) *A History of the County of Cambridge and the Isle of Ely, Volume III*, London: Victoria County Histories

Robinson, L. (ed) (1990) *Court Rolls of Manor of Wakefield, 1651–2*, Yorkshire Archaeological Society: Wakefield Court Rolls Series, VIII

Rodgers, C. P. (1999) 'Environmental management of common land: Towards a new legal framework?', *Journal of Environmental Law*, vol 11, no 2, pp231–255

Rodgers, C. P. (2007) 'A new deal for commons? Common resource management and the Commons Act 2006', *Environmental Law Review*, vol 9, no 1, pp25–40

Rodgers, C. P. (2008) *Agricultural Law*, 3rd edition, West Sussex: Tottel Publishing

Rodgers, C. P. (2009) 'Nature's Place? Property rights, property rules and environmental stewardship', *Cambridge Law Journal*, vol 68, pp550–574

Rodgers, C. P. (2010) 'Reversing the tragedy of the commons? Sustainable management and the Commons Act 2006', *Modern Law Review*, vol 73, pp428–453

Ross, A. (2009) 'Modern interpretations of sustainable development', *Journal of Law and Society*, vol 36, no 2, pp32–54

Royal Commission (1958) *Royal Commission on Common Land 1955–1958: Report*, P. P. 1958, Cmnd 462
Rural Planning Services (1985) *The Future of Rural Common Land – A Report to the Department of the Environment*, RPS Case Study 22
Sabine, G. H. (1965) *The Works of Gerrard Winstanley*, New York: Russell & Russell
Schama, S. (1996) *Landscape and Memory*, London: Fontana Press
Schlager, E. and Ostrom, E. (1992) 'Property rights regimes and natural resources: A conceptual analysis', *Land Economics*, vol 68, no 3, pp249–262
Searle, C. E. (1993) 'Customary tenants and the enclosure of the Cumbrian commons', *Northern History*, vol 29, pp126–153
Shannon, W. D. (2009) *Approvement and Improvement in Early-Modern England: Enclosure in the Lowland Wastes of Lancashire, 1500–1700*, PhD thesis, Lancaster University, UK
Shaw Lefevre, G. (1894) *English Commons and Forests*, London: Cassell
Shaw-Taylor, L. (2002) 'The management of common land in the lowlands of southern England', in M. De Moor, L. Shaw-Taylor, and P. Warde (eds) (2002) *The Management of Common Land in North West Europe, c. 1500–1850*, Turnhout: Brepols, pp59–85
Short, B. (1999) 'Conservation, class and custom: Lifespace and conflict in a nineteenth-century forest environment', *Rural History*, vol 10, no 2, pp127–154
Short, C. (2008) 'The traditional commons of England and Wales in the twenty-first century', *International Journal of the Commons*, vol 2, pp192–221
Short, C. and Winter, M. (1999), 'The problem of common land: Towards stakeholder governance', *Journal of Environmental Planning and Management*, vol 42, no 5, pp613–630
Silvester, R. J. (2004) 'The commons and the waste: Use and misuse in mid-Wales', in I. D. Whyte and A. J. L. Winchester (eds) *Society, Landscape and Environment in Upland Britain*, Birmingham: Society for Landscape Studies, pp53–66
Silvester, R. J. (2007) 'Landscapes of the poor: Encroachment in Wales in the post-medieval centuries', in P. S. Barnwell and M. Palmer (eds) *Post-Medieval Landscapes,* Macclesfield: Windgather Press, pp55–67
Smout, T. C. (2000) *Nature Contested: Environmental History in Scotland and Northern England since 1600,* Edinburgh: Edinburgh University Press
Steers, J. A. (1936) 'Some notes on the North Norfolk Coast from Hunstanton to Brancaster', *The Geographical Journal*, vol 87, no 1, pp35–46
Steers, J. A. (ed) (1960) *Scolt Head Island*, Cambridge: W. Heffer & Sons
Straughton, E. (2008) *Common Grazing in the Northern English Uplands, 1800–1965: A History of National Policy and Local Practice with Special Attention to the Case of Cumbria*, Lampeter & Lewiston: Edwin Mellen
Suggett, R. (2005) *Houses and History in the March of Wales: Radnorshire 1400–1800*, Aberystwyth: Royal Commission on the Ancient and Historical Monuments of Wales
Summerfield, G. (ed) (1990) *John Clare: Selected Poetry*, London: Penguin
Sydenham, A. (2006) *Commons and Village Greens – The New Law,* Dorchester: Lime Legal
Tarlow, S. (2007) *The Archaeology of Improvement in Britain, 1750–1850*, Cambridge: Cambridge University Press
Thirsk, J. (2007) *Food in Early Modern England*, London: Hambledon Continuum
Thomas, K. (1969) 'Another Digger broadside', *Past and Present*, no 42, pp57–68
Thomas, K. (1983) *Man and the Natural World: Changing Attitudes in England 1500–1800*, London: Allen Lane
Thompson, E. P. (1991) *Customs in Common: Studies in Popular Culture*, London: Penguin
Turner, M. (1980), *English Parliamentary Enclosure: Its Historical Geography and Economic History*, Folkestone: Archon Books

Turner, M., Beckett, J. and Afton, B. (2003) 'Agricultural sustainability and open-field farming in England, c.1650–1830', *International Journal of Agricultural Sustainability*, vol 1, no 2, pp124–140

Tyler, G. (2002) *Sheep, Steam & Shows*, Chapel-le-Dale: Committee of the Ribblehead Sheep Show

United Nations (1992) *Report of the United Nations Conference on Environment and Development 1992*, New York: United Nations General Assembly

United Nations (2002) *Report of the WSSD*, UN Document A/CONF 199/20

United Nations (2005) *World Summit Outcome, Resolution A/60/1*, Adopted by the General Assembly on 15 September 2005, New York: United Nations General Assembly

Wade, R. (1994) *Village Republics: Economic Conditions for Collective Action in South India*, San Francisco: ICS Press

Wade Martins, S. (2004) *Farmers, Landlords and Landscapes: Rural Britain, 1720 to 1870*, Macclesfield: Windgather

Ward, A. (1997) 'Transhumance and settlement on the Welsh uplands: A view from the Black Mountain', in N. Edwards (ed) *Landscape and Settlement in Medieval Wales*, Oxford: Oxbow Monograph 81, pp97–111

WCED (World Commission on Environment and Development) (1987) *Our Common Future*, The Bruntland Report, Oxford: Oxford University Press

Welsh Assembly Government (2006) *Scheme Guidance for Tir Gofal, Document from the 2006 Application Pack: A Guide to the Scheme* (English version), http://wales.gov.uk/depc/publications/environmentandcountryside/farmingandcountryside/farmingschemeinformation/agri-env/tirgofal/documents/tirgofalschemeguidance/schemeguidancetirgofale.pdf?lang=en

Welsh Assembly Government (2007) *Rural Development Plan for Wales 2007–2013*, Wales

Welsh Assembly Government (2010) *GlasTir: New Sustainable Land Management Scheme for Wales*, http://wales.gov.uk/docs/drah/publications/100407glastirinserten.pdf

Whyte, N. (2009), *Inhabiting the Landscape: Place, Custom and Memory, 1500–1800*, Oxford: Windgather Press

Williamson, T. (2006) *East Anglia (England's Landscape Volume 2)*, London: HarperCollins for English Heritage

Wilmot, S. (1990) *The Business of Improvement: Agriculture and Scientific Culture in Britain, c. 1700–c. 1870*, Historical Geography Research Series No 24

Wilson, O. and Wilson, G. (1997) 'Common cause or common concern? The role of common land in the post-productivist countryside', *Area*, vol 29, no 1, pp45–58

Winchester, A. J. L. (1984) 'Peat storage huts in Eskdale', *Transactions of the Cumberland & Westmorland Antiquarian & Archaeological Society*, vol 84, pp103–115

Winchester, A. J. L. (1987) *Landscape and Society in Medieval Cumbria*, Edinburgh: John Donald

Winchester, A. J. L. (2000) *The Harvest of the Hills: Rural Life in Northern England and the Scottish Borders, 1400–1700*, Edinburgh: Edinburgh University Press

Winchester, A. J. L. (2002) 'Upland commons in northern England', in M. De Moor, L. Shaw-Taylor, and P. Warde (eds) *The Management of Common Land in North West Europe, c. 1500–1850*, Turnhout: Brepols, pp33–57

Winchester, A. J. L. (2006) 'Village byelaws and the management of a contested common resource: Bracken (*Pteridium aquilinum*) in Highland Britain, 1500–1800', Digital Library of the Commons, http://dlc.dlib.indiana.edu/archive/00001772/

Winchester, A. J. L. (2007) 'Baronial and manorial parks in medieval Cumbria', in R. Liddiard (ed) *The Medieval Park: New Perspectives*, Macclesfield: Windgather Press

Winchester, A. J. L. (2008) 'Statute and local custom: Village byelaws and the governance of common land in medieval and early-modern England', Digital Library of the Commons, http://dlc.dlib.indiana.edu/archive/00004046/

Winchester, A. J. L. and Straughton, E. A. (2010) 'Stints and sustainability: Managing stock levels on common land in England, c. 1600–2006', *Agricultural History Review*, vol 58, no 1, pp29–47

Wmffre, I. (2009) 'Toponymy and land-use in the uplands of the Doethïe valley (Cardiganshire)', in H. James and P. Moore (eds) *Carmarthenshire and Beyond: Studies in History and Archaeology in Memory of Terry James*, Carmarthenshire Antiquarian Society Monograph Series, vol 8, pp270–283

Wood, A. (1997) 'The place of custom in plebeian political culture: England, 1550–1800', *Social History*, vol 22, no 1, pp46–60

Woodward, D. (1998) 'Straw, bracken and the Wicklow whale: The exploitation of natural resources in England since 1500', *Past and Present*, vol 159, pp43–76

Wordsworth, W. (2004) *Guide to the Lakes*, Ernest de Sélincourt (ed) with Preface by Stephen Gill, London: Frances Lincoln

Wrightson, K. (2007) 'The "decline of neighbourliness" revisited', in N. L. Jones and D. R. Woolf (eds) *Local Identities in Late Medieval and Early Modern England*, Basingstoke: Palgrave MacMillan, pp19–49

Cases and Legislation

Cases

Anon Yearbook 37 Henry VI 34
Beckett (Alfred F.) v. Lyons [1967] Ch. 449
Besley v. John [2003] EWCA Civ. 1737
Bettison v. Langton [2001] 3 All E.R. 417
Box Parish Conservation Body v. Lacey [1979] 1 All E.R. 113
Cole v. Foxman [1618] 74 E.R. 1000
Earl de la Warr v. Miles [1881] LR ChD 535
Hampshire County Conservation Body v. Milburn [1991] 1 A.C. 325
In the Matter of Creeks Foreshore and Salt Marshes, Burnham Overy, Burnham Norton and Brancaster Norfolk (1980) 25/D/105-11
Paine & Co. v. St. Neots Gas and Coke Co. [1939] 3 All E.R. 812
Re Lustleigh Cleave, Lustleigh, Devon (no 1) [1978] 209 /D/114–130
Re The Black Mountain, Dinefwr, Dyfed [1985] 272/D/441, 16 D.C.C. 219
Re Thornham Common, Thornham North Norfolk District (1975) 25/D/79–95
Samborne v. Harilo [1621] 123 E.R. 1162
Smith v. Bensall (1597) 75 E.R. 1034; [1597] Goulds. 117
Southern Water v. NCC [1992] 3 All E.R. 481
Tehidy Minerals Ltd. v. Norman [1971] 2 Q.B. 528
Tyrringham's Case [1584] 4 Co. Rep. 36a (76 E.R. 973)

Legislation

Act Concerning the Breeding of Horses, 1540, 32 Hen. VIII, c. 13
Administration of Justice Act 1977
Commons Act 1876, 39 & 40 Vict., c. 56
Commons Act 1899, 62 and 63 Vict., c. 30
Commons Act 1908, 8 Edward 7, c. 44
Commons Act 2006
Commons Councils (Standard Constitution) (England) Regulations 2010, SI 2010/1204
Commons Registration Act 1965
Commons Registration (England) Regulations 2008, SI 2008/1961
Commons (Severance of Rights) (England) Order 2006, SI 2006/2145
Commons (Severance of Rights) (Wales) Order 2007, SI 2007/583 (W.55)
Countryside and Rights of Way Act 2000
Environmental Stewardship (England) Regulations 2005, SI 2005/621
Inclosure (Consolidation) Act 1801, 41 Geo. 3, c. 109

Inclosure Act 1836, 6 & 7 Will. 4, c. 115
Inclosure Act 1845, 8 & 9 Vict., c. 118
Malvern Hills Act 1884, 47 & 48 Vict., c. 175
Metropolitan Commons Act 1866, 29 & 30 Vict., c. 122
National Parks and Access to the Countryside Act 1949
National Trust Act 1907
National Trust Act 1971
New Forest Act 1877, 40 & 41 Vict., c. 121
Open Spaces Act 1907
Wildlife and Countryside Act 1981

Index